Hard work and education once insured achieving the American Dream – equality of opportunity, comfort, and success. While not everyone shared equally, the Dream became a guideline for our culture. Today, in a world filled with doubt and uncertainty, the Dream appears to be in jeopardy.

Authors:
Paul Stich
George Habib

Editor:
Wayne Garnsey
Judith Shuback – *Associate Editor*

Cover Design, Illustrations, and Artwork:
Eugene B. Fairbanks

N&N Publishing Company, Inc.
18 Montgomery Street Middletown, New York 10940
phone: 1 800 NN 4 TEXT email: nn4text@warwick.net

Special Appreciation

Dedicated to our students, with the sincere hope that

ECONOMICS – STAReview
Crosscurrents of the American Dream

will further enhance their education and better prepare them to participate in the world's economic systems.

Special Credits

To the many teachers who have contributed their knowledge, skills, and years of experience to the making of our text, we thank you.

To these others, our researchers and readers, our deepest appreciation for their assistance in the preparation of this manuscript.

David Bennett
Cindy Fairbanks
John Farrell
Kenneth Garnsey
Fran Harrison
Joanne Stich
Maureen Stich
Gloria Tonkinson

To the directors, librarians, and research staffs of these fine NY libraries, we extend our gratitude for their cooperation, excellence, and professionalism:

East Fishkill Public Library, Hopewell Junction
John Jay High School Library, Hopewell Junction
State University Library, Albany
Thrall Library, Middletown
Vassar College Library, Poughkeepsie

N&N Publishing Company, Inc.
18 Montgomery Street Middletown, New York 10940
phone: 1 800 NN 4 TEXT email: nn4text@warwick.net

Cat # 910 Soft Cover Edition: ISBN # 0-935487 80 8

1 2 3 4 5 6 7 8 9 0 BMP 2008 2007 2006 2005 2004 2003
Printed in the United States of America, Book-mart Press, NJ

SAN # 216 - 4221

Table of Contents

INTRODUCTION

WHAT IS HAPPENING TO THE AMERICAN DREAM

Historical Economic Forces

IS THE DREAM GONE?

Has the freedom to choose and freedom from want disappeared? Is the **American Dream** (equality of opportunity, comfort, and success) gone?

Not everyone agrees. The problems facing the generations of the 2000s are daunting, but this is a better educated generation. Slightly more than 24% of this generation now completes 4 years of college (Michael Lee Cohen. *The Twenty-something American Dream: A Cross-Country Quest for a Generation.* 3). They have enormous knowledge and power they have not yet begun to use. The American Dream is as real for them as it has been for previous generations. It is a potent and long-standing part of our nation's secular faith. Chasing "the Dream" is an act of devotion that all people, regardless of their sectarian beliefs, can perform (Cohen. 6-8).

The Dream Requires Economic Literacy

What is wrong then? Why does the upcoming generation have doubts about the promise of the future? Studying economics can provide answers – a degree of economic literacy is necessary to really grasp what the American Dream is. Of course, studying economics as a subject by itself is a new experience for most students. Yet, as consumers, workers in part-time jobs, and students of history and society in general, most young adults have more economic knowledge than they realize.

Economics is a part of life. There are economic causes behind nearly everything that happens. Of course, political and social events also change the economic pattern of life. It is all integrated. Taking economics out of that integrated pattern of life and studying it all by itself is a little unnatural. However, to see how important it is to the whole society, it has to be separated and analyzed.

The Dream Requires Historical Perspective

Most students beginning to study economics do not realize it, but they already have a fair knowledge of economic history. If students start from what they know, they can see the pattern of modern economic history evolve.

Occupations and businesses related to the automobile grew in the 1920s and 1930s despite the roller coaster nature of the business cycle. ©PhotoDisc

Students are aware that the United States was just emerging as an industrial power when their great grandparents were children. Before World War I, Britain, France, and Germany were far ahead of the United States in production and industrial development. The Great War's devastation in Europe took a heavy toll on the more advanced nations. Limited participation in the War gave U.S. industry a great boost. Production technology developed before the War (e.g., Ford's refinement of the assembly line) and accelerated during the War.

However, in those days before the electronics revolution, even the advanced technology took a decade or more to affect everyday life. For example, by 1916, Ford's factories could churn out inexpensive cars, but the public did not really get on the road until 1925. Electricity could be

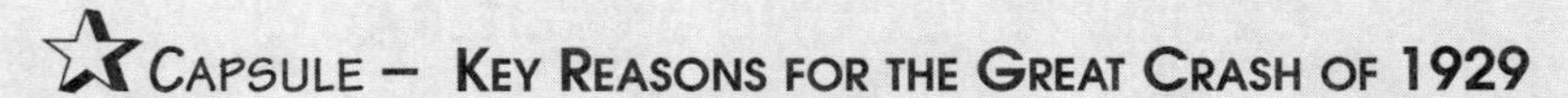

CAPSULE – KEY REASONS FOR THE GREAT CRASH OF 1929

- Wealth was flowing into the hands of only 5–10% of the population.

- American manufacturers were overproducing massive amounts of goods. As the years went by, the number of people who could afford to buy goods actually declined. The number of those who could consider themselves middle class stagnated.

- Wages had not kept pace with the GDP (Gross Domestic Product). Farmers', miners', and textile workers' incomes were declining from the mid-1920s. The number of poor Americans grew rapidly after 1925. Consumer purchasing began to level off.

- Government saw some of the signs, but the Harding-Coolidge-Hoover Administrations were locked into a laissez-faire philosophy and refused to "tamper" with income taxes, interest rates, or make use of the federal government's regulating powers.

- Congress had raised tariffs, sealing American markets off from other nations. Without U.S. dollars circulating, buying American goods and paying debts to U.S. bankers became impossible. World trade dried up. In the Fall of 1929, business declines caused public confidence to falter. Edgy stockholders began to sell shares rapidly. The wave of selling turned into a panic. The unstable economy collapsed.

generated on a very large scale in 1900, but U.S. businesses and homes did not use it extensively until the 1920s.

When World War I ended, following a year-long depression (normal while society readjusts from being at war), the economy boomed. During the War, consumers could not (or would not) purchase much. In addition, the government siphoned money away from consumers with the sale of war bonds. In the 1920s boom, consumers bought cars, real estate, electric appliances, indoor bathrooms, and radios. Investors (about 10% of the population) bought stock in the companies that processed the raw materials and produced the finished goods cthat onsumers were buying. Many investors made fortunes. It was the "Roaring Twenties." It was a time of very fast and very furious living. Then in 1929, to the shock of millions, it fell apart.

The economic collapse led to great hardship. It showed that the economy is reflective of human existence. Economics is an aspect of human behavior, it is not even-tempered. It is neither steady nor perfectly predictable. (This is a good point to remember when some economists get carried away quantifying human behavior with numerical formulas.)

Immediately after the 1929 collapse, people accepted official explanations by economists and politicians that this was a normal "correction phase" (reorganization) for an overheated economy. Americans had long accepted the idea that their economy needed no socialistic tampering by government. This is what classical economists called **laissez-faire**. In 1929, the people expected no government moves (now called **fiscal policy**) to aid the ailing economy.

At first, there was no sense that the Dream was in jeopardy, but as the Great Depression deepened, and the years went by, the American public became more disgruntled, dissatisfied, and disenchanted.

The Dream Requires a Proactive Government

By 1933, nearly one-fourth of all workers were unemployed. Many more were **underemployed** (working, but for lower wages and fewer hours). After four years, the people's mood changed. They sensed this was no ordinary correction phase. They were desperate for some action – government action to "prime-the-pump" or "jump-start" the economy. The American public took a leap of faith. In 1932, they voted for a political change which promised government action to revitalize the economy – and the Dream. They voted for Franklin Roosevelt and his ***New Deal***.

President Roosevelt experimented with the new economic role for government. The government borrowed money for programs to stimulate new programs (see the chart below). The country grudgingly accepted **deficit spending** (financing expenses by borrowing because of limited revenues). *New Deal* programs put the unemployed to work on civil projects and created new civil service jobs. These jobs preserved peoples' self-respect and gave them money to demand goods and services, thus

☆ Capsule – *The New Deal's 3 Rs*

"Priming the Pump"

President and Advisors Suggest Fiscal Policy Legislation.
Congress Enacts Recommended Fiscal Legislation.

RELIEF Immediate Action To Halt The Economy's Deterioration	**RECOVERY** "Pump – Priming" Temporary Programs To Restart the Flow Of Consumer Demand	**REFORM** Permanent Programs To Avoid Situations Causing Contractions and Insurance for Citizens Against Economic Disasters
Bank Holiday	Agricultural Adjustment	Securities and Exchange Commission
Emergency Banking Act	*National Industrial Recovery Act*	Federal Deposit Insurance Corporation
Federal Emergency Relief Act	Home Owners Loan Corporation	Social Security Administration
Civil Works Administration	Works Progress Administration	National Labor Relations Board

"priming the economic pump." Among the nation's priorities, survival replaced the sacred principle of laissez-faire. From that point, the people came to expect government would deal with broad economic problems such as poverty, unemployment, and all other economic problems.

Besides this change in public philosophy, the *New Deal* also made some permanent economic changes which placed government squarely in the lives of all Americans. Social Security and watchdog agencies were created to avoid the problems of the 1920s. The Securities and Exchange Commission watched the stock markets on Wall Street while the Federal Deposit Insurance Corporation watched the banks.

While the *New Deal* kept faith in the American Dream alive, the fact remains that it did not cure the Great Depression. It was the massive World War II military spending that began in 1940 that made the economy boom again. When the War ended, government continued to play a critical role in the economy. (Today, government is responsible for over one-third of all spending in the United States.)

Acceptance of the *New Deal* did not mean that everyone agreed with this new role for government. Traditionally, the heartbeat of a free market economy is the interaction of consumers and producers. Any government economic role alters the market and is always controversial.

As most wars end, economic activity slows. After World War II, as the nation converted to peacetime production, the government moved again to shore up the Dream. Under Truman's *Fair Deal*, the federal government continued spending to help the returning veterans go to school and buy homes under the ***G.I. Bill***. This legislation stimulated the economy through the normal post-war sag. This policy also accelerated the movement of the population out of the cities to where land was available – the suburbs. Life in the suburbs demanded autos. This stimulated another major industry in the late 1940s. More cars on the roads led to demand for more expressways, beltways, and freeways. The suburban life also gave rise to demand for more shopping centers, government offices, schools, and recreation facilities. As a result, the construction industry boomed in the 1950s.

The move to the suburbs following WW II increased demand for cars, homes, expressways, shopping centers, schools, and recreation facilities. ©PhotoDisc

There was foreign stimulation, too. World War II destroyed most of the productive facilities in Europe and Asia. Orders for American goods flooded world markets. The Marshall Plan and other U.S. government decisions to keep occupation troops and send aid to Europe and Japan intensified the flood of demand. The defense industry continued high production during the Korean War and with American allies throughout the Cold War.

The Dream Requires the Control of an Overactive Government

As in all human endeavors, there can be too much of a good thing. The government had moved to preserve the Dream in the 1930s and 1940s. In the 1950s, all this government generated demand over-stimulated the economy. Business could not meet all the government demand and simultaneously provide for consumer demand. **Aggregate supply** (total production) of goods and services was stretched to the limit. At the same time, **aggregate demand** (total consumption) grew rapidly because high employment gave a greater number of consumers more to spend. The imbalance in aggregate supply and aggregate demand made prices rise. **Inflation** (too many dollars chasing too few goods) became a chronic problem.

Throughout the 1960s, President John Kennedy's *New Frontier* and President Lyndon Johnson's *Great Society* kept the expansion (and inflation) rolling with tax cuts and higher government spending. Medicare, urban renewal, and the "War on Poverty" made high levels of deficit spending fashionable. The added expense of the war in Vietnam sent government spending sky high. The pace of inflation increased. The Dream seemed jeopardized again, and this time big government was the problem instead of the solution.

President Richard Nixon fought with Congress to slow down spending for government programs in the 1970s. Withdrawal from Vietnam also cut military spending. As the economy slowed, unemployment rose, and a recession hit. The economic picture worsened in the middle of the 1970s when OPEC (Organization of Petroleum Exporting Countries) began restricting oil supplies. Prices shot up, and many workers lost their jobs and income. Economists called the problem **stagflation** (inflation and recession hitting at the same time). Under Presidents Gerald Ford and Jimmy Carter, the economy weakened even more. In the late 1970s, the Iranian Revolution and the Iran-Iraq War cut oil supplies and generally inflated prices again.

By 1980, most Americans had a powerless feeling that the Dream was about to die. Their way of life was being destroyed by **hyperinflation** (prices rising by more than 10% annually). It was fueled by out-of-control government expenses and soaring oil prices.

With promises to control inflation by cutting deficit spending and taxes, Ronald Reagan won office and the Republicans captured the Senate in 1980. President Reagan's advisors tried a **supply-side** stimulation approach (government policies aimed at giving business and investors more incentive). They proposed to cut federal government spending and shift public programs to private business. This policy was dubbed "Reaganomics" by the media.

Supply-siders claimed that cutting taxes for industry would renew the desire of the wealthy class to invest. They theorized that capital development would surge. Supply-siders declared that investment of untaxed surplus capital in industry would spur growth, which would lead to new jobs. Those working in these new jobs would reduce unemployment claimants and create new taxpayers.

With these aims in mind, Reagan supporters pushed a series of broad tax cuts through Congress. One problem was that they also wanted to increase government spending to strengthen national defense. The defense companies and their stockholders did very well, but the goods produced did not help nonmilitary consumers. However, the rise in defense spending cancelled the effect of other government spending cuts that the supply-siders managed to get from Congress.

In the early 1980s, another recession hit the country before supply-side policies took hold. The Federal Reserve launched its own campaign against inflation by forcing bank interest rates up. However, the high interest rates cut investment and lending so much that businesses cut production and workers. The recession worsened, and unemployment soared above 10 percent.

The supply-siders' tax cuts did lead to some new investment in industrial technology but failed to contribute to significant growth. Much of the extra money went to foreign investment. Diminishing federal funding for state programs led states to cut expenditures for education, health, cultural, and other social programs, diminishing the quality of life.

The supply-siders also led a drive to reduce down government regulation of industry. Deregulation helped to cut business costs and increased profits, but it also led to higher consumer prices for telephone, cable TV, and utilities. Banking deregulation led to more services, but to cover new costs, banks raised interest rates for consumer loans, eventually slowing down consumption.

Supply-siders deregulated cable TV, telephone, and utilities which cut business costs and opened the market to new technological advances, but raised consumer prices in the long run. ©PhotoDisc

The Dream Requires Even-Handed Government Policies

As a result of the supply-siders campaign, only one group actually began to enjoy the American Dream again – "the rich." With generous tax breaks, the rich had more money to lend and invest. They profited from the Federal Reserve's policies of keeping interest rates high. However, the lavish media coverage of their conspicuous life-style created an impression on the general public. Even TV dramas such as *Dallas*, *Dynasty*, and *Falcon Crest* glorified the rich. There was a misperception the Dream was easily attainable for everyone.

However, the rich were a small group. *U.S.A. Today* reported that less than 2% of the population had incomes over $100,000 in 1987 (Moore. 1). In *The Politics of Rich and Poor*, a 1990 analysis of what went wrong with the Reagan Era, author Kevin Phillips says the 1980s was "a second Gilded Age" (see "Stool" illustration below). Phillips showed that middle and lower income groups could not really share the Dream (Phillips. 9). They could not afford to borrow at such high interest rates. Amid what appeared to be a general growth in prosperity, their standard of living declined. The gap between rich and poor grew larger. In the 1980s, Americans maintained their standard of living by going deeper in debt and putting more family members to work. In a special 1991 edition of *Fortune* magazine, Thomas Stewart said that the proportion of debt to after-tax income rose 84% for the average American family ("The New American Century," 17). The Dream was elusive for the majority.

Supply-side deregulation allowed large businesses to engage in complicated mergers and buy outs of competitors. There was a great deal of short-term gain. These moves enhanced corporations' market power and stock dividends. **CEO** (corporate Chief Executive Officer) salaries and benefits ran into the millions. In 1987, *Forbes* magazine stated that the

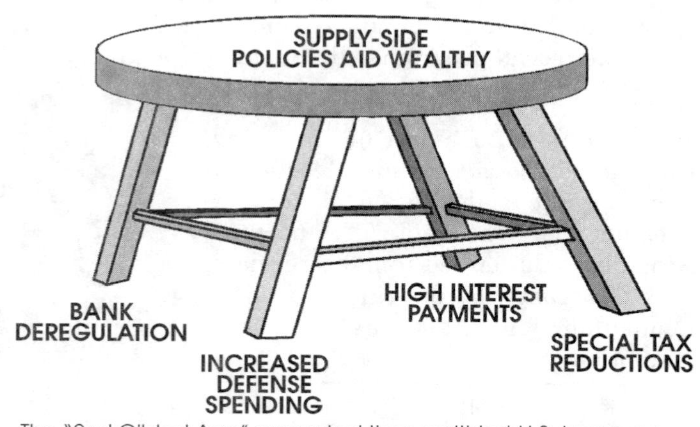

The "2nd Gilded Age" supported the wealthiest U.S. taxpayers through President Regan's policy of Supply-side Economics.

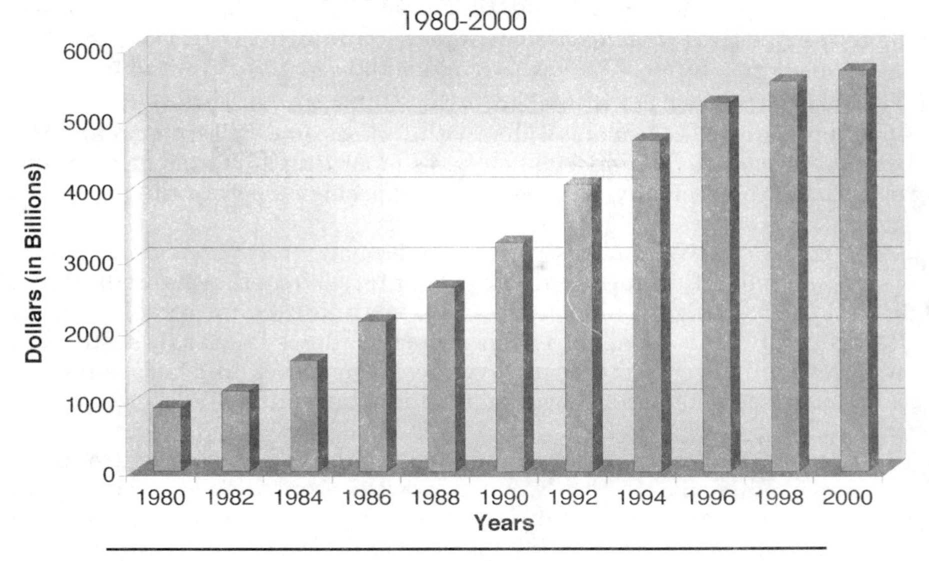

average annual corporate CEO salary was $762,253 (Phillips. 176). The corporate takeovers and investor trading made a few speculators very wealthy. However, some trade practices led to Wall Street scandals and banking collapses. In some cases, the short-term gains led to long-term structural damage that carried into the 1990s. In the long run, none of them led to **real growth** (net increase in jobs, higher productivity, or lower prices). Wealth did not "trickle down" to all of the American people as the supply-siders hoped.

Amid all the supply-side reforms, Reagan and Congress lost their appetite for cutting government spending. The combination of less tax revenue and massive government spending sent the national debt soaring beyond $4 trillion in the early 1990s (see graph above). The government's voracious need to borrow, coupled with the Federal Reserve Bank's "tight monetary policy" to hold down inflation, made money scarce and expensive. Interest rates (the price of loans) soared, too. Average Americans could not manage the credit cards, mortgages, and auto loans. Only the rich had large amounts of disposable income to spend or to lend the government (in the form of bonds). They got richer, but the general lack of consumer demand meant a slowdown of production, and layoffs began.

For all the government action, the Dream once more seemed beyond the reach of average Americans. On top of the national debt problem, came a persistent international trade imbalance. Phillips points out reduced taxes for the rich increased their disposable income (*Forbes*. 4). While they did invest, they also began spending lavishly, especially on personal imported goods. A good deal of their money left the country for

BMWs, Mercedes, Volvos, and Porsches. This upsurge of competition from Western Europeans, Japanese, and new Pacific Rim industrial countries slowed U.S. domestic job growth.

These problems continued into the 1990s under President George Bush and threw the economy into another recession. Bill Clinton and the Democrats won election in 1992 on basis of cutting government debt and revitalizing the economy, but the economic problems persisted.

During Clinton's administration, the economy recovered while unemployment and inflation remained low. Interest rates remained stable, despite new banking and real estate scandals (some involving the President and First Lady). The prosperity allowed federal, state, and local governments to increase revenues from taxes and fees allowing them to reduce debts and show annual budget surpluses.

International trade deficits remained high as Americans continued to buy imported goods. As the "wonder-growth" economies of Asia (Japan, Singapore, Taiwan) faltered in the late 1990s, Clinton shored up these countries (and Mexico) by buying up some of their currencies, and providing loans.

Congressional reforms diminished the federal economic role in welfare and pared down military spending, leading to greater deficit reductions.

The new millennium began with President George W. Bush convincing Congress that budget surpluses would allow a 10-year $1.35 trillion tax cut and still allow for increased military spending. Yet, growth slowed in 2001, especially in high tech industries, and the country moved into a recession. Despite Federal Reserve stimulus actions to lower interest rates, unemployment reached a nine-year high in 2001.

By mid-2001, the economy was further shaken by the exposure of fraudulent accounting scandals which led to the collapse of several large corporations, such as Enron [$63.4 billion], Arthur Anderson LLP [accounting firm], and WorldCom Inc. [$9 billion]. There were major corporate bankruptcies including Texaco [$35.9 billion], Financial Corp. of America [$33.9 billion], Pacific Gas and Electric [$21.5 billion, and Kmart Corp. [$16.3 billion].

Without warning, the terrorist attacks on the World Trade Center's Twin Towers in the heart of New York City's financial center on September 11th, 2001 ended the lives of almost 3,000 persons. The attacks also had widespread effects on the U.S. and world economies. The collateral damage from the attacks further weakened struggling businesses, such as in the travel and entertainment industries, and deepened and extended the recession making recovery more difficult.

THE DREAM REQUIRES AN ACTIVE, ECONOMICALLY LITERATE PUBLIC

This is the economic situation in which the upcoming generation must function. A *Business Week* article said members of the new generation feel "paralyzed by social problems they see as their inheritance" and that they "...[desire to] avoid risk, pain, and rapid change...." (Zinn. "Move Over Boomers..." 14 December 1992, 192)

In *The Twenty-something American Dream*, Michael Lee Cohen debates this negative image of his generation presented by the media. He claims many young people are confused, because the old ways of resolving the problems have broken down. The upcoming generation feels political parties, labor unions, and large corporations are no longer useful mechanisms for channeling their social concerns (Cohen, 300). These young people see political parties as historical artifacts that provide some members with money and some privileges, but they do not see parties as agents of change. They feel labor unions are corrupt and do not work for a service economy as they did for a manufacturing economy. Large corporations are "stateless, self-preserving institutions" treating employee loyalty as peasant foolishness (Cohen, 301). Cohen repeats the famous quote of a recent G.E. Chairman, "Loyalty to a company, it's nonsense." (Cohen, 301)

Does this mean there is no American Dream for the upcoming generation? Hardly, there are plenty of "end-of-the-civilization" doomsayers out there, but the fact remains that the United States is the dominant global economic power. Japan is an important economic power, but the quality of life in Japan still falls behind that in the United States. *Fortune's* Thomas A. Stewart showed Japan's 2000 per capita **Gross Domestic Product** (GDP: total value of all goods and services produced inside the country) was $24,000. He indicated the figure for the United States was $36,200. ("The World in Focus," *Junior Scholastic* 10/15/01) Still, the pessimists who say the Dream is dead or gone make Americans take stock in themselves. Cohen says, "Dissenters and doubters force us to constantly reconsider and redefine the Dream and revitalize it in the process" (Cohen. 307).

SUMMARY

What students must recognize from recent economic history is that there is still a horizon of opportunity that a new generation can seek. Studying economic decision-making is the way to begin that quest. Studs Terkel has been listening and writing what Americans say and think about themselves for decades. In his 1980 book, *American Dreams: Lost and Found*, he mentions a housewife who didn't like the word "dream." She said, "It's not a dream, it's possible. It's everyday stuff." (Terkel xxv)

ASSESSMENT • QUESTIONS • APPLICATIONS

1 The subheadings of this chapter show that preserving the American Dream involves certain requirements. Explain why the Dream requires each of the following:
   a an awareness of recent history
   b a degree of government involvement
   c control of an overactive government
   d an economically literate public

2 Consider this quote:
"There never has been one American Dream on which we must all agree. The belief there ever was a single, clearly defined American Dream is just a sentimental longing for a time of perfect consensus that has never existed in this nation. The dream of creating a shining city on a hill and the settling of the West came at the expense of those who had been here for centuries. The post-war dream of a suburban paradise excluded racial minorities and consigned women to very restrictive roles."

– Michael Lee Cohen. *The Twentysomething American Dream*: pages 306-307

   a Is the American Dream only for the rich? Why, or why not?
   b Is the Dream only good for one sex, race, or ethnic group? Why, or why not?
   c Why does it seem difficult to define the American Dream?

3 For this question, think globally. Economics is universal in nature. Everyone has a struggle for survival. In a group, discuss how similar economic expectations are in other places.
   a Do you think a Mexican or Canadian (or Nigerian, or Thai, etc.) "Dream" exists? Using facts, explain your position.
   b Choose a country. Look in a world cultures text, encyclopedia, almanac, or the Internet. Find out how the Dream in other countries might be similar to or different from the American Dream.

4 The American economy is basically a market economy where consumer and producer choices determine its direction. Following the Great Depression, the entry of government as a major force in the American economy altered the system.
   a How did government become a major economic force, and what were some of the programs initiated?
   b Why was it necessary for government to play a major role in the economy?
   c Explain why you are for or against the government role in American economic life.
   d Do you see government as preserving the Dream or jeopardizing it?

5 Supply-side stimulation of the economy in the 1980s was a departure from economic policies the government had followed since the 1930s.
   a Why did supply-side advocates feel there was a need for a change?
   b List and explain the basic ideas behind supply-side strategies.
   c Evaluate the success of supply-side policies of the 1980s.

Assessment Project: Household Financial Profile

Student Task

Write a brief sketch of the financial status of a household that you create. Your "adopted" household must be realistic but should be completely fictional. For example, you could choose a "statistically typical" American family of four: head of household, spouse, and two children. Or, choose a single parent household, two–salaried, or one–income family.

This project can be completed by yourself or jointly with a classmate. As a guide, you may use computer software for home budgeting such as Home Office's *M.Y.O.B. Accounting*, Kiplinger's *Simply Money*, Intuit's *Quicken*, Andrew Tobias' *Managing Your Money*, or one of the other personal financial management computer programs. However, you must submit a *Household Financial Profile* in hard copy. Your instructor will provide this form from the Teacher Supplement. Keep in mind that the household you create will become the basis for several other assessment activities throughout this book (e.g., budgeting, major purchases, paying taxes). You should refer back to this *Household Financial Profile* for basic data.

Procedure

After creating your "adopted family" for this assessment, complete the following:

1 Fill-in completely the data requested on the *Household Financial Profile* chart (from your instructor). You may need parental, teacher, or other professional help. Again, this data will be used for this and other "household" projects that follow in other Issues.

2 Write a descriptive essay of the household. In other words, put your *Household Economic Profile* into sentence form. As you write, keep in mind these questions: (1) Do you have a economic basis for a functional family? (2) Does an overview of your profile identify the household as "lower, middle, or upper" income? (3) What are the feasible

prospects (goals) for this family and the American Dream? In "real life," a financial profile can be used to determine net worth, which is needed for things such as a new home purchase, college financial assistance, or starting an entrepreneurial enterprise.

3 Identify and list your informational sources for this assignment. Include library and interview sources.

EVALUATION

The criteria for the evaluation of this project are itemized in the grid (rubric) that follows. Choice of appropriate category terms (values) is the decision of the instructor. Selection of terms such as "minimal," "satisfactory," and "distinguished" can vary with each assessment.

Household Financial Profile Evaluation Rubric

(Refer to teacher's supplement for suggestions of scoring descriptors for evaluation.)

Evaluation Item
Item a: (1) Does the report show understanding that while different socioeconomic (as well as national, ethnic, religious, racial, and gender) groups have varied perspectives, values, and diverse practices and traditions, they face the same global economic challenges?
Item b: (5) Does the report analyze problems and evaluate decisions about the economic effects caused by human, technological, and natural activities on societies and individuals?
Item c: (6) Does the report present ideas in writing (and orally) in clear, concise, and properly accepted fashion?
Item d: (7) Does the report employ a variety of information from written, graphic, and multimedia sources?
Item e: (8) Does the report show monitoring of reflection upon, and improvement of work?

ISSUE 1

Living in a Global Economy

Why must economic choices be made?

Pro-lifers keep up the fight
March decries 22 years of legal abortion, 1B
Pyne defense gains concession, 1B
Pan Am misconduct affirmed, 3A
Marist gears up to face Rider, 1C
Bruins' rookie stifles champs
Goalie holds off late surge by N.Y. 1C

Poughkeepsie Journal

Steinhaus keeps focus on economy
New incubators top initiatives

IBM work force halved since '92

Earnings rebound to $2.9B

Downsizing nets profit

Region weathered worst of the storm, experts say

Demand strong for mainframes

Scarcity...Basic Choices
Downsizing the Dream

Back in April, it all looked very sweet. Kelly Fagan received a thick envelope from Springfield College in Massachusetts. (Seniors know that thin envelopes from colleges often mean rejection.) Springfield accepted her for a five-year program in physical therapy. Kelly was in seventh heaven for a week. And yet, it got better! Kelly's boyfriend Matt received a thick envelope from the University of Hartford. He was accepted as a marketing major in the School of Business. The two schools were separated by only an hour on Interstate-91. They would be able to see each other on weekends. For Kelly, the hard work was paying off, and the dreams of the past few years were coming to fruition.

Of course, Kelly knew the real work was just beginning. She had always been a good student. That would be no problem. It was the financial side that concerned her the most. Kelly's Mom and Dad were in their forties and both worked. Dad was a production supervisor at "Big Blue" – IBM. He had worked there for nearly twenty-five years. Mom was a dental hygienist now. She had gone back to school for training when Kelly's younger brother and sister entered grade school. At first, Mom worked for Dr. Hartman part-time, then a year ago she went full-time. The Fagans' lived in southern Dutchess County, New York. While it was not exactly an upscale community, it was not a cheap place to raise a family, either. Kelly knew Dad's salary allowed them to get by, but saving for the three kids' education required Mom's income.

When Kelly talked to her parents about her dreams, they said they would manage. Together, they had checked the colleges and had many discussions on the finances involved. Springfield was not the least expensive, but it was a good school. With an education loan and a small scholarship, it was within their means. For Kelly, everything was working out. Life was indeed sweet.

It has been said that the only thing certain about life is its very uncertainty. Kelly was about to find out the solemn truth of that statement. The bitterness broke through a few days after Kelly acknowledged her acceptance at Springfield. She had stayed late to watch some friends on the girls' softball team at practice. The house was quiet. She assumed the family was out shopping as she headed toward the kitchen. The light over the sink was the only illumination. Out of the corner of her eye, she saw a shadow move, and she froze.

"Hello, Kel," her Dad said. She relaxed a bit, but knew his tone had an edge to it.

"Why are you sitting alone in the dark, Dad?"

"Mom took the kids to the mall for a burger. I needed some time alone." He motioned for her to sit down. Kelly had an eerie feeling the news was not going to be good.

"You know the company has been making cuts in operations because of slow sales in mainframes and PCs?"

"I heard you and Mom talking about it." Kelly's voice was quiet and quivering. "Some kids at school have been concerned about their parents' jobs in the past couple of months. Is something wrong with your job? Why didn't you tell me?"

"With all my seniority, I was pretty sure nothing would happen. There were rumors; we didn't want you to worry." He paused. "Kel, they let me go. I have almost a year's salary coming, and my other benefits will continue for a while. We will survive, but we will have to adjust."

"Adjust how, Dad?"

"It may be rough for a little while. We will cut down on household expenses and cancel the cabin at the lake this summer. There may be an opening for me in a company that some of the executives are trying to organize. There is one thing, however." Again Kelly's Dad paused. "Your college."

This was it. Kelly had a sick feeling in the pit of her stomach. Her father reached for her hand. "Mom and I hate to do this, but we think it may be better for us all if you gave Dutchess Community College a try for

a year. If all goes well, we may have the resources for Springfield. I know it hurts, Kel, but we need your help on this one."

Before he finished his sentence, tears welled in Kelly's eyes. She felt so helpless. She heard him yell her name as she dashed upstairs, but things were just a blur at that point. She wasn't mad at him, but the bitterness was there and growing.

* * * * * *the end* * * * * *

A Global View

In recent decades, the powerful domestic forces outlined in the introduction have dramatically reshaped our economic life. Yet, Americans also feel greater and greater influence from abroad.

Our lives are linked to the rest of the world in so many ways. On the most basic level, there is the accepted presence of millions of products from other countries. Think how different today's auto market is from that of twenty years ago. However, it is not just what and how much we buy from others that shapes our environment. There is also the awareness that goods and services flow through a vast network of lightning communications and new transportation structures. They shrink time and space, and therefore they integrate humanity's needs and wants.

For example, to continue to grow and modernize, the economies of China and India require broader economic relations with foreign markets, and we are a vital part of those markets. As such interdependence expands, lives change everywhere – usually in quiet, almost imperceptible ways.

On the surface, increased economic activity yields more product availability and a better life for expanding nations. At the same time, it means greater competition for the limited resources available. As international consumers, investors, producers, borrowers, and lenders, we become more and more aware of the goals of other people competing for resources. The concept of scarcity becomes more critical every day. It steadily alters our lives on a global basis. Understanding scarcity and the basic nature of economic choices – and their consequences – becomes more and more critical as globalization occurs.

Basic Choices

Graduation is always a bittersweet trade-off. On the sweet side, the general education is over, and an adult world beckons. A young person is ready to move on to work or more intensive preparation for a career. Now, the quest for the American Dream really heats up.

These young Americans are ready to move on to work or more intensive preparation for a career. The quest begins for the American Dream. ©PhotoDisc

Graduation also has a bitter side. It is the last time to shout and laugh and embrace many friends in the comfort of protected halls and classrooms. The place and the good times pass on to others, and going back is impossible.

For Kelly Fagan, the balance was not there. The bitterness outweighed the sweet. The quest for the Dream was turning sour before it began.

A deep recession, tougher competition, and some serious management misjudgments in the 1990s left IBM with nearly $5 billion in losses. The company cut twenty-five thousand positions from its 300,000 work force worldwide. In 1993, it cut another 75,000, and our fictitious Mr. Fagan's job as a production supervisor would have been one of them (*Poughkeepsie Journal*. March 28, 1993, 2E). In middle life, his quest for the Dream was also turning sour.

The situation is disturbing, but in a market economy, it is not unusual. The U.S. economy has more than 280 million consumers and 70 million businesses interacting every day. It is not a perfect system that provides for every need and want of every person. Mistakes and misjudgments are always possible in economic situations. In reality, someone is always getting hurt. When you consider it – linking the United States in with 192 other nations' economic systems, each different in some way – it is astonishing that more people are not disillusioned about the Dream.

Everything Begins with Scarcity

Asking people to define economics reveals quite a few mumbling something about money. Money is certainly an economic concern, but by now, it is apparent there is a little more to the subject. Economics is really about people making decisions which affect each others' lives. It is really about **scarcity**. There are limits on every resource humans use to meet their needs. Productive resources include:

- Natural resources (land, water, trees, minerals…)
- Human resources (labor, talent, organizational skills…)
- Capital resources (tools, computers, machinery, financial investment...)
- Information resources (research, Internet, "information highway")

By combining these basic resources, people produce the goods and services that sustain them and make living comfortable – even pleasurable.

However, this presents a problem. It is the most basic, timeless, and universal problem that exists. Looking back at the list, it seems simple enough. In fact, most people would not see any problem at all, but they have not studied economics. There is a very large, persistent problem – *all of these resources are limited in some way*. Scarcity means there is simply not enough of any of these resources to supply all humankind's demands. There never has been enough, and there probably never will be. Scarcity is a basic fact of life.

Growing up in a developed industrial country, students rarely bump into scarcity. Or do they? Kelly Fagan did – there was not enough money to go to Springfield College. Her father did also – there were too many workers and not enough work. The company laid him off. Unusual? Take a good look around. Read the newspapers. Watch TV. Listen to conversations at the lunch counters. There have been famines, recessions, and even the Great Depression. These are major events, but ordinary people face scarcity every day. "Making ends meet" means dividing the household income to cover basic expenses (see Figure 1.1). There are difficult situations and personal tragedies. Confidence in the American Dream gets shaken every day.

On community levels, schools, roads, or police sometimes cannot be funded. Nationally, adequate defense is desirable but costly. At the same time, people want government to take care of the unemployed, the homeless, the poor, the elderly, and the terminally ill. It all cannot be done at once. Scarcity forces decisions on priorities, and trade-offs occur. Viewing things on a global scale, scarcity becomes more and more evident. Consider all the starvation in places where water and arable land are scarce.

Essentially, scarcity affects everyone in a variety of ways. It forces humankind to make the most of limited resources.

Coping with Scarcity

How can scarce resources be allocated (used) properly? That is not an easy question. Actually, it is three questions in one:

- What to produce?
- How to produce?
- Who gets what is produced?

Put two or three people together sharing some limited resources – an argument ensues. Put a few thousand people together with limited resources – a war ensues. (Throughout history, societies have warred over land, water, oil, gold?) As old and ever-present as the condition of scarcity is, coping with it is never simple.

Economics is about the search for ways to deal with scarcity. **Economics** is the study of how people cope with scarcity. If there are not enough resources to fulfill everyone's needs and wants, people have to make choices that flow from compromise and sacrifice. Satisfaction, happiness, and even survival hinge on how well people make choices about scarcity.

All choices cost something. Economists call this **opportunity cost**. Deciding to use a resource in one way costs the opportunity to use it for

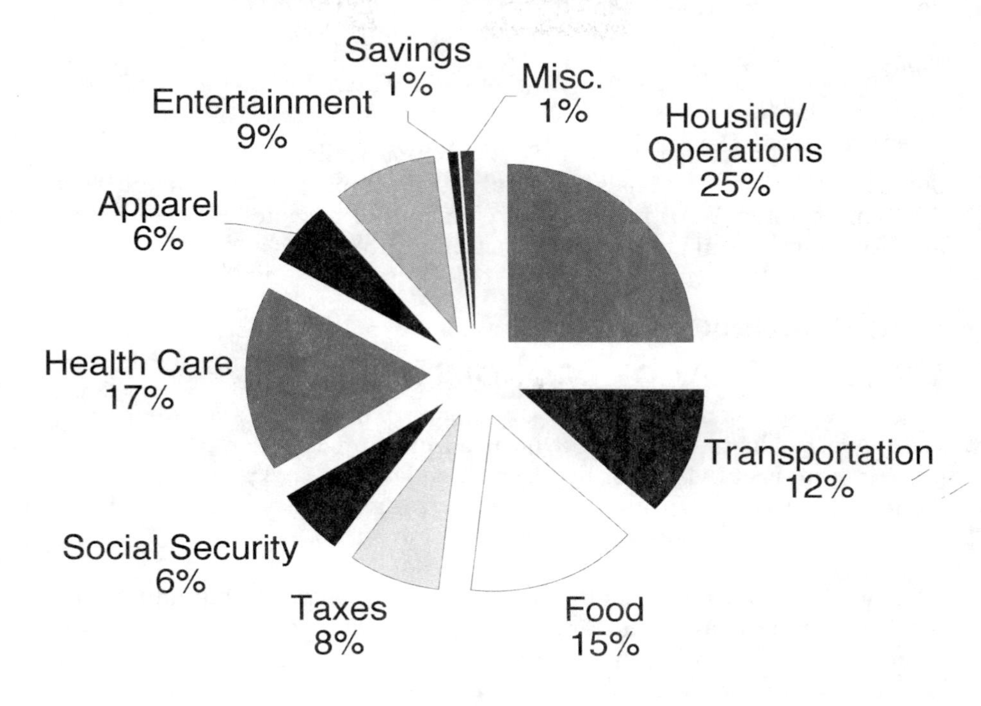

Figure 1.1 No two households divide their incomes alike, but this graph, based on the U.S. Commerce Department's 2000 U.S. Census data, allows for some general comparisons. A family budget would reflect these general expense categories. Decisions have to be made daily in every household as to how scarce resources (income) will be used to meet these demands. Keeping expense records helps with comparisons and decisions.

something else. Sometimes the opportunity is only temporarily lost – until more money, other resources, or technological alternatives become available. Sometimes the opportunity is permanently lost. Using irreplaceable minerals, nonrenewable energy, labor, time, and money to develop the Stealth Bomber may cost the society the opportunity to have a new medical research facility – perhaps forever.

Money is spent, but economics is about more than money. This choice involved lost opportunities for better health care that might have saved lives in the future. These are the trade-offs that scarcity demands.

Simple scarcity forces a choice. Consider having only $15.00 and being in the mood for a movie and a pizza. Choosing the movie is fine, but it costs \$8–\$9, and the opportunity to get a pizza is also sacrificed. There are dozens of such routine trade-off situations in daily life. Consumers, businesses, and governments constantly face the dilemma of opportunity cost. Sometimes, those costs are minimal. Sometimes, they are awesome. Do the benefits outweigh the burdens?

An economic model can clarify what opportunity cost might mean to business. Economic models allow analysis of complex situations and make decisions clearer. With models, the elements of a choice can be systematically analyzed, and opportunity cost illustrated.

AN ECONOMIC MODEL: CIRCULAR FLOW OF ECONOMIC ACTIVITY

In a simple sense, economics is about give and take between those who have products and those who need or want them. Exchanges take place in a market (wherever buyers and sellers meet). A general economic model which can help us see the pattern or market exchanges is the Circular Flow of Economic Activity (see Figure 1.2).

The flow shows a circulation of resources between individuals and economic institutions and embodies the concept of incentive. In the model, individuals offer their services and productive resources such as land and money (capital) to businesses so they can produce products in **factor markets** (where productive resources are exchanged). They receive remuneration which they spend to sustain their lives in **product markets** (where goods and services are offered). This model allows us to see the basic flow of economic energy in most modern societies on a very simple, but realistic level.

ANOTHER ECONOMIC MODEL: GETTING THE "HOLE" PICTURE

The idea of an economic model is to clarify a situation. Melissa and Jason are going to start a donut shop, "Holier Than Thou." They have limited resources – two bakers, butter, flour, sugar, ovens, etc. With all the resources, they know they can produce 1,000 donuts a day. They also know that producing only one kind of donut will soon bore customers. (Their competitor down the block offers 10 varieties.) They see that they can divide their resources and produce two basic kinds – regular and filled. By changing the toppings and fillings of the two types, they can offer a wide range of donuts.

The question is, how to divide the scarce resources. They make up a simple chart (see Figure 1.3 on page 28) which helps them see the possibilities.

c Survey your parents, teachers, or other adults to see if they think the numbers you have arrived at in parts *a* and *b* are realistic. How would some of the people you interview rearrange the budget? Find out why. Write a brief essay relating your estimates and survey findings. Discuss what this tells you about scarcity and economic decision-making.

QUESTIONS CONTINUED ON NEXT PAGE.

HOUSEHOLD EXPENSES

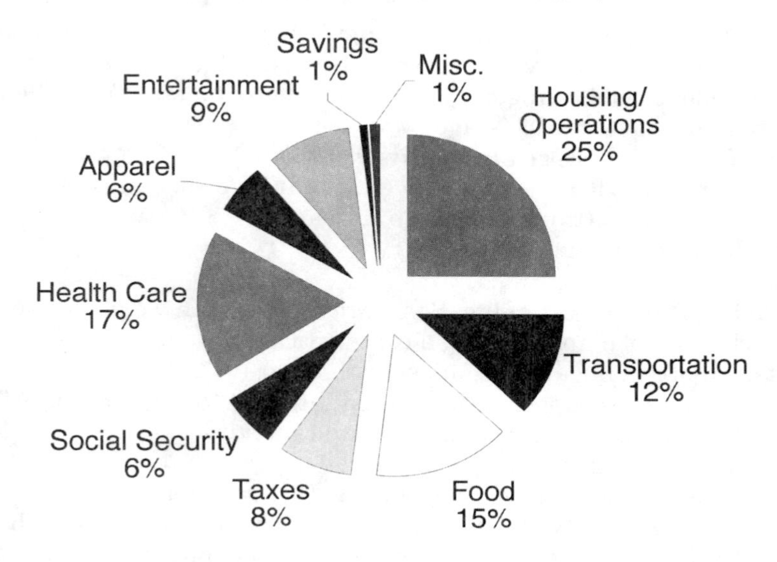

U.S. MEDIAN HOUSEHOLD INCOME (SEPT 2001)

Source: U.S. Census Bureau (1996 Dollars)

Region	Income
U.S.	**$42,168.00**
NORTHEAST	**45,106.00**
New England (ME, NH, VT, MA, RI, CT)	45,208. 00
Middle Atlantic (NY, NJ, PA)	44,777. 00
MIDWEST	**44,646. 00**
East North Central (OH, IN, IL, MI, WI)	44,389. 00
West North Central (MN, IA, MO,ND, SD, NE, KA)	40,959. 00
SOUTH	**38,410.00**
South Atlantic (DE, MD, DC, VA, WV, NC, SC, GA, FL)	37,720. 00
East South Central (KY, TN, AL, MS)	34654. 00
West South Central (AR, LA, OK, TX)	32,595. 00
WEST	**44,744.00**
Mountain (MT, ID, WY, CO, NM, AZ, UT, NV)	35,356. 00
Pacific (WA, OR, CA, AK, HI)	46,360. 00

2 A number of factors make the American Dream difficult to achieve. In later chapters, many of the following factors will be studied in detail. However, in thinking about success in life, it may be good to begin considering their impact now. Income levels vary considerably, sometimes through personal choice, sometimes through market forces, and sometimes through social and political conditions.

a How do education and type of occupation affect income?
b How do age, sex, and location affect income?
c How do taxes and inflation affect income?
d How does personal financial management affect living conditions?

3 The American Dream is neither singular nor static. Goals change at different stages in life. How would success and happiness be viewed at each of the following periods in life? Identify a specific goal a person might have at each stage:

a Young adult stage (age: early twenties)
b Early married stage (late twenties through early thirties)
c Parenthood (thirties through fifties)
d Retirement (sixties plus)

4 Trade-offs are a part of life. Some are routine, and we make them quickly (for example, buying a concert ticket for a favorite group instead of getting an oil change for the car).

a Consider the opportunity cost situation at the Holier Than Thou Donut Shop. Is it more complicated than it looks? What trade-offs have to be made?
b Consider the trade-off Kelly Fagan's Dad is asking her to make in the opening story. What will it really cost? What could the results be?
c Brainstorm some of the more serious economic choices ahead of you at different stages of your life (career, relocation, a home, family needs, retirement).

5 Recall an event in your past when you were disappointed because you were unable to get what you wanted. Describe the experience in a brief essay. Then complete the following:

a In a small group, each member should read their own essay to the group.
b By consensus, the group should select one essay to use as a skit with roles and a narrative.
c As a group, rewrite the chosen essay as a playwright would. Rewrite passages into dialogue to be spoken by the actors, and do not forget to add stage directions.
d Perform the skit for the class. A narrator should ask the class to identify the scarcity, trade-offs, and opportunity costs involved.
e The entire class should rate the best skits based on the portrayal an understanding of the concept of scarcity.

6 Brainstorm some everyday personal choices.
   a Think about trade-offs on car repairs, entertainment, clothing, personal care, and savings. Discuss their trade-offs, advantages and disadvantages, benefits and burdens, and long-term and short-term consequences.
   b Make a production possibility graph for any two of these items using the amount of money you might have available to spend on them in a week or a month.

ASSESSMENT PROJECT: THE HOUSEHOLD BUDGET

STUDENT TASK

Set up a budget for the household created in the Introduction chapter. Use the sample *Monthly Budget Information Form* (from your instructor). As a guide, you may use computer software for home budgeting, such as Home Office's *M.Y.O.B. Accounting*, Kiplinger's *Simply Money*, Intuit's *Quicken*, Andrew Tobias' *Managing Your Money*, or one of the other personal financial management computer programs. However, you must submit a Monthly Budget Information report in hard copy.

PROCEDURE

1 Transfer the starred (*) items from your *Household Financial Profile* chart used in the Introduction project. (Remember, they are annual figures, so in this project you will have to divide by 12 to get monthly figures.)

2 Fill in remaining data by looking in stores, financial newspapers and magazines, using library resources, or interviewing family and friends. Make a list of all your sources.

3 Once your Monthly Budget Information Form is completed, subtract your Total Expenses from your Net Income, and determine if you are in a surplus or deficit situation.

4 Analyze your results. Consider these questions in a written analysis: Am I living "below, within, or above my means"? If there is a surplus, how best can I utilize that surplus to become more efficient? If there is a deficit, why and how can I remedy it?

5 (This step must be audited and approved by your instructor.) Based on your analysis, you may find it necessary to make adjustments to your original *Household Financial Profile*.

Note: You can not just "play around" with the numbers, delete dependents, give yourself a big raise, or hit the lottery.
All adjustments must be "real life" possibilities. Consider the consequences carefully. You may have to cut back or drop certain expenses. You could raise your income with a second job. However, you must support in writing why you make these decisions (used in later stages of this ongoing project).

Evaluation

The criteria for the evaluation of this project are itemized in the grid (rubric) that follows. Choice of appropriate category terms (values) is the decision of the instructor. Selection of terms such as "minimal," "satisfactory," and "distinguished" can vary with each assessment.

Household Financial Profile Evaluation Rubric

(Refer to the teacher's supplement for suggestions of scoring descriptors for evaluation.)

Evaluation Item
Item a: (1) Does the work show understanding that while different socioeconomic (as well as national, ethnic, religious, racial, and gender) groups have varied perspectives, values, and diverse practices and traditions, they face the same global economic challenges?
Item b: (5) Does the work analyze problems and evaluate decisions about the economic effects caused by human, technological, and natural activities on societies and individuals?
Item c: (6) Does the work present ideas in writing (and orally) in clear, concise, and properly accepted fashion?
Item d: (7) Does the work employ a variety of information from written, graphic, and multimedia sources?
Item e: (8) Does the work show monitoring of, reflection upon, and improvement of work?
Item f: (9) Does the work show cooperative effort and respect for the rights of others to think, act, and speak differently?

ISSUE 2

THE UNITED STATES ECONOMIC SYSTEM I

Why are there different economic systems?

CAPITALISM ON QUEUE - A LINE OF OPPORTUNITY

Nedezhda left the apartment near R'azanskij Prospekt early. "Nedda," as her family called her, knew the lines were always there, but they lengthened at dawn. "Queuing up" was what they called it. The British had used it to describe the waiting on the ration lines during World War I. Some people, shut out the day before, simply camped on the street all night. Bread, toilet paper, milk – it did not matter what you needed, the queue was a way of life in Russia ever since Nedda could remember. The waiting took forever. The only things that moved with any speed on a queue were rumors.

The queue began just a block from Pavelec Station. The conversations were always the same. People carped endlessly about the Gorbachev and Yeltsin reformers' failures. They broke down the communist command system. The reformers lack of knowledge of how markets function led to the confusion and supply problems.

Deep down, people knew they had spent most of their lives waiting on lines. The old system had not produced what they needed, either. The government planners were incapable of allocating resources. Under the communists' Gosplan, the government used to regulate raw materials and tell the factory managers what products to make and how much to produce. The central planners rarely brought all the pieces together. Sixteen to twenty percent of all the resources went to military production. Supplies of everyday goods always fell short of demand.

Now, converting state farms and factories to privately owned ones created many problems. Supply shortages kept prices high. Yet, the greatest frustration was not being able to get basic items once you resigned yourself to paying the high prices. Half the population was working, the other half was queuing up.

Of course, Westerners had moved in to assist. The Canadians built a new McDonald's near Smolenskaya Square. It offered hamburgers and created a few new jobs, but who made enough to go there even once a month? Besides, the hour you spent on the Big Mac line was time taken from the potato line.

"What a life!" Nedda grumbled to no one in particular. "You work, you sleep, and queue up the rest of your life. An American can breeze into a supermarket or a mall, choose from thousands of items in an hour or so, and have the rest of her day off for fun."

"I love these lines," said a voice from behind her.

"Spare me the sarcasm," Nedda said over her shoulder. Then she turned to see if she knew the speaker. She was a little surprised. He was a young man, perhaps nineteen, with a leather jacket, expensive high tops, and was wired to a portable CD player clipped to his jeans.

"No, actually I'm making money just standing here," he said. "My name is Aram. I am from Orel in the south. I came here looking for work after I finished school. The jobs we were assigned never materialized after the reforms began."

"If you have no job, then you have no money. What are you doing on line? And by the way, where did you get all those clothes you're wearing?" Nedda asked.

"Oh, I have money, and I made it right here," Aram said. "You just said you'd rather be doing other things than standing in line. It is different for me. I'm getting paid to be here."

"I thought that it was illegal to buy things for others."

"Nope. Not anymore. No one ever enforces that rule anyway. Actually, I am an employer. I have five other people who work for me waiting on lines for others." Aram produced a business card which read, "Right on Queue. Aram Vedev, Purchasing Agent."

"You mean this is what you do for a living?"

"Yes, this is my regular line. I come here with about a dozen orders every day. Many people are willing to pay me and my associates to wait for them and deliver the goods later in the day. That gives them time for second jobs or for recreation. You know, many of my clients have started their own businesses. They could never do it if we didn't queue up for them. Say, you wouldn't want to work for me would you? I have an opening on the produce lines over on Mira Prospekt. You charge customers an additional ten percent of the price of whatever goods you buy. At the end of the day, I take ten percent of your profits."

Nedda considered it. “Everything you do depends on whether people think they can afford your service. Your success also depends on what goods are available. How can you manage not knowing how much you will make from one week to the next? Besides, when would I have time to wait in line for my needs?”

Aram’s eyes lit up. “Markets change, you change. As far as your needs, we have something special going. All my comrades ... oops, I mean associates, buy a little extra on their lines. We have a small warehouse in the Vychino District. I brought my sister up from Orel to manage it. At the end of the day, we meet there, turn in our money, get paid, and buy what we need. How’s that for on-line capitalism?”

* * * * * *the end* * * * * *

Introduction

Opportunity and success seem universal. People such as Nedda and Aram in the story lived behind what British Prime Minister Winston Churchill once dubbed, "The Iron Curtain," or what became known as the "Communist World." Like Americans – past and present – pursuing the Dream, these people have hope for a better life.

People everywhere must constantly make very similar choices about scarce human, natural, information, and capital resources. Every society must decide WHAT will be produced, HOW it will be produced, and for WHOM it will be produced. Yet, people see life from different viewpoints, have different experiences, and evolve different values. How they set priorities – and how they order them – can vividly portray those differences.

Economists use economic analysis to make choices about resources seem clear and scientific. Of course, the use of charts and graphs to quantify and clarify resources is helpful and even comforting. It is important to have facts and figures to guide decision-making. Still, it is not unusual for two people to look at the same situation, data, charts, or graphs and come to different conclusions.

Figure 2.1

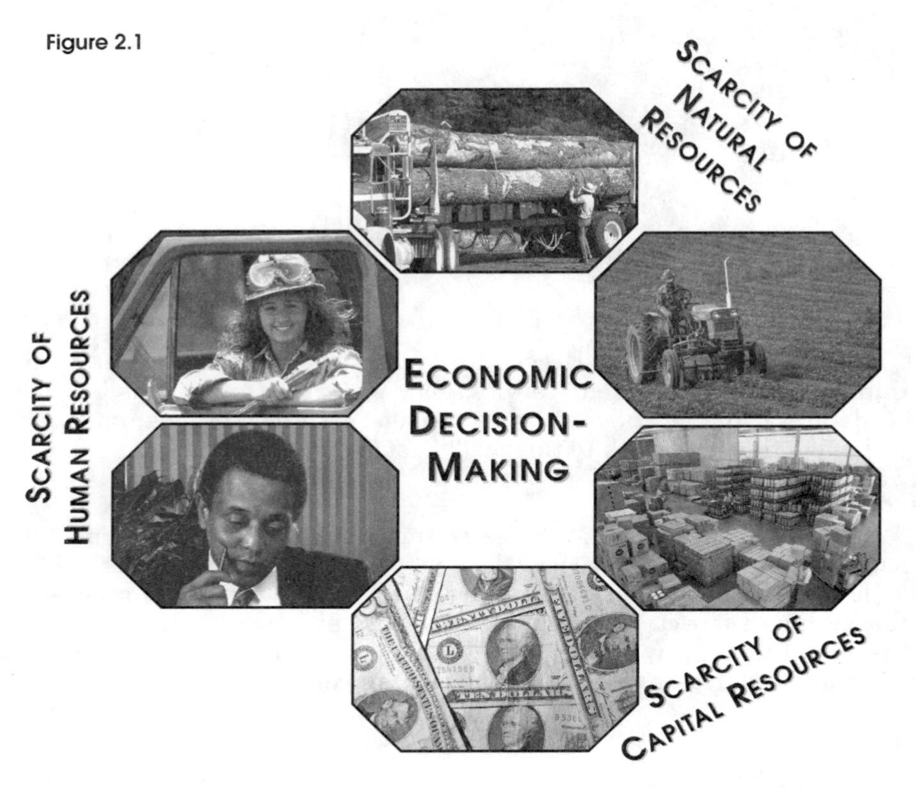

Economic Systems Reflect Experience and Culture

If individuals differ, then groups of people differ, too. Attitudes and values evolved from diverse cultural characteristics such as tradition, religion, history, conflicts, and prejudices. They alter the way people see and do things. If these characteristics change the way people think and act, they obviously influence the way people make decisions. This includes decisions about using available human, natural, and capital resources (see Figure 2.1 on page 38).

While scarcity poses the same basic questions (What to produce? How to produce it? For whom will it be produced?), societies approach economic decisions differently. One nation's view of using precious resources may not be satisfactory in the eyes of another. Naturally, disagreements occur within all nations and societies. Still, one political or cultural mindset prevails for a time as to economic priorities. In extreme cases, revolutions and civil wars can erupt if there are enough opponents of the prevalent mindset.

To a person thinking about all this, it may be easy to shrug and say something like, "Well, to each his own ..." or, "Let each society work out its own system. What's the harm?" Often in the distant past, when most societies were primitive and isolated, there was no reason for concern. However, it has been many centuries since the world was like that. Neighbors having strongly different systems run into serious conflicts over resources. There are prominent economic factors in nearly every conflict humankind has ever seen, right down through the "Cold War" of the late 20th century. If people are to achieve a better way of life, how different people answer the same basic economic questions matters very much.

Basic Systems: Tradition, Command, and Market

Most early societies evolved their economic decision-making approach from past practice, customs, and religion. Economists call this approach a **traditional system**. All economic activities merely followed patterns set earlier. Traditional systems did not respond well to change. If an emergency occurred such as a typhoon or drought, there were no guidelines for coping. Usually, village or clan elders commanded people to follow new procedures and adjustments. When the crisis faded, people went back to the old ways. Traditional systems did not allow for growth because there was no experimentation. They were unchanging. Traditional systems were labor-intensive, **subsistence level** economies. This meant that all the energy of the society was devoted to producing bare essentials without a surplus.

Labor intensive, subsistence level economies are commonly found in less developed countries (LDCs). Here, Mossi women are cultivating by hand outside of Biba village, the Toma region, Burkina Faso, Africa. ©1994 David Johnson

Not until there was contact with other societies and observations of different ways of doing things did any real change emerge. In Western society, not until the Commercial Revolution in the 14th century did the pace of change accelerate enough to break down the traditional system of feudalism. Tradition could not guide people when they arrived at situations no one had ever experienced. As the pace of change gained momentum, entirely new patterns of decision-making emerged.

Essentially, two new basic patterns emerged: command and market. They still exist as opposite ends of the economic decision-making continuum (see Figure 2.2). At one end are **command systems**. They result when governments attempt to control resources and decision-making. In 14th century Europe, as localized feudal systems disintegrated, national monarchs became strong and tried to control decision-making.

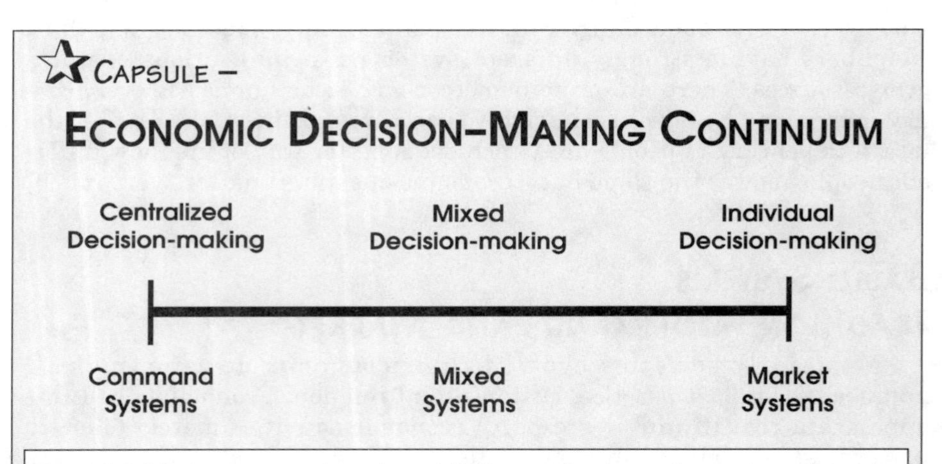

Figure 2.2 Modern economic systems fall along a simple continuum based on who is answering the three basic questions about allocation of scarce resources (WHAT to produce?, HOW to produce? For WHOM is it produced?). Most systems mix government (centralized) decision-making with individualized decision-making. Traditional systems are not shown on the continuum because there is no conscious dynamic of decision-making – traditions dictate the activities and allocations. If a storm were to disrupt the normal flow of activities in a traditional system, a village leader or council would have to consider the situation and consciously reallocate resources. At that point, tradition fails, and a command structure has temporarily replaced tradition.

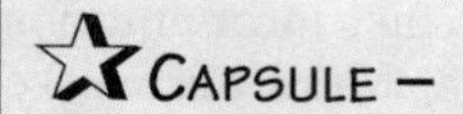

CHARACTERISTICS OF BASIC ECONOMIC SYSTEMS

Traditional (example: strong in India)

Decision-making:	*Problems:*
Custom, religion, and tradition determine many economic decisions.	Unable to deal with change; labor-intensive, subsistence level of production; no surpluses to trade and obtain development capital.

Market – "Capitalist" or "free enterprise" (example: United States)

Decision-making:	*Problems:*
Individual decision-making, consumer demand, and producer supply combine to make basic economic decisions; private property and profit are vital; minimal government involvement (laissez-faire) is desirable.	Inequality between income levels (classes); subject to unpredictable fluctuations of business activities; early capitalists tended to exploit workers to cut costs and maximize profits; some government regulation is usually needed for fairness.

Command (example: China)

Decision-making:	*Problems:*
Central planning agency makes basic economic decisions of what to make, for whom, and for how much; government controls most of the resources and means of production.	Lack of personal incentive to improve quality of life often leads to inadequate production and poor quality; strong centralization limits flexibility of decision-making.

Mixed (example: Socialism in Great Britain)

Decision-making:	*Problems:*
Government planning agency makes some of the economic decisions; market and private businesses make other decisions; government owns some of the means of production; extensive social welfare program.	The high cost of extensive government social welfare programs results in high taxes and reduces work incentives, initiative, and creativity.

However, the pace of change eventually became too fast for monarchs to systematically control merchants and tradespeople. More and more independent management of economic resources occurred. As Adam Smith showed in his famous tract, *The Wealth of Nations* (1776) (see profile on Adam Smith, page 43), the individual drive to use resources for **profit** (personal gain) is a powerful force. While complete independence from government was impossible, in isolated places such as the colonies of North America, independence of decision-making flourished, and new economic structures called **market systems** grew.

History indicates that there were powerful political and social forces at work in the 17th and 18th centuries which moved the American settlers toward independence. At the same time, a long neglect by British officials of their system of economic command allowed the American colonists to enjoy a great deal of independent economic decision-making. While many debated his thesis, historian Charles A. Beard made a strong argument in the 1930s in *Rise of American Civilization* that it was this powerful force of economic freedom that moved the Americans to revolt against the British command structure. What emerged in the United States after independence was a modified market economy. It held very dear the concept of minimizing government interference in individual decision-making, or what will later be discussed as *laissez-faire capitalism*.

Mixed Modern Systems

As humankind moved into the modern era, most economic structures became mixtures of the two pure systems. In *every* system, the activities of government alter economic decisions, usually for security and order. So, there is really no such thing as a *pure* market system.

It is clear that no government can make all the decisions for everyone about everything. Consequently, there is no such thing as a *pure* command system. This does not mean that there have never been attempts at total control. The totalitarian dictatorships of modern times (Hitler's Nazism, Mussolini's fascism, and Stalin's and Mao's communism) were economic command structures that left little decision-making to individuals. Numerous countries still have dictatorial governments in which little freedom of individual economic decision-making exists.

Tradition is still an economic force in the U.S. Evidence for this is that many retail stores depend on the weeks around Thanksgiving, Hanukkah and Christmas for 50% of annual sales. ©PhotoDisc

Of course, these positions are not "carved in stone." Economic philosophy is often a matter of individual priorities and personal beliefs. Both parties believe in the importance of all the basic economic values. Democrats want to keep the economic atmosphere free and growing, but they want it to occur in a stable and just fashion. Republicans want equal opportunity for all and want people to be secure, but they do not want to see freedom, competition, and initiative diminished by overwhelming government restrictions or regulations.

Because there is a universal desire to satisfy all the basic values, the two parties are not always clear in their stands on issues. There is usually compromise. Some Americans are confused by the parties. Many citizens choose not to join either major party because the lines are not clear. However, parties hold the power on how much command will be mixed into our basic market structure. Participating in some party activities is a way citizens have of influencing the mix.

SUMMARY

These ideas provide some notion of the nature of the American mixed market structure or capitalist economy. Every society evolves its own mixture of market, command, and traditional economic decision-making elements. It is a dynamic process. Mixtures change according to internal and external conditions. There are always conflicts inside societies over economic decisions.

There are also conflicts among societies. No society stands alone. Nations are interdependent. The actions of one nation influence others. The world recently entered a new era without the burden of the Cold War. The collapse of communism in Europe and the demise of the Soviet Union changed the setting of global economic conflict. Former communist nations searched for new systems of making economic decisions. Formerly command-dominant societies sought more personal control of individual and household decision-making. Aram's story at the beginning of this section illustrated this. While this new freedom conflicts with security-oriented traditions in many societies, it has been strengthened by global communications. People have greater knowledge of societies different from their own. They also have greater levels of education. Communication and education cause people to reexamine their systems in a new light and modify them. Expectations rise. In the long run, has the reordering of values brought the world into a period of greater understanding or greater conflict?

ASSESSMENT • QUESTIONS • APPLICATIONS

1 Think about the story of Nedda and Aram.
   a Explain what difference in attitude you see between the two?
   b Which person represents the values needed most for survival in a market economy? Explain why.

2 Think about the basic six economic values: efficiency, freedom, growth, justice, security, and stability.
   a Based on your own judgment, list these six economic values in order from most important to least.
   b Explain why you placed each value where you did as you listed them.
   c Compare your order with that of others.
   d After listening to others' ideas, would you change your priority order? If so, why and how? If not, why not?

3 If you are setting up a hypothetical household, go back to the financial role you have set up for yourself in the assessment tasks. Think about your values and how a person in your position would view public policies.
   a Where do you think your circumstances place you on the political spectrum? (1) Liberal, (2) Conservative, (3) Democrat, (4) Republican, (5) Independent. Why?
   b Make a reason list of the way you feel about key economic issues: (1) education, (2) financial security (minimum wage, unemployment compensation, pensions, medical insurance, etc.), (3) consumer protection, (4) business regulations, (5) environmental regulations, (6) transportation, (7) farm and business subsidies. Why does the order of your list reflect your values?

4 Most economies fall along the decision-making continuum as mixing some market and some command.
   a How would you classify your household on the continuum. Why?
   b How would you classify the United States on the continuum. Why?
   c Some traditions influence economic decision-making even in modern economic structures. Give several examples.

5 Like most modern economies, the United States mixes market and command approaches to decision-making.
   a Give three examples of market decision-making in the United States
   b Give three examples of command decision-making in the United States
   c Research and report on some of the difficulties encountered by Russia in trying to change its economic system in the 1990s.

6 While the United States mixes market and command, basic decision-making rests with buyers and sellers.
   a Explain the importance of self-interest in the United States market.
   b Give an example of decisions formerly made by individuals now made by government.
   c In what way does self interest conflict with a value such as economic justice?

7 Consider the broad economic value structure (at the end of this Issue) used to classify the Republican and Democratic Parties. Analyze your own ranking of the six basic economic values (question 2). Then, based on your analysis, complete the following.
   a Toward which party does your value structure lean? Explain.
   b Where does this leaning put you in relation to others in your household? Your fellow students? Your community?
   c Does your ranking of the six basic economic values influence personal economic decisions? Explain.

Assessment Project: Free Market System

Student Task

Research and present a position in a class debate. Resolved: Only a market system will allow the Russian people to survive as a nation.

Procedure

1 In order to have a balanced presentation, a lottery system should be used to assign the prospective debaters to a position (pro or con).

2 Instructor assigns 2 or 3 individuals to each pro team and con team.

3 Each team meets to brainstorm their approach, key arguments, terms and phrases to be used during the debate and determine the library research needed.

4 Members of each team research the items determined by the decision-making session (Step 3) and required for support of arguments. It is important that any point of position (argument) have factual backing. Debates are not just opinions.

5 Each team meets after the research to discuss their findings, organize the approach, outline the delivery, and develop team's debate notes and strategy.

6 On the scheduled day of the first debate, a lottery should be used to choose which teams will be opponents in the actual class debate.

7 The debate.
- 5 minutes for the oral presentation of the pro position.
- 5 minutes for the oral presentation of the con position.
- 2 minutes for rebuttal for each position.
- 5 minutes for peer evaluation.

EVALUATION

The criteria for the evaluation of this project are itemized in the grid (rubric) that follows. Choice of appropriate category terms (values) is the decision of the instructor. Selection of terms such as "minimal," "satisfactory," and "distinguished" can vary with each assessment.

Debate: Russian Economic System
Evaluation Rubric

(Refer to the teacher's supplement for suggestions of scoring descriptors for evaluation.)

Evaluation Item
Item a: (1) Does the presentation show understanding that while different socioeconomic (as well as national, ethnic, religious, racial, and gender) groups have varied perspectives, values, and diverse practices and traditions, they face the same global economic challenges?
Item b: (5) Does the presentation analyze problems and evaluate decisions about the economic effects caused by human, technological, and natural activities on societies and individuals?
Item c: (6) Does the presentation present ideas orally in clear, concise, and properly accepted fashion?
Item d: (7) Does the presentation employ a variety of information from written, graphic, and multimedia sources?
Item e: (8) Does the presentation show monitoring of reflection upon, and improvement of work?
Item f: (9) Does the presentation show cooperative work and respect for the rights of others to think, act, and speak differently?

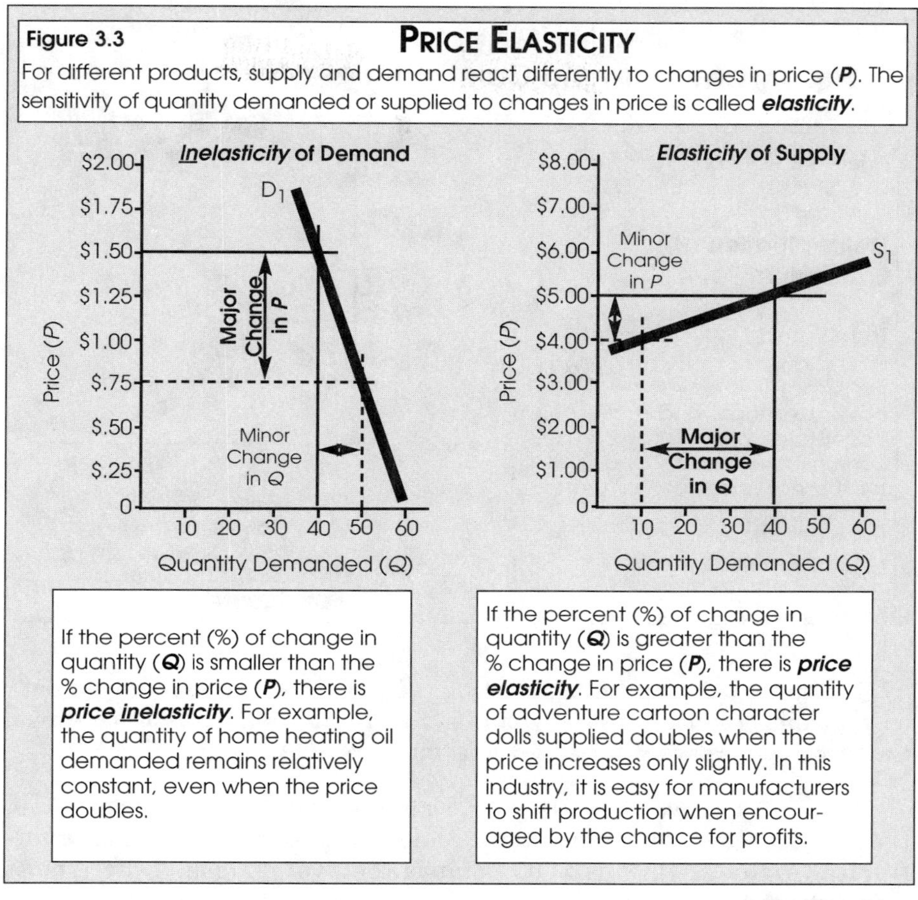

Figure 3.3 **PRICE ELASTICITY**

For different products, supply and demand react differently to changes in price (***P***). The sensitivity of quantity demanded or supplied to changes in price is called ***elasticity***.

price. With other products, consumers will react dramatically to changes in price. The same is true for suppliers. They may be limited in what they can produce. Even if some of their other costs decline, the suppliers may not be able to get more land or minerals. Economists refer to the relationship of Q to P as **elasticity**. Elasticity is the sensitivity of changes in quantity demanded (or supplied) to changes in price. See Figure 3.3 above for a discussion of price elasticity.

VISUALIZING HOW DEMAND AND SUPPLY DETERMINE PRICE

Economists create **economic models** to show the result of forces behind supply and demand. First, they create numerical lists, called **schedules**, to visualize the laws of supply and demand. When they plot the numbers from the schedule onto a graph, they produce supply and demand **curves**. For example, in Figure 3.1 on page 59, plotting the demand schedule numbers on a graph produces a demand curve [D_1]. It shows that as price drops, Carturo's customers will buy more.

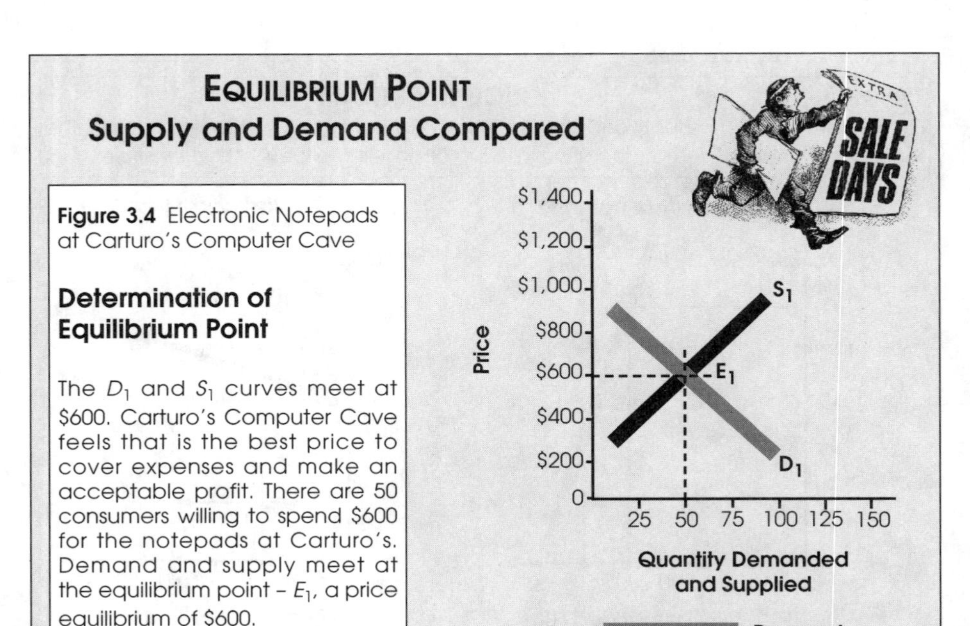

In Figure 3.2 on page 59, plotting the supply schedule numbers data on a graph produces a supply curve [S_1]. It shows that as price drops, Carturo's owners want to sell fewer computers.

Figure 3.4 above shows that by combining the two sets of data from the schedules onto one graph, the D_1 and S_1 curves intersect at an **equilibrium price** [E_1]. This $600 point is the average point where most transactions take place.

At this equilibrium point on Figure 3.4, there are enough consumers with $600 willing to buy the 50 electronic note pads Carturo's owners are willing to offer at that price. At $600, the market is in balance. Economists also call it the "market clearing price." It is the point of compromise. There are enough consumers who choose to pay $600 to clear the shelves of what Carturo's chooses to offer.

ABOVE AND BELOW THE EQUILIBRIUM MARKET PRICE

Will there be stores that sell and consumers that buy above and below the equilibrium point? Of course. Above the equilibrium, small local stores with few customers have to sell each item at higher prices to cover operating costs and still make a profit. Many consumers will grudgingly accept higher prices to save time and energy instead of going miles out of their way to a mall. A glimpse at the supply-demand graph Figure 3.4 shows that producers would love to sell twice as many at $1000 (a price $400 above the equilibrium at Carturo's). Yet, no consumers are willing or capable of buying at the high price. Essentially, producers will not sell any (or very few). This means that at $1000, producers would have a surplus of 100. Producers have to reduce the price to attract enough buyers to sell all their stock.

Another example would be the difference that people pay for items when they run into a local "convenience store" for a few items. To get a lower price, they know they would have to travel farther and wait in line longer at a major supermarket. In a remote area, consumers will usually accept higher prices per item rather than travel long distances to shopping malls or urban stores.

One historic example is Sears, Roebuck Co. It built a major business in the late 1800s by offering the convenience of mail order to the farmers of the Great Plains. To get items they needed, farmers accepted the company's extra charges for shipping. Of course, convenience is still what makes direct mail (e.g., L.L. Bean, Chadwicks, Lands' End) and telemarketing (QVC Network) popular and profitable today.

Below the equilibrium, big discount chains (e.g., Wal★Mart, *K*-Mart, Best Buy, Circuit City) will accept lower profits per item, because they can sell more on a national scale. Making money by selling more for less profit is called **volume selling**. Another look at the Figure 3.4 supply-demand graph shows that there are 75 consumers who would buy at $400 (a price $200 below the equilibrium at Carturo's). These consumers will probably go a distance to shop at discount stores.

Yet, only a few big-time suppliers are willing to accept a low profit by selling at $400. For smaller stores, it is simply not worth their while. That low a profit margin is a **disincentive**. In general, fewer products are available at that low price in the market. At $400, the Figure 3.4 graph shows 75 consumers but only 25 items available. The gap between demand and supply is 50 units. Low supply in the face of high demand means a **shortage** occurs. A consumer has to search far and wide for a "bargain price" such as $400. That margin of profit discourages the average producer. As a result, supply is low – there is a shortage.

BALANCING SUPPLY AND DEMAND

Equilibrium prices mean the market is in balance. Producers who have a surplus of products at high prices will lower their prices, but they will be discouraged. Many producers may accept lower profits for a short time, but they drop out of that market for the long run. On the other hand, producers who sell below the average price will attract consumers and sell out fast. Eventually, they realize they can raise prices and still sell out.

The market never stands still. The signals people get from the market interaction of supply and demand change their current and future behavior. A consumer who cannot afford something may accept a substitute or save for a future purchase. A producer who has to cut prices to get rid of surplus goods today may plan to cut workers' hours, wages, and benefits – or close a plant altogether.

In either case, the mix of the consumers' and producers' decisions alters the market. Millions of consumers' and producers' decisions intermix daily. The result is a complex, ever-changing market.

CHANGES IN SUPPLY AND DEMAND

Economics is about people making and changing decisions. Since they change often, the market is always changing. An equilibrium price shows the market is in balance – for the moment. Blink for a second, and it all changes.

As mentioned previously, the amount of demand can change because of changes in the forces that determine demand: income levels, consumer tastes, and availability of substitutes. For example, if people in a community have more money due to a recovery or a local factory hiring, disposable income increases. More income would expand the capacity of the people to demand a product at every price level. The left side of Figure 3.5 shows why economists say these forces cause demand to "shift right." (demand generally increases).

On the right side, Figure 3.5 also shows that the amount of supply can change because of changes in the forces that determine supply: resource costs, technology, and taxes. Suppose all coat makers cut workers' wages. With labor costing less, coat makers would be able to produce more coats for the same price as before. They can produce more of every kind of coat at every price level. Economists would say this reduction in wages caused supply to "shift right." (supply generally increases).

With all the interplay of forces shifting the amounts of supply and demand, prices inevitably change. The curve on the left of Figure 3.6 shows what happens when market demand increases (shifts right) and supply remains the same. The equilibrium price increases.

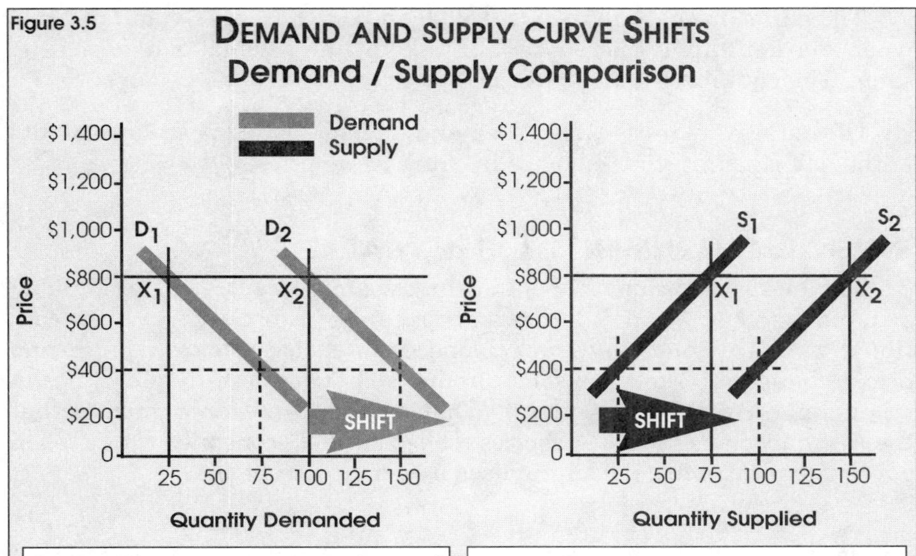

On the D_1 curve, consumers demand 25 items at $800 ($X_1$), but because of a SHIFT (D_1 to D_2) on the D_2 curve, they demand 100 at $800 ($X_2$). Note the equivalent change at the $400 price level. At every price along the D_2 curve, consumers demand more items.

On the S_1 curve, producers supply 75 items at $800 ($X_1$), but because of a SHIFT (S_1 to S_2) on the S_2 curve, they produce 150 at $800 ($X_2$). Note the equivalent change at the $400 price level. At every price along the S_2 curve, producers supply more items.

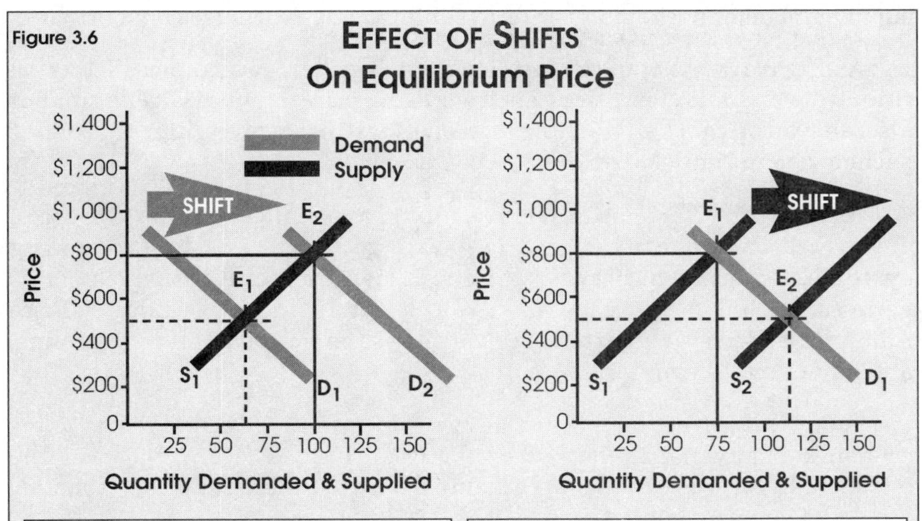

When the supply (S_1) remains constant, but the demand shifts right (increase D_1 to D_2), price increases from E_1 (62 items at $500) towards E_2 (100 items at $800). To restate, increased demand with constant supply leads to price increases.

When the demand (D_1) remains constant, but the supply shifts right (increase S_1 to S_2), price decreases from E_1 (75 items at $800) towards E_2 (112 items at $500). To restate, a constant demand with an increase in supply leads to lower prices.

The curve on the right of Figure 3.6 on page 65 shows what happens when market supply increases (shifts right) and demand remains the same. The equilibrium price drops.

Of course, the forces behind demand and supply can also cause shifts to the left, causing other changes in equilibrium price.

When Governments Enter Markets

The most basic element behind the dynamic interplay of supply and demand is *free choice*. Producers and consumers exercise free choice continually. All this blending and reblending of choices makes equilibrium prices change. Markets for some products change more frequently than others (e.g., toys, clothing styles). What is important to recognize is that the *free* interplay of peoples' choices makes market economies work. When government intrudes, it compromises free choice in the market.

Issue 7 discusses the role of government in detail. Still, it is worth noting here that when government becomes a major buyer or seller of goods, it changes supply and demand conditions in the market.

On rare occasions, government imposes price limitations. These laws or actions are sometimes necessary, as in times of national security, to alter the behavior of producers and consumers (sometimes intentionally). Of course, such government interference disrupts the natural interplay of supply and demand. Rigid floors and ceilings cause surpluses or shortages.

As Figure 3.7 shows, the market changes when government decrees a **floor** (lower limit) for prices such as farm price supports. Government also alters the market when it decrees a **ceiling** (upper limit) for prices such as urban rent controls.

In wars, these actions are necessary to force reallocations of resources. To fairly distribute artificially scarce goods, governments set up **rationing systems**. Government agencies strictly issue ration coupons which act as permission slips for purchases. In World War II, the U.S. Office of Price Administration used an extensive control system for meat, butter, gasoline, and other strategic materials.

Today, all governments are active forces in the market. They alter economic behavior in many ways. Political battles often rage over the effects of government actions. It is important to understand the economic impact of government actions.

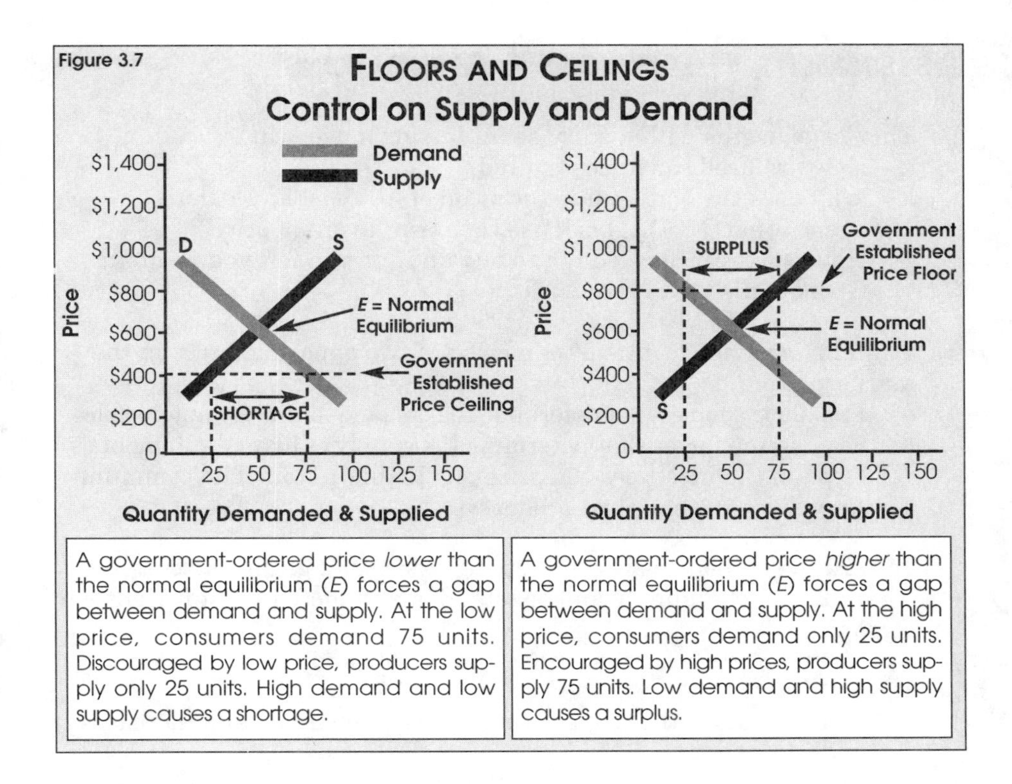

Figure 3.7 **FLOORS AND CEILINGS**
Control on Supply and Demand

A government-ordered price *lower* than the normal equilibrium (*E*) forces a gap between demand and supply. At the low price, consumers demand 75 units. Discouraged by low price, producers supply only 25 units. High demand and low supply causes a shortage.

A government-ordered price *higher* than the normal equilibrium (*E*) forces a gap between demand and supply. At the high price, consumers demand only 25 units. Encouraged by high prices, producers supply 75 units. Low demand and high supply causes a surplus.

SUMMARY:

Freedom of choice is part of the American Dream. Freedom of choice drives decision-making about supply and demand. Consumers and producers make endless choices. Those choices synthesize into market prices. Of course, in modern day America, government rules and regulations modify some choices. We all want government to safeguard fairness and to protect consumers, workers, and the environment. Yet, we sacrifice some freedom of choice for such economic security. To achieve the American Dream, each generation has to balance its freedom of choice and its need for security. Issue 7, on the role of government, explores this challenge to freedom in detail.

Finally, there is another element driving producers' choices – competition. Competition raises problems for producers, forcing short- and long-range decisions. Yet, it also keeps the market in balance to some extent. Issue 4 deals with competition in more detail.

ASSESSMENT • QUESTIONS • APPLICATIONS

1 This issue begins with a story about buying a used car.
   a How are used car prices figured?
   b Why does the National Association of Automobile Dealers Association (NADA) book use the term "average price"?
   c Have you ever decided not to buy an item you felt you wanted? Give details.

2 Equilibrium price results from a clash of two opposing forces in the marketplace.
   a Explain the forces that determine the demand for luxury automobiles.
   b Explain the forces that determine the supply of luxury automobiles.
   c Explain the messages the price of a luxury automobile communicates to consumers and producers.

3 Toward the end of this issue, there are ideas and graphs discussing what makes total supply and/or total demand increase (shift right) on a graph.
   a List the causes for the increase in supply and the increase in demand.
   b Identify some other causes for increases in supply and increases in demand.
   c Reverse the situation. Think of what causes there might be for both lines to shift left (decrease in aggregate supply and a decrease in aggregate demand).
   d Mix the situation. Suppose supply shifts right, and demand shifts left. Draw a graph to show this. What happens to the equilibrium price? Make a list of what might cause demand to decrease while supply increases.
   e Reverse the situation just discussed in *d*. Suppose demand shifts right, and supply shifts left. Draw a graph to show this. What happens to the equilibrium price? Make a list of what might cause supply to decline while demand increases.

4 Freedom of choice is important in a market, but wars sometime limit freedom of choice.
   a Why do wars create shortages of goods?
   b In World War II, the U.S. government attempted to do this through a rationing system. Research how the OPA (Office of Price Administration) operated during World War II. Defend your position as to why the WW II rationing system was a success or failure.
   c After World War II, the U.S. government removed economic regulations. Why did it take several years for supply and demand to reach equilibriums in many markets?

5 Government actions alter the market.
   a Explain how taxes change demand in the market.
   b Explain how taxes alter supply in the market.
   c Explain how a local government ceiling on rents for senior citizen apartments could change the supply of apartments.
   d Explain how a local government ceiling on rents for senior citizen apartments could alter the demand for apartments.

6 Government actions affect the market.
   a Research and report on how federal government price supports (floors) on wheat could alter the supply of wheat.
   b Research and report on how federal government price supports (floors) on wheat could alter the demand for wheat.

ASSESSMENT PROJECT: MAJOR APPLIANCE PURCHASE

STUDENT TASK

Produce a 3-5 page report on making a major household purchase. The task can be done on its own or as part of the Hypothetical Household Portfolio. In the latter form, the purchase must be reconciled with budget and goals set up in prior household assessments.

PROCEDURE

1 Assume that you wish to buy a major appliance, entertainment equipment, or piece of furniture in the $500-$1000 range.

2 Go to back issues of *Consumer Reports*, *Consumer Reports Annual Buying Guide*, *Consumers' Digest*, and *Consumer Guide*. Find out which makes and models are recommended. Make a list of them. Also, list any other product or buying recommendations of which *Consumer Reports* thinks shoppers should be aware.

3 Visit two different retail stores that sell the item(s) you want, and talk to a salesperson.

4 Tell the store personnel you must obtain the following information on an official dealer invoice (or on their store stationery): *a*) the delivered price; *b*) extra charges and taxes that add to the cost of delivering the item; and, *c*) financial arrangements for purchase, including the down payment, the A.P.R., and the total finance charge for all the years payments will be made.

5 Write a 3-5 page report which: *a*) summarizes the background information from *Consumer Reports* and other sources; *b*) discusses the two sets of dealer information (including prices); *c*) presents your analysis of the information (including from which dealer you would buy and why); and *d*) weighs the purchase against household budget and analyzes its consequences.

Evaluation

The criteria for the evaluation of this project are itemized in the grid (rubric) that follows. Choice of appropriate category terms (values) is the decision of the instructor. Selection of terms such as "minimal," "satisfactory," and "distinguished" can vary with each assessment.

Major Appliance Purchase Evaluation Rubric

(Refer to the teacher's supplement for suggestions of scoring descriptors for evaluation.)

Evaluation Item
Item a: (1) Does the report show understanding that while different socioeconomic (as well as national, ethnic, religious, racial, and gender) groups have varied perspectives, values, and diverse practices and traditions, they face the same global economic challenges?
Item b: (5) Does the report analyze problems and evaluate decisions about the economic effects caused by human, technological, and natural activities on societies and individuals?
Item c: (6) Does the report present ideas in writing (and orally) in clear, concise, and properly accepted fashion?
Item d: (7) Does the report employ a variety of information from written, graphic, and multimedia sources?
Item e: (8) Does the report show monitoring of, reflection upon, and improvement of work?
Item f: (9) Does the work show cooperative effort and respect for the rights of others to think, act, and speak differently?

ISSUE 4

THE ENTERPRISE SYSTEM

How do people organize in a market?

THE ACTION ZONE: BREAKING INTO THE MARKET

It was a little on the dark side. Just one of those dismal December days that reminds you that winters are mild but very gray around here. Turning off the main highway, I caught a glimpse of a ship's mast. Near a rock outcropping, a pool of gray water reflected the clouds overhead and castle turrets. Castle turrets? A pirate ship? I wondered if I'd driven onto the back lot of a film studio.

This was *The Action Zone*. The new entertainment center was less than a year old, but very popular. Miniature golf, bumper cars, water slide, video arcade – a kids' dream of civilization. It was all there on the edge of beautiful downtown Jacksonville, North Carolina.

My name is Alex Pierce. What brought me there was a research project for my marketing class at Coastal Carolina Community College. Professor Hodges said he wanted us to find out what motivates an entrepreneur. My younger brother said his friends "spent major bucks" at *The Action Zone* this summer. Ahead was a modern white building with neon signs. Behind the building, bulldozers, jackhammers, and back hoes were chomping at layers of shale. I parked and made for the building.

Inside, it was quiet. Yet, the place was ablaze with light and color. There were video games of every size and shape. Beyond the blinking and buzzing was a snack bar. I asked the young woman behind the counter for the owner, Bonnie Wright. After getting my name, she led me through a balloon fringed party room, and we stepped outside. She pointed towards the hard hats and Caterpillar assaulting the rock. So, I walked that direction.

"They make a racket, don't they?" A young woman in slacks and a denim jacket came toward me. "Hi, I'm Bonnie Wright. How can I help you?"

"Hello, Alex Pierce," I said, extending my hand. "I called last week to see if I could interview you for a college paper, remember?"

"Oh sure. You go to Coastal, right? Have you been here before?"

"No, and this is a surprise. Mom said when she and Dad were first married, they lived in those garden apartments across the road. There was nothing but a liquor store and a falling rock zone on this side. Now, I take the back roads to school, so I haven't been out on the main highway for a while. This place is amazing, and it looks like you're expanding, too."

"We didn't expect to put in the batting cages so soon, but business is booming!"

"Wait a second," I said. "We're on the same planet, aren't we? The big corporations are downsizing. Unemployment is way up. The economic recovery claims seem a myth around here – and you say business is great?"

"It is! We've nearly paid our initial construction loan. Look, let's back up a bit. I know this will sound strange, but it was the recession that started this business. Let me explain." We sat down on the back of a big green recycled-plastic tortoise bench. "In high school, I worked for a caterer. He did lawn weddings. After high school, my friend Beth and I started our own catering service. We did business lunches, office parties, and company picnics. It went well for about four years. When the recession began, companies started to cut their expenses. As our business dried up, we tried to figure what was happening. What would people spend their money on when they had less?"

"The basics – food, shelter, and clothing," I quipped.

Bonnie looked at me the way Professor Hodges does sometimes. "I believe I once read, 'Man does not live by bread alone.' Alex, no matter how bad it gets, people still want to feel alive. They want entertainment, but not expensive entertainment. We asked ourselves what people did for fun back in the Great Depression. The movies became popular, and amusement parks blossomed, but miniature golf was very hot!

"There are plenty of theaters here, but no small amusement parks. About 300 miles away, there are a few gigantic ones. But, you have to go up to Virginia or way down to Georgia. Still, that makes for half a day's ride.

"Besides, spending the day at the big parks is very expensive. From here, you spend hours traveling and bucking the crowds. You wait on lines for rides, food, and even bathrooms. Then comes the long ride home with cranky kids. It takes the fun out of the whole thing. Actually, these pleasure outings can be a pretty grueling experience for a family."

"Got it," I said. "You can offer excitement without the long ride and the lines."

"Now you've really got it, Sherlock," she laughed. "Everyone likes miniature golf. We planned fountains, waterfalls, ships, and haunted houses. It is really fun. The bumper boat ride over there is another winner. Next spring, we will have the batting cages ready. What better place for a kid's birthday party? This room holds almost sixty people. Even in winter, we offer packages in the video arcade. It is very busy. In fact, we have a party this afternoon."

"Wow! How did you ever figure all this out? That is what Professor Hodges really wants us to find out. How does a business person decide to supply a service?"

"Buy me a hot dog?" Bonnie questioned. I nodded as she grabbed my arm and started walking. Without missing a beat, she continued, "Well, once Beth and I had the idea, we hit the library and found some trade organizations. They gave us information on trade shows where we talked to owners and equipment suppliers. We went on trips to the shore and the mountains. We talked to people who ran small entertainment centers. Research is part of the game.

"While we collected facts, I started talking to my Dad. He has been in business for himself all his life. I guess that is where I get my independent streak. He had this piece of land, or should I say, rock?"

That reminded me that it felt good to get off that tortoise shell. "How did you know the demand was there?"

"What really sold us on the location was that we contracted for a report from a marketing consultant. A friend of Dad's at the Chamber of Commerce suggested it. It was expensive, but it said there were 40,000 people within a 5-mile radius. It also said the average age of those people was 38. That means teens, young adults, young couples, and little kids. That's an awful lot of young people in their earning years. The market was there... Want mustard on yours?"

"Thanks, and heap on the relish." I said, as I handed over a five-dollar bill. "Where did you get the money to get it going?"

"Family, Dad liked the idea from the start. He said he would give us part of the money for a share of the profits. He wanted to be a silent partner. Beth's Aunt Carolyn agreed to a similar arrangement. We run the business itself... Napkin? Even in the recession, our local bank agreed to take a chance and give us the rest. Of course, we had to sell them on the idea. Dad and Aunt Carolyn co-signed and put up their houses as collateral. Still, we got the money. Four million other little decisions, contracts, leases, and here we are!" She looked at my shirt. "Oops."

I looked down. "I guess I need that napkin. I'd better get this interview back on track. "Professor Hodges says enthusiasm is the entrepreneur's main weapon. You are certainly well armed, but it doesn't sound all that simple."

"It's not simple at all," Bonnie said. "You lose sleep, your stomach churns, and you always wonder if you're making the right moves."

"I know the demand is here, but…" I said.

Bonnie raised an eyebrow. "But what?" she asked, dabbing mustard from her upper lip.

"Professor Hodges says a business person has to be satisfied with the profit margin to want to keep supplying the demand."

"Like any business, we have to cover our utilities, mortgage, business loans, supplies, and payroll for thirty workers. After all that, we are making a 5% profit."

"That doesn't sound like very much." Although what I was really thinking was they must be getting a much bigger profit on these lousy hot dogs. Of course, I didn't say it out loud.

"Some people might not be happy. Still, we see potential. Next week, we start looking for land down in Holly Ridge for *The Action Zone 2*. We are taking the profits and reinvesting. What does that tell you? Want another dog?"

On my drive home, I began to understand that a good plan is not enough to be a successful entrepreneur. It takes energy, persistence, and stick-to-it-ness. She made a profit on me, didn't she!

***** *the end* *****

Introduction

Owning a business is part of the American Dream. It has the values of independence and self-reliance embedded in it. The "rags-to-riches" stories made famous by 19th century writers such as **Horatio Alger** permeate our culture. Alger made a fortune publishing tales about good, hard-working souls. He elevated the idea that anyone with a dream and determination can succeed to American folklore. Of course, there is a little more to it than that. Yet, the idea has strong allure.

Producers such as Bonnie and Beth form a partnership to go into business. Bonnie and Beth supply entertainment at *The Action Zone*. Consumers respond because the entertainment is offered at a lower price than distant, big amusement parks. The last chapter showed acceptable prices keep the whole market in equilibrium. Understanding how producers arrive at those prices is important in learning economics. So is understanding how and why people go into business. Organizing and making economic decisions is critical in a market economy. Successful merchants, manufacturers, and service businesses do not emerge randomly. Owners build them very carefully, day by day.

Basic Types of Business Organizations

There are three basic ways to organize a business: proprietorships, partnerships, and corporations (see Figure 4.1 on page 77). The key is who owns them. Basic business operations (e.g., production, marketing, finance, personnel) may be delegated to salaried managers (who are employees). Still, an owner makes the life and death decisions. All of the responsibility remains in the hands of the owner(s).

Proprietorships

72% of all businesses. Proprietorships are unincorporated businesses owned by a single person. They are almost always small businesses: shops, groceries, restaurants, farms, gas stations. It should be noted that lawyers today advise some form of incorporation for even the smallest businesses because of the legal protection corporations afford. (Incorporation laws vary from state to state.) These incorporated businesses may still be run by one or two owners. (For purpose of discussion here, we classify businesses by *who* is making the day-to-day decisions and earns the profits.)

Business Organization

Above: With many large corporations downsizing, laid-off workers are turning in record numbers to "home businesses," often as partnerships among a few former colleagues from the same firm. High tech telephone communications and powerful personal computers have reduced the need for the traditional office.

Left: Although the number of small family farms is decreasing while large corporate farms increase in size and number, there are still 2.4 million American farms. About 86% are proprietorships, 10% partnerships, and 4% corporations.

Right: The corporate structure allows for sizable national and international operations such as this meat packing firm. ©PhotoDisc

Figure 4.1

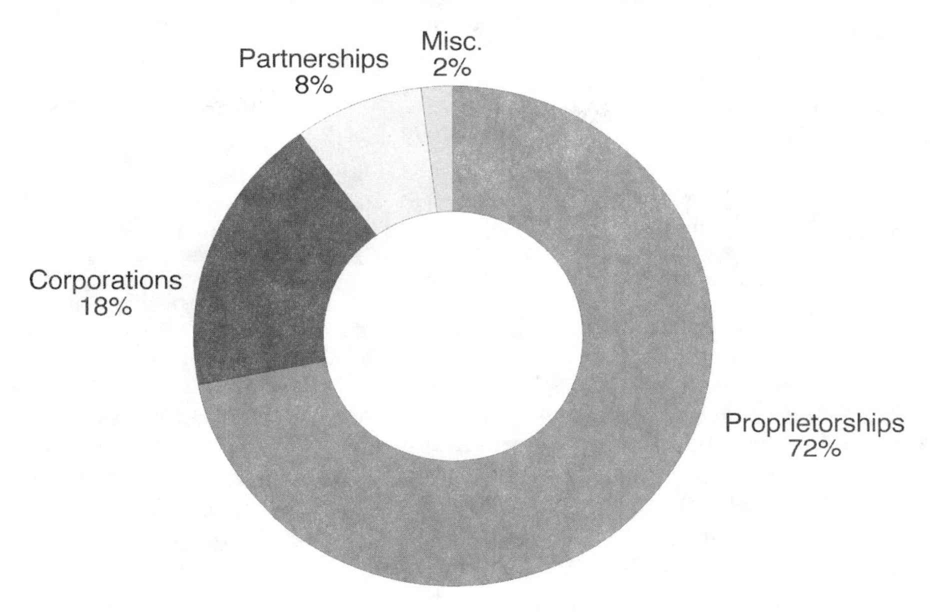

Source: *Statistical Abstract of the United States* 1992,U.S. Department of Commerce

Most U.S. businesses are small proprietorships (shops, family owned and operated stores, and skilled trades such as plumbers and electricians). Corporations are fewer in number. Still, because of their sheer size and massive advertising, corporations are better known and draw in more than 90% of sales in the nation.

PARTNERSHIPS

8% of all businesses. Partnerships are unincorporated businesses owned by two or more people. There is no limit on the number of partners. Usually they are small in size, having only two or three individuals involved. Law firms and accounting offices commonly organize as partnerships. Depending on the size, the day-to-day operation may be divided up among the partners.

Alex Pierce discovered *The Action Zone* is a partnership. Bonnie Wright and friend Beth are **general partners**. They share the operating responsibilities. Bonnie's father and Beth's aunt are **limited partners** since they do not actively run the business but share the profits.

Figure 4.2

TOP TEN U.S. CORPORATIONS (REVENUE)

Source: *World Almanac*, 2001

Company	Revenue (in millions)	Industry
Exxon-Mobil	$210,392	petroleum
Wal☆Mart Stores	$192,295	retailing
General Motors	$194,600	automobiles
Ford	$180,600	automobiles
General Electric	$129,800	electronics
Citigroup	$111,800	finance
IBM	$ 88,396	computers
AT&T	$ 65,891	communications
Verizon	$ 64,707	communications
Philip Morris	$ 63,276	food and tobacco

CORPORATIONS

18% of all businesses. A corporation has thousands (or even millions) of owners. In a **closed corporation**, ownership shares (stocks) are limited and privately held. In a large **public corporation**, stocks can be sold to the public through stock markets. A board of directors, acting as the elected representatives of the stockholders, sets general policy. The board hires a **CEO** (**Chief Executive Officer**) who assembles a management staff and conducts daily operations.

There are 3 million corporations in the United States. Most are small with only a few stockholders. Only about 2,000 are large corporations with billion dollar assets such as those that

The Dow Jones Industrial average includes 30 of the nation's largest corporate stocks. In 2000, it had a high of 11,722.98 and a low of 876.03

Figure 4.3

Direct and Indirect Stock Ownership by U.S. Families

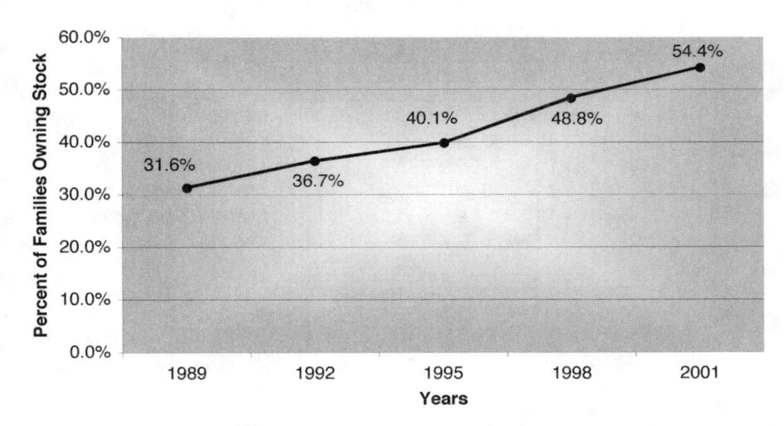

Stock investment patterns reflect general confidence in the growth of the Gross Domestic Product (GDP, aggregate performance). In general, long-term investors get better yields on stocks than most other types of investments.

annually make the *Forbes 1000* or *Fortune 500* lists (see Figure 4.2). They make up less than 10% of all business organizations. These large corporations generate 90% of the sales.

A key element is legal protection for owners. *A corporation exists as an individual in the eyes of the law.* It is responsible for debts and other legal problems. If the business fails, the corporation **liquidates** (sells) its assets. It pays its creditors and bond holders. Stockholders are *not liable* for any other unpaid debts. Stockholders lose only the value of their investment. Unlike proprietors and partners, their personal property is not liable.

Diminished legal risk makes stock investment attractive to people. Proprietorships and partnerships rest on risking the limited personal capital (e.g., savings, loans, gifts) and property. Corporations offer an investor small risk. They can raise millions by offering thousands of inexpensive shares for sale. Shareholders earn income **dividends** (portions of the profits) for their investment, but can lose only the value of their shares.

The shareholder can sell the stocks on the market. If the company is doing well, the value of the stocks **appreciates** (rises). Selling appreciated stocks returns a profit over the original purchase. Of course, corporations do fail, and stocks do **depreciate**. Bankruptcy can make stocks worthless. An investor has to shop carefully, read financial news, and watch stock listings to protect the investment. Figure 4.3 shows that careful investment, over long periods, yields the most impressive gains – a fact that has helped build strong public support for corporate stock investment.

Tradeoffs With Different Business Organizations

Figure 4.4 — and the Advantages and Disadvantages of Each

Type	Advantages	Disadvantages
Proprietorship	• owner close to customers and workers • owner receives all profits • one manager's point of view	• owner assumes all risks • limited operating capital • owner bears total responsibility for management
Partnership	• more capital can be raised • risks are shared • more management ideas	• profits must be shared • unlimited liability for owners • dissolves if one partner leaves
Corporation	• increased capital through sale of stocks • losses limited to investment • increased number of managers • can transfer ownership • larger growth possibilities • research facilities possible • risks shared	• state and federally regulated • subject to corporate taxes • management removed from customers and workers

Advantages and Disadvantages of Ownership

The table in Figure 4.4 gives an overview of the advantages and disadvantages of the different types of businesses. Owners' goals and dreams move them toward the different types. Ease of getting capital, financial and legal liabilities, and psychic rewards define the choice.

Financial and Legal Liability

Proprietors usually want to support themselves and their families and be their own boss. If they run into financial or legal trouble, lawsuits could not only destroy the business, but their personal money and property can be lost, too. Partners also stand to lose everything when trouble looms. Partners share the ownership, but the liability for each partner is the same as if they were proprietors. Only in a corporation is the personal wealth and property of owners separated from that of the business, and there are even exceptions to that generalization.

Capital Formation

When it comes to getting money to start or expand a business, there are great differences among the business types. Proprietors and partners stake their personal wealth and property to get capital. A proprietor in need of operating or expansion funds stands alone before the banker. In a partnership, the banks can look at the creditworthiness and collateral of several individuals. Their collective credit and property give them a greater chance for funding. Yet, partners are still limited to their personal ability to raise funds.

Capital formation is one of the big advantages for corporations. They get start-up funds from many stockholders investing small amounts of money. There are regulations on how much stock can be put on the market, but corporations can get capital two other ways: borrowing and bonds. Unlike proprietors, large corporations are not at the mercy of local banks. They can put together loan packages from many sources, perhaps nationwide. Also, corporations can sell bonds on the market. Individuals or institutions (pension funds, insurance companies) buy these **corporate bonds**. Bondholders lend corporations money at interest for a short period. They become creditors of the corporation. If the corporation fails, bondholders must be legally paid just like banks. Stockholders in a bankrupt corporation suffer the loss of the value of their investment, but not the bondholders.

Psychological Rewards

Beyond financial gain, there is a powerful attraction in the emotional compensation an owner-operator receives. For many, owning a business is part of the American Dream. The independence and self-reliance attract them. Some individuals thrive on the constant challenge of "making it" alone. They enjoy being free to make their own decisions. They find satisfaction building a business. They enjoy being in control of their destiny. These are **psychological rewards**.

Psychological rewards (also called psychic rewards) obviously motivate sole proprietors. In partnerships, they are less important. Individuals form partnerships to grow, take advantage of broader capital formation, or to diminish the work load. Yet, partners give up some control and independence in the process.

Individuals who own shares of corporations receive few, if any, psychic rewards. Unless they are on the board of directors, they make no decisions. Stockholders receive financial rewards (dividends), but no noticeable psychic ones.

Franchises

Among the fastest growing businesses in today's market are franchises (see Figure 4.5 on page 82). They are an interesting mix of the three basic types. By definition, a franchise is a license to conduct a business under another person's name. A large franchising corporation

AVON

Holiday Inn

Figure 4.5

Top U.S. Franchisers
(based on number of units in operation, 2000)

Company	Product
Subway	submarine sandwiches
McDonald's	hamburgers
7-Eleven	convenience store
Burger King	hamburgers
Taco Bell	mexican food
Coverall Cleaning Concepts	commercial cleaning
KFC	chicken
Jackson Hewett	tax service
Pizza Hut	pizza
Jani-King	commercial cleaning
Dunkin Donuts	doughnuts
Jazzercise	fitness center
Jiffy Lube	auto oil-change service
GNC Franchising	vitamins/nutrition supplement

(e.g., fast food giants McDonald's, Subway, Burger King) grants a franchisee permission to market its products. A franchisee could be a sole proprietor, a group of partners, or another corporation. Franchise sizes vary. One might be a large undertaking such as a group of Holiday Inns; another might be a small door-to-door operation such as Avon cosmetics.

The franchisee runs the business and gets many of the psychic rewards and most of the profits. Yet, there is a difference. The franchisee is not independent. Psychological rewards are limited. The franchise agreement is a contract to do things the franchisor's way. It sets very definite rules on operations. In many cases, no other products can be offered except the franchisor's. The franchisor requires certain equipment, building designs, uniforms, supplies, operating hours, promotions, and periodic inspections. On the other hand, the franchisee gets nationally known brands, national advertising, mortgages, training, and legal advice. Economists estimate that nearly one half of all business starts are now through national franchises.

Growth: Mergers and Combinations

No matter which form of business, growth is a common goal. Proprietors usually wish to increase their profits by offering new products or services. Growth may mean hiring new employees, moving to a bigger shop, or staying open later. Still, proprietors bump into limits. There is just so much one owner/operator can do. Also, there is a limit on a single owner's ability to raise capital.

Horizontal Combination

The horizontal merger is the most logical type. One corporation combines with, or takes over, another in the same industry.

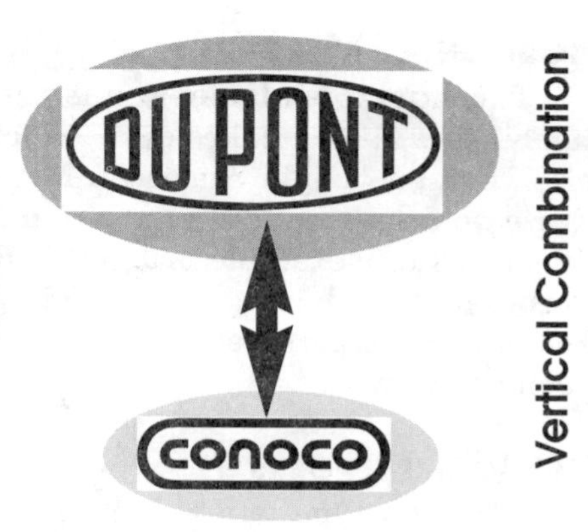

A second way to combine is through a vertical merger. In this case, a corporation may buy another in a related phase of its business.

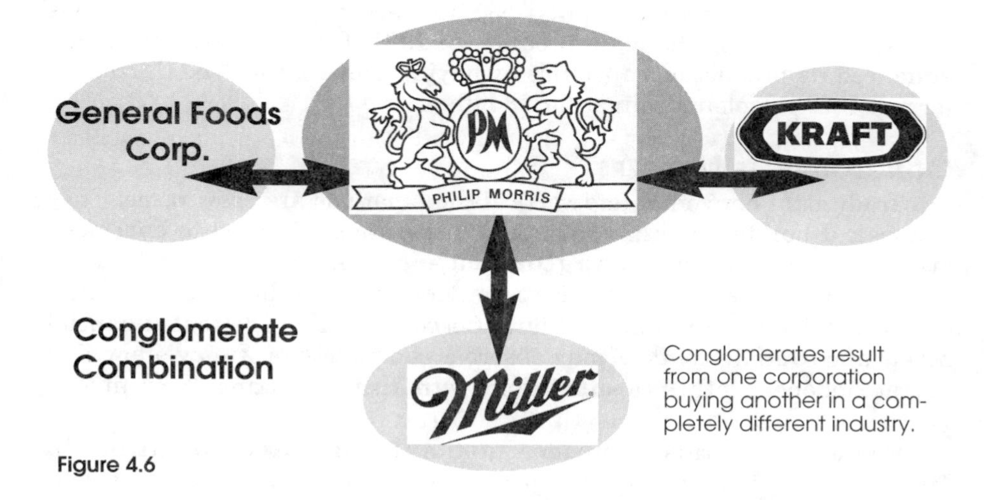

Conglomerates result from one corporation buying another in a completely different industry.

Figure 4.6

People form partnerships to overcome some of these limits. Additional owners mean management tasks can be shared, or additional sites can be opened. Partnership also means expanded capacity to form capital. Even so, there are limits on the capacities of partners, too.

Corporations have the greatest capacity to grow. Their potential to raise capital is clear. They can grow by merging with other corporations. A **merger** takes place when one company acquires (buys) another or when two join to form a new company. Mergers enable corporations to expand from local, to regional, to state, national, or even international scope. There are several types of mergers or combinations. Economists classify mergers as horizontal, vertical, and conglomerate (see Figure 4.6).

Horizontal Mergers

The **horizontal merger** is the most logical type: one corporation combines with – or takes over – another in the *same* industry. For example, Chrysler bought American Motors in the early 1980s. The Jeep and Eagle vehicle lines and production facilities were added to the Chrysler line. A historic example is John D. Rockefeller building the Standard Oil Corporation by buying up competing oil refining companies. These were horizontal mergers because the companies were all engaged in similar business activities.

Vertical Mergers

A second type is a **vertical merger**: in which a corporation buys another in a *related phase* of its business. This saves money and adds to productivity. In the 19th century, Andrew Carnegie built the Carnegie Steel Corporation by buying mines (ore supplies) and railroads (cut costs of shipping ore to his steel mills). Vertical mergers combine operations that go into making the main product. In 1981, DuPont (petrochemicals) enhanced its production capacities by buying Conoco, then the thirteenth largest U.S. petroleum refiner for $8 billion.

Conglomerate Mergers

Traditional horizontal and vertical combinations are easy to see. They are logical building blocks that allow corporations to grow to enormous size. The third type, a **conglomerate merger**, is not as logical. Conglomerates result from one corporation buying another in a *completely different* industry. *Corporation X* buys *Corporation Y* to add to its financial assets and overall profits. *X* may absorb *Y* completely, or *X* may allow *Y* to operate independently as a **subsidiary** with *X* simply taking *Y's* profits.

Companies do this to broaden profits through **diversification**. In 1989, when *TIME* Inc. saw its growth in publications slowing, it ventured into another field. It diversified by buying motion picture giant Warner Communications for $14 billion. *TIME*-Warner became a new conglomerate.

Diversification helps a corporation insulate itself from the ups and downs of its main market. By the 1980s, U.S. tobacco sales were in serious decline. In 1986, tobacco giant Philip Morris spent $5 billion to acquire General Foods. In 1989, PM spent $13 billion to acquire Kraft Foods. In between, it bought Miller Brewing Co. Through conglomerate mergers, PM quickly became one of the largest tobacco, food, and beverage corporations in the world.

Critics charge that conglomerate mergers do little to help the economy grow. Borrowing for mergers adds to the purchasing corporation's debt. It uses scarce capital that could have been used to improve its productivity. Conglomerate mergers may add to the profits of a purchasing corporation, but they do not expand production or add jobs. In fact, purchasing companies commonly downsize their new subsidiaries.

Competing in Different Market Structures

The mechanics of supply and demand were studied in Issue 3. Supply and demand do make markets run, but market structures vary. The nature of products, ease of entry, and the number of firms in a particular market alter the behavior of competitors. For example, Bonnie's *The Action Zone* offers consumers an alternative amusement to a long ride to big parks. PepsiCo drives to beat Coca-Cola. Ford strives for quality. Big or small, businesses compete with others. There are few exceptions to this fact of economic life. To survive and grow, owner/managers must know their market and be aware of competitor's moves.

Competition takes many forms. Price is the first form that comes to mind. Producers seek ways to offer a product at a lower price to lure customers away from other firms. Still, there are other forms of competition. **Nonprice competition** includes promotions, packaging, sponsorships, quality, and service.

Figure 4.7 on page 87 illustrates the four basic market structures. Ranging from most competitive to least competitive, they are: perfect competition, imperfect competition, oligopoly, and monopoly.

Perfect Competition

Perfect Competition is the simple supply and demand models studied earlier in Issue 3. The products are identical and easy to produce. Raw agricultural products such as wheat, corn, and oats are examples. There are many sellers and buyers. The interaction of supply and demand sets the price. Price competition is so intense that there is little nonprice competition (e.g., advertising, location, contests). Sellers cannot afford it.

Although *Perfect Competition* does not really exist in a "non-perfect" economy, the concept of perfect competition can be demonstrated in the farmer's market or the thousands and thousands of small roadside produce stands where competition is high, product is abundant and similar from stand to stand, and where overhead is low, so are the profits. ©PhotoDisc

Imperfect Competition

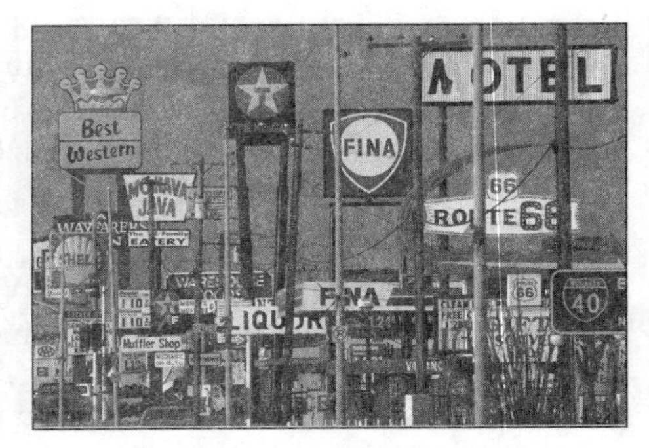

Commonly, *Imperfect Competition* is illustrated in the business practices that exist among small entrepreneurial shops. However, this market structure is easily observed at the thousands of "strips" that guard the entrances and exits of the interstate highway system, in suburban mini-malls, and at the outer limits of cities and towns all over America. ©PhotoDisc

Imperfect Competition is also close to the basic supply and demand model. The products are very similar and relatively easy to produce. Firms are often small operations such as hair cutting, dry cleaning, restaurants, and clothing factories. There are many sellers and buyers in this market structure. For the most part, interaction of supply and demand sets the price. Price competition through sales is intense, but there is some nonprice competition. This includes advertising, contests, coupons, convenient location and hours, free parking, etc. Competitors spend time and energy making their business distinct from others.

(Note: Economists also refer to this structure as "monopolistic competition." The term is a bit confusing for students. It refers to the fact that there is *one basic product* in this market, but the competition among many suppliers is intense.)

Bonnie and partners' *The Action Zone* mini amusement complex fits into this type of market. She competes not only with other small entertainment facilities, but also with big, far off complexes. In addition, she must position herself as an alternative to other entertainment businesses such as movies.

Oligopoly

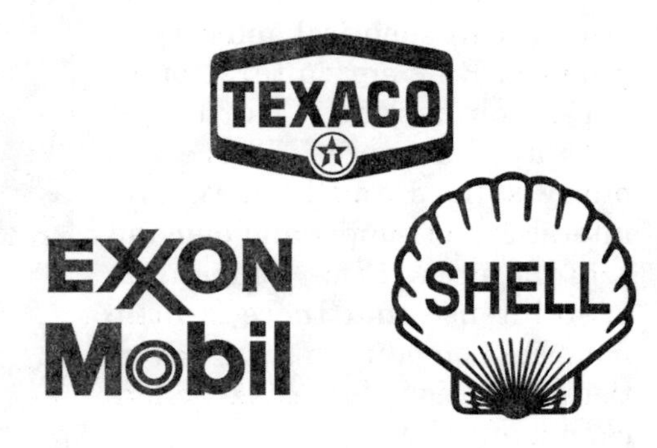

Oligopoly is where the basic market model radically changes. In this market structure, there are few sellers, the products are similar, but production is complex, large-scale, and expensive. This market includes athletic shoes, autos, beers, breakfast cereals, chemicals, soft drinks, electric appliances, and petroleum refining. These expensive, highly mechanized, high tech industries, are not easy to enter. Therefore, the number of suppliers is very limited. While supply and

Figure 4.7

TYPES OF MARKET STRUCTURES

Perfect Competition

- many small sellers / many buyers
- identical products little nonprice competition
- market sets prices

Imperfect Competition

- many small sellers / many buyers
- Slightly different products
- Strong nonprice competition
- sellers have some control of prices

Oligopoly

- few large and some small sellers / many buyers
- Slightly different products
- strong nonprice competition
- sellers have some control of prices

Monopoly

- single seller / many buyers
- unique products
- no substitutes
- no competition;
- seller sets prices

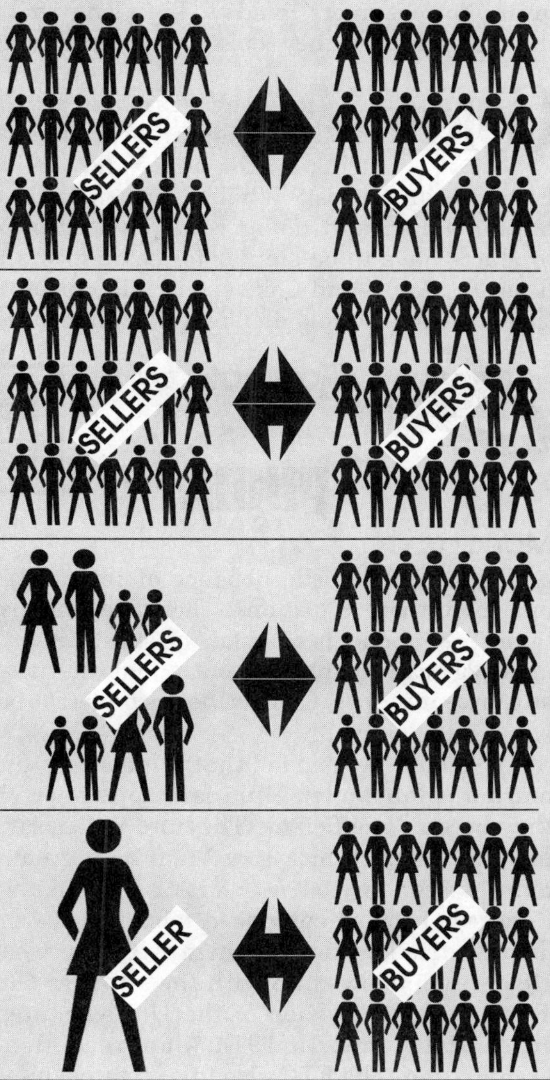

demand do influence the price, sellers are so few and so big, they have the power to alter supply.

Today's oligopoly markets are like "shared monopolies." Producers are not big enough to dictate prices, but they control a substantial percent of sales. They keep within range of their competitors with products so that price competition is often minimal. No one wants to "break out of the pack" for fear a price war would ruin them. Oligopolists usually solidify their "market share turf" and go along with the other oligopolies.

Yet, oligopolists employ fierce and expensive non-price competition to protect their market shares. Their advertising aims at creating brand name loyalty in consumers' minds to keep long-time customers. Ads do not always mention price, but they tout quality, performance, image, and comparisons.

Coke

Does the brand loyalty approach work? Announce loudly in a group of friends that one manufacturer's cola drink is "the best," and the arguments can last for hours. Friends can be lost. Whole families pride themselves on buying Pepsi and never consider any other brand. The products have to be similar for competitors to stay in business. Yet, Pepsi and Coke spend millions on ads and promotions to convince cola drinkers that their product has no equal.

Monopoly

Monopoly is the absence of competition. In a pure (unregulated) monopoly, there is just one seller. The lone firm can act as an economic dictator. The product is singular (no substitutes), and many people need it. The monopoly can completely control quantity available (supply). It can charge any price it wishes. Competition is undercut before it can get on its feet.

It should be obvious that a monopoly undermines the basis of a free market. Monopolies eliminate consumer choice. Without competition, they become inefficient. They are not motivated to grow or improve the product. Adam Smith saw them as a great evil capable of destroying a market economy (*Wealth of Nations*, 1776). In the Progressive Era, the U.S. Congress became convinced monopolies were ruinous to economic freedom. It tried to control them with the weak ***Sherman Antitrust Act*** (1890) and followed up with the stronger ***Clayton Antitrust Act*** (1914). The Antitrust Division of the United States Justice Department prosecutes violations. In 1914, Congress also set up the Federal Trade Commission. The FTC also investigates unfair competition.

Yet, the government does allow some monopolies. Local phone service, cable TV, and electric companies are examples. Their services are critical. Common sense shows hundreds of utility companies constantly stringing and unstringing wires would be dangerous and chaotic. Therefore, local, state, and federal agencies license and control these monopolies. They must ask permission from government agencies (public service commissions) to raise rates or alter production (see Issue 7 for details on antitrust suits).

SUMMARY

Since their inceptions, public utilities such as electric, telephone, and cable TV have been government regulated *monopolies*. With the breakup of AT&T, regulated competition in the utilities began. ©PhotoDisc

The modern market economy is a complex place. Owning and operating a business is a challenge. A business owner has to set goals and select a type of organization to achieve them. They have to understand what kind of market structure they enter, and how to compete in it. Bonnie Wright and partners launched *The Action Zone* in an imperfect competition market structure. Consumers can choose from many other entertainment facilities, small and large. Bonnie and Beth put ads in the paper, circulated coupons, and ran promotions. They selected a high traffic area. Still, they needed a colorful, lighted sign and the mansions, ships, and castles of their miniature golf course to beckon consumers from the road.

Demand patterns change. Competitors come up with new ways to lure customers away. Organizing a business and competing in an ever changing market is no easy way to make a living. Yet, it is an exciting and essential part of the American Dream. If people did not venture into business as a natural part of the American Dream, from where would products and jobs come?

The high tech industries such as computer hardware and software are dominated by a few companies. For many years IBM "owned" the computer industry. When PCs began replacing the mainframes, Apple and others increased competition. In 1995, 70+% of all PCs worldwide were running on an operating system and software developed by Microsoft. While attempting to contain the growth of this giant through an antitrust suit, *U.S. of America v. Microsoft Corporation*, Judge Sporkin said in reference to the proposed $1.5 billion purchase of financial giant Intuit, makers of *Quicken* (accounting software), "it is a potential threat to the nation's economic well-being." "(If he allowed it) the message will be that Microsoft is so powerful that neither the market nor the Government is capable of dealing with all its monopolistic practices." ©PhotoDisc

ASSESSMENT • QUESTIONS • APPLICATIONS

1 In the opening story, college student Alex Pierce interviewed Bonnie Wright for a report on entrepreneurs.
   a List some main points you think Alex would include in his report.
   b What other ideas about entrepreneurs would you advise Alex to add to his report?
   c Why would Professor Hodges assign a report such as this to someone beginning a study of economics?

2 The opening story's dialogue between Alex Pierce and Bonnie Wright demonstrates that all businesses must engage in several activities. They include production, marketing, finance, and personnel management.
   a Using the four categories of business activities, list examples of Bonnie performing these functions.
   b Besides the examples you found in the story, what are some other activities Bonnie would have to perform to start and maintain her business?
   c Which activities are most important for a new business? Explain your choices.

3 One way to go into business today is to buy a franchise. Suppose you were considering a franchise. Pick one of those listed in this Issue or another one that interests you.
   a Investigate buying the franchise. Get some facts. Contact the franchisor in writing or by phone.
   b Make a list of advantages and disadvantages. Would you go into this business? Explain your decision.

4 Corporate combinations allow tremendous growth in some markets.
   a What are some advantages and disadvantages to producers of having large corporations merge?
   b What are some advantages and disadvantages to consumers of having large corporations merge?
   c Mergers often allow corporations to survive in oligopolistic markets. Explain why. Is there any danger in oligopolistic mergers?

5 Think about the meaning of free enterprise. The different market structures studied in this chapter show that not every business operates under the same rules.
   a Do monopoly market structures violate the idea of free enterprise? Explain your opinion. Is it fair for the government to make a monopoly break up?
   b Some economists call oligopolies "shared monopolies." Do oligopoly market structures violate the idea of free enterprise? Explain your opinion.

c Suppose two camera companies take years to build themselves into giant firms controlling 70% of all sales in the country. Is it fair for the government to sue to break these companies up? Is the government interfering with their freedom, or are they interfering with small entrepreneurs trying to create new camera companies? Explain your opinion.

6 There are four basic market structures.
  a Identify the four and name a product or service your household purchases from each.
  b Explain the differences among the four types.

Assessment Project: "Pre-Starting" a Business

This project can be completed in one of the following business types:

- Proprietorship (one student)
- Partnership (two students)
- Corporation (small group of students)

Student Task

Become an entrepreneur; brainstorm and research your idea for a business. Then, design a plan for starting that business. This is not a formal "Business Plan"; instead, it is an exercise that realistically addresses the questions: What's involved? How much does it cost? Where will I secure the funding? How, when, and where do I get started? Will I need employees? What kind and how many?

Procedure

1 Select a type of small business that interests you. Keep in mind the following: the community needs and resources, local competition, funding possibilities (family assistance, private, commercial, or public), type of business (proprietorship, partnership, or corporation).

2 Write a plan for setting up your business. Include:
- a list of personal goals
- a description of the business (what it does, location, legal status [permits, regulations], equipment needed)
- description of the market, competition, and a marketing plan
- projections of start-up and normal operating costs
- projections of net income and profit
- explanation of how management functions will be done
- description of personnel, try to write the plan so that a potential backer would want to lend you money to reach your goal. Include of list of sources used to guide you in making the plan.

3 Develop an implementation calendar, a month-by-month listing of actions to be taken, while assembling the resources needed for your business.

4 Make a summary analysis of your plan, being a specific as is possible. Answer the questions listed above in the Student Task part of this Project.

Evaluation

The criteria for the evaluation of this project are itemized in the grid (rubric below) that follows. Choice of appropriate category terms (values) is the decision of the instructor. Selection of terms such as "minimal," "satisfactory," and "distinguished" can vary with each assessment.

One-Year Business Plan Evaluation Rubric

(Refer to the teacher's supplement for suggestions of scoring descriptors for evaluation.)

Evaluation Item
Item a: (1) Does the business plan show understanding that while different socioeconomic (as well as national, ethnic, religious, racial, and gender) groups have varied perspectives, values, and diverse practices and traditions, they face the same global economic challenges?
Item b: (5) Does the business plan analyze problems and evaluate decisions about the economic effects caused by human, technological, and natural activities on societies and individuals?
Item c: (6) Does the business plan present ideas in writing (and orally) in clear, concise, and properly accepted fashion?
Item d: (7) Does the business plan employ a variety of information from written, graphic, and multimedia sources?
Item e: (8) Does the business plan show monitoring of, reflection upon, and improvement of work?
Item f: (9) Does the work business plan show cooperative work and respect for the rights of others to think, act, and speak differently?

ISSUE 5

LABOR AND BUSINESS IN THE UNITED STATES

Can workers survive?

LABOR AND THE AMERICAN DREAM

"...They never told us what was real..."

The song opens with a blaring whistle, the kind once sounded in industrial towns when a shift ended. It is a sound reminiscent of the booming success of textile mills, car manufacturing plants, and the great steel mills of the past. Billy Joel's *Allentown* first creates an image of people going to work, giving an honest day's labor for an honest wage. Then, it shifts the listener to images of deserted factories and mills.

"Well, we're living here in Allentown, and they're closing all the factories down. Out in Bethlehem, they're killing time, filling out forms, standing in lines."

It is a familiar theme of melancholy: wistful memories of another generation living the American Dream accompanied by anguished disillusion.

"While our fathers fought the Second World War – spent their weekends on the Jersey Shore ... But the restlessness was handed down, and it's getting very hard to stay!"

There is wrenching frustration in the song. It lashes out at those who nurtured the Dream but had no answers when the Dream began to fade.

"All the promises our teachers gave – if we work hard, and we behaved. So the graduations hang on the wall, but they never really helped us at all, because they never told us what was real ... but they've taken all of the coal from the ground, and the union people go away."

The bitter tone builds on the misery of young people caught in an economic debacle which robbed a generation of a future.

"Every child had a pretty good shot to get as far as their old man got, but something happened on the way to that place they threw a ... right in our face."

Amidst the despondency, there seems to be hint of hope that moving away might be the answer – the eternal hope is that there is still a place where the Dream can be recaptured.

"Well, I'm living here in Allentown, and its hard to keep a good man down, but I won't be getting up today. It's getting very hard to stay and live here in Allentown."

***** *the end* *****

INTRODUCTION

Is the American Dream an impossible dream in towns where tens of thousands of people are being "surplused," "downsized," and just plain "let go"? Or could it simply be a time to recover, retrain, reeducate, and find different routes to the economic goals?

Job Security Is Elusive

Hard work has always meant advancement in the workplace. The ethic of doing one's best led to promotions and a better life for one's family. But, something has happened to that belief (see sidebar on opposite page on downsizing). As hard as it may be to accept, it is possible that a company struggling to compete in the marketplace must adjust to survive. This often means workers lose their jobs. However, many economists suggest that something is wrong when a company such as Proctor & Gamble, making considerable profits, decides to dismiss 40,000 workers to broaden its profit margins and dividends. Where is the concern for those employees that have helped create the corporate profits?

Lifetime job security was once an accepted tradition in this country. Many companies attached a great value to their workers. Now, after the massive layoffs of the early 1990s, most companies say they see little new hiring in the 1990s. They claim they must make staff reductions and strive for higher efficiency with those who remain. Good or bad, it is a trend in all kinds of companies, big, small, and everywhere between. The industrialized world has producers striving for higher productivity, struggling with cutthroat competition, and adopting technological changes. All this makes jobs the centerpiece of economic, political, and social debate. It does not matter from which side one approaches the world's jobless woes – it is getting worse. *Newsweek*'s Scott Sullivan says we are "...squandering our people" as millions of unemployed cannot find work while millions more work on temporary status in jobs that offer no benefits (14 June 1993, 46).

The above sign was too often seen during the mid-1990s as major corporations downsized producing a "trickle down" effect of more job layoffs from secondary businesses. ©PhotoDisc

Sullivan proposes that economists and policymakers consider this: "What if there really were no more jobs than we have right now? What if the increasing unemployment of the last 20 years presaged (foreshadowed) a long period in which it would be cheaper for developed countries to keep half or more of their citizens jobless from cradle to grave?" He observes that "... with the most persistent unemployment in modern times, the possibility of a society not based on work as we know it remains a bold and mostly discounted hypothesis." (Sullivan. 47) Yet, what options are there?

☆ CAPSULE – DOWNSIZING AND THE FUTURE OF WORK

The recent wave of corporate downsizing has done more than swell the ranks of the retired and the unemployed. The restructuring of America's large corporations has changed the nature of careers and advancement inside their walls. According to *Newsweek* financial columnist Jane Bryant Quinn, people are bumping into barriers and ceilings in their careers much earlier and at much younger ages than in the past. "Almost everyone stalls eventually, but the unrest seems more general today. Able boomers, "thirty-somethings," ready for promotion, see jobs above them being snuffed. With few places to go they are topping out younger and at lower levels than they expected. Older generations weren't stopped until they reached their late 40s." (Quinn. "A Generation Topped Out." *Newsweek*. 20 September 1993, 42)

"Downsized companies need to think about how to encourage talent that can no longer advance," writes Quinn. She says more enlightened corporations are looking at two ways to do this. The first is lateral transfers to broaden employees' experience that can offer challenges and also avoid burn-out. She says, "Some 60 large companies now do without the traditional career ladder completely. Take General Electric. It used to have twenty- nine well defined professional pay grades ... it has replaced them with six occupational bands with varying levels of responsibility (Quinn. 42)."

A second way of encouraging talent is performance pay. This may be the most fundamental change that will affect the future of work in America. Raises will no longer come at regular intervals or by individual effort. Companies will reward teams of workers as they innovate new production techniques. Quinn says, "Twenty-one percent of firms in a recent survey give workers more incentive pay – like $2000 each to a team that launches a new product on time (Quinn. 42)."

In this respect, downsizing places added emphasis on the need for greater job skills. The old rules of career advancement through individual effort have changed. Individuals have to have talent for cooperative problem-solving and decision-making.

THE CHANGING NATURE OF WORK

The song *Allentown* presents the changing nature of the workplace in the world today. If the workplace changes, so must the worker. As a factor of production, human resources must not only be preserved, they must be helped if future generations are to have their "piece of the pie." Tough global competition inspires rapid technological change. That creates high productivity but fewer jobs. Increasing unemployment and insecurity haunt the world's most prosperous nations. It appears the only salvation for workers is training.

This is not a new situation. By the mid-1800s the nature of work changed markedly. Before the Industrial Revolution, America did not have large-scale unemployment. On farms and in small shops, workers labored hard and did most operations by hand, but they directly provided for their families. With factory work and division of labor, the Industrial Revolution created great urban markets that separated the worker from the customer. An economic and social insecurity arose not much different from that which we face today. The small business, with easily predictable markets, gave way to firms that mass-produced for both domestic and foreign markets with no guaranteed sales.

Of course, mechanization made it easier to produce more, and surpluses meant growth. How bad could that be? As with most major movements in human existence, the Industrial Revolution had positive and negative effects. There were surpluses, and they did improve the standard of living. Still, large-scale producers risked fortunes to outstrip their competition. They overproduced, creating gigantic surpluses that led to periodic price declines and, eventually, unemployment. Small businesses suffered and societies went through wrenching changes. For the first time, societies went through protracted recessions and depressions. Factory workers lacked control over their livelihood. Their entire existence hinged on decisions made in corporate offices by unseen management and owners. The Dream seemed more elusive than when Americans struggled in a less high tech and more agrarian society.

Although all this seems familiar today, it was new a century ago. We are used to workers losing jobs through factors beyond their control. Still, time has not made it any easier on the individual. Workers fear a lack of demand for the products they produce. It always means suffering. With their skills not in demand unless their industry recovers, workers have only one other option – to learn a new set of skills. Imperfect as it is, this is the only survival option. The issue of the changing nature of work has to be confronted.

What Is Labor?

There comes a time when everyone has to go out and earn a living. In economic terms, when that happens, a person becomes a factor of production – a human resource. He or she places an ability to produce in the market. The worker offers time, education, and skills for wages and benefits.

Like everything in the market, the forces of supply and demand decide how well the sale of a person's labor goes. The **demand for labor** is why many companies want to hire at different **wage rates** (amount one gets paid for one's labor), as shown on curve D_1 of Figure 5.1 on page 99.

As the demand for a product changes, so does the demand for the labor that produces it. Economists call the demand for labor a **derived demand** – demand for labor depends on aggregate consumer demand in a market (see Figure 5.2).

Demand for workers for the cold, remote North Slope pipeline in Alaska led the employer to offer wages at 200 to 300 percent above the national average wage for oil field workers. Figure 5.3 on page 100 shows demand for labor "shifting to the right." In this situation, the shift from curve D_1 to curve D_2 means more workers are needed by industry at every wage level.

The more consumers buy of what labor makes, the better off workers are. On the other hand, if consumer demand shrinks, workers' jobs and wages are at risk.

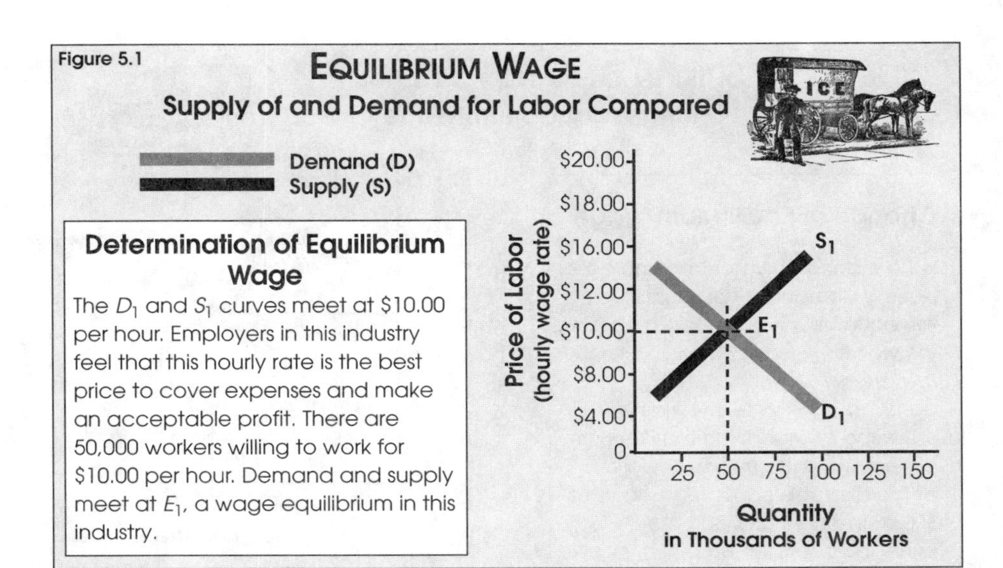

The market for labor is also dependent on workers' ability to be productive. **Labor productivity** refers to how much profit a worker creates for an employer. Employers commonly ask:

- Is the amount of money workers are paid going to come back into the company plus a bit more?
- Does the worker's effort enhance the company's income to go beyond the cost of production?

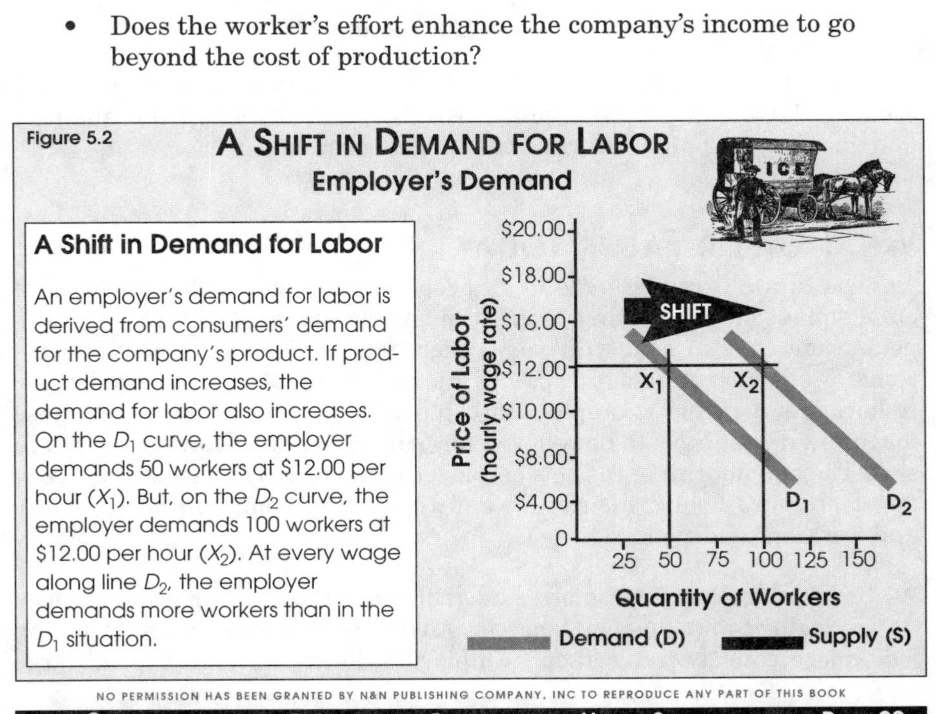

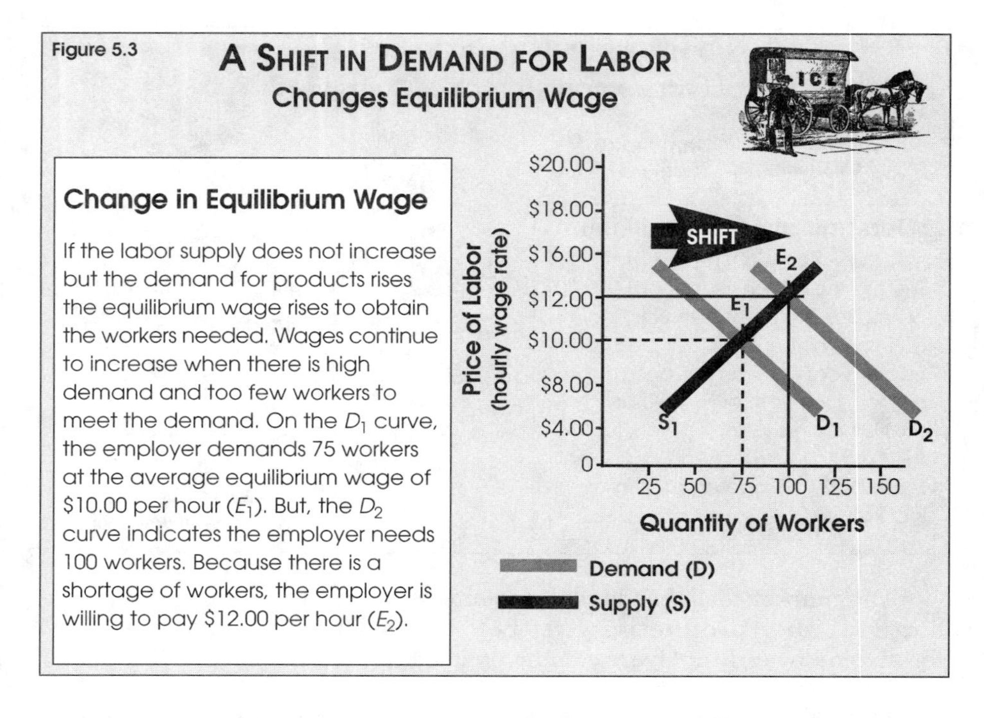

In order for an employer to succeed, the business must support this formula:

REVENUES minus (–) **COSTS** equals (=) **PROFITS**

Profits lead to expansion of production, which is necessary for job security. Labor productivity, joined with capital, increases the quantity and quality of supply. That generally means growth.

WHAT LABOR FACES TODAY

The **labor force** is made up of people over 16 years of age who have employment or are seeking it. As a member of this labor force, a young person now has to deal with very different situations than past generations. Modern technology replaces human labor at a very rapid pace. Robotics is a prime example. Once placed on an assembly line, these machines do not have to be relieved for "coffee breaks." They do not call in sick. They do not threaten their employer with strikes or slowdowns. They do not require health insurance, and they never complain about safety and working conditions.

Today's workers need more education than those of a generation ago. As technology and cheaper labor in other countries take manufacturing jobs, more education is critical. Employers do not want to expend large

Figure 5.4

A Shift in Supply of Labor

An Increase in the Number of Workers

A Shift in the Supply of Labor

An increase in available workers, due to reasons such as increasing immigration, more women and men entering the workforce because of the need for two incomes in family, and/or layoffs in other industries, shifts the S_1 curve to S_2.

On the S_1 curve, there are 100 workers willing to work at $12.00 per hour ($X_1$). But, on the S_2 curve, there are 150 workers willing to work at $12.00 per hour ($X_2$). At every wage along line S_2, more workers are available than were available in the S_1 situation.

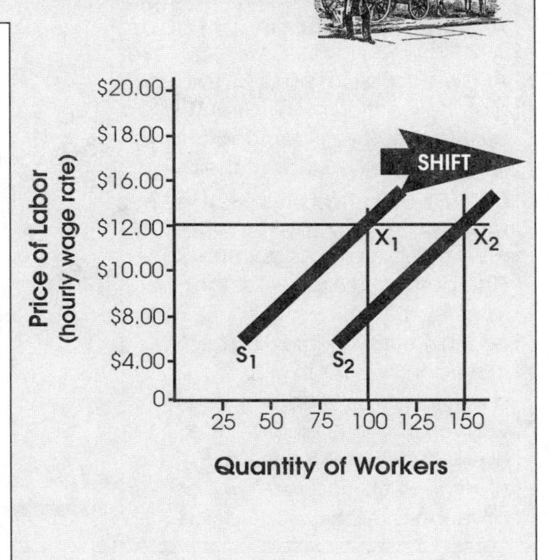

sums of money to train new workers. Today's workers must get the schooling necessary to compete with the others in the labor market.

Career employment will be very different in the coming generation. Twenty years ago, workers retired from life-long jobs. To remain employed or seek advancement, today's worker may switch jobs several times. (Experts predict 10 to 12 switches on the average.)

If regional and global trends such as the European Union and NAFTA continue, political borders may no longer be economic barriers to immigration. People will freely cross national boundaries seeking employment wherever they can find it. It could increase the number of workers in the U.S. labor market. This could shift the supply curve of labor to the right (see Figure 5.4).

If the supply of labor shifts right, but demand for labor remains constant, Figure 5.5 on page 102 shows the equilibrium wage drops (E_1 to E_2). This increase in the labor force makes competition for the few jobs more intense.

Demand for products triggers employers' demand for more workers. If the number of workers remains the same and the demand for the goods increases, Figure 5.3 (on the previous page) shows that the equilibrium wage will rise (E_1 to E_2). The imbalance of supply of labor and demand for labor may drive the average wage up or down in a certain field.

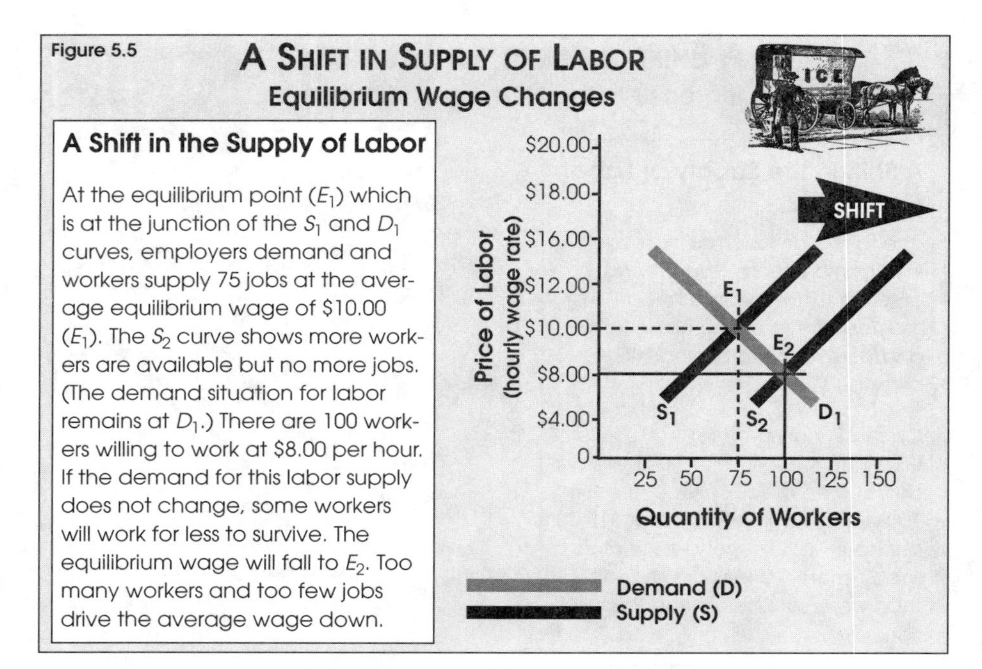

LABOR UNIONS: WORKERS' SELF-DEFENSE

Unionism simply means workers **organizing** (joining with other workers) to protect their employment and improve their lot in life. Forms of unionism can be traced back to the Middle Ages and the formation of guilds. In this country, various skilled workers came together in trade organizations early in our history.

Yet, it was not until the heavy industrialization of the late 1800s that brought national action to create labor unions. In 1869, a national organization effort began with the **Knights of Labor** seeking to create one big union for all workers. By 1886, it reached its peak with a membership of 700,000 workers. In that year, the Knights were involved in a series of national strikes that culminated in the bloody **Haymarket Riots** in Chicago. The police accused the Knights of provoking the riots. The Knights' membership declined after losing the confidence of the public and many workers.

In the same year, **Samuel Gompers** began another effort to organize the skilled workers in this country. This immigrant cigar maker began to build the **American Federation of Labor** (**AFL**). The Knights could not draw workers to common political causes. Gompers succeeded by avoiding politics. The AFL pursued those goals most important to the membership: higher wages and better working conditions. By aiming at these basic economic goals and steering clear of political involvement, Gompers built a popular union that had more than four million members by the 1920s.

Yet, even the AFL left a significant void in organizing workers. It unified only small local organizations of skilled tradesmen. It did not accept unskilled industrial workers, women, or African Americans.

In 1935, United Mine Workers President **John L. Lewis** began efforts to provide a place for all those groups shut out by the AFL. Passage of the ***Wagner Act*** (*National Labor Relations Act*) in 1935 aided his efforts. This federal law ensured workers the right to secret ballot referendums to select a bargaining agent. This made the organization of unskilled workers possible, and Lewis formed the **Congress of Industrial Organizations** (**CIO**). In 1955, after a long period of hostility, these two rival national unions joined to create the **AFL–CIO**, the largest affiliation of labor organizations in the country. In 2000, the AFL-CIO had 13.3 million members.

A few of the other AFL-CIO affiliated labor organizations include: the **ILGWU** (International Ladies' Garment Workers' Union – 150,000 members), the **International Brotherhood of Teamsters** (with 1.5 million members), the **UAW** (United Auto Workers – 746,000 members), the **United Steelworkers of America** (700,000 members), and the **NALC** (National Association of Letter Carriers – 313,000 members).

Besides the AFL-CIO, there are more than 100 national unions that function independently. They have no affiliation, are self-governing, and act in their self-interests. These groups represent approximately 3.3 million workers. A few of the better known independents include: the **ANA** (American Nurses Association – 200,000 members), **NEA** (National Education Association – the largest independent union with 2 million members), **UMW** (United Mine Workers – 240,000 members), and the **International Longshoremen's and Warehousemen's Union** (45,000 members).

Recent Declines in Union Power

Until recently, the objectives of unions were simple. They sought **collective bargaining agreements** (contracts) for better wages, pensions, safe working conditions, job security, better fringe benefits, and grievance procedures to assure contract enforcement. The historical data in Figure 5.6 shows that after World War II, union membership amounted to about 25% of all workers. By 1990, it had dropped to about 16%. By the year 2000, it stood at 13.5%.

Why the decline? First, things are very different today. There are changes taking place in the union movement because of changes at work and in the workplace itself. Manufacturing jobs once made up more than 33% of nonagricultural jobs. Today the number has dropped to less than 20% of nonfarm work. It was in factories, mills, and plants that unions

Figure 5.6

UNION MEMBERSHIP

PERCENT OF THE AMERICAN LABOR FORCE

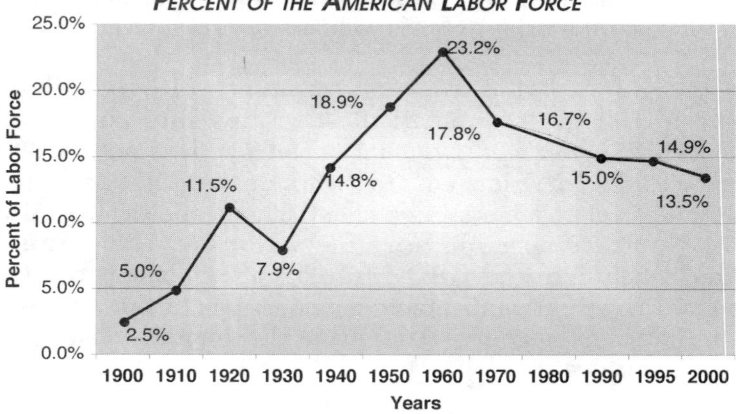

Source: Bureau of National Affairs, 2001

found their strength. As these workplaces closed or were converted to modern technology, unions could do little to stop the job losses. Members saw fewer reasons to pay local, state, and national dues to ineffective unions.

Second, unions are partially victims of their success. Laws entitle most workers to what early unions fought to get for their members (e.g., workers' compensation, minimum wage, and safety laws). Unions gained enough power in the mid-20th century to have their contracts become benchmarks for entire industries. To be competitive for labor, employers had to match or improve the contract provisions. Some employers wanted to avoid unions altogether, so they offered workers better wage and benefit packages than those unions received. When the economy boomed and labor was scarce, workers found they could often get better wages and benefits without unions.

Third, beyond collective bargaining, the "heavy weapons" used by unions to get their objectives became less effective. If union leaders call a **strike** (work stoppage), employers replace union workers with the many nonunion people just waiting to get a job. When a union promotes a **boycott** (refusal to buy product or service of an inflexible employer), people generally ignore it and continue to purchase whatever they want to satisfy themselves. Most consumers and some workers willfully (or ignorantly) cross **picket lines** (lines of striking workers in front of workplaces demonstrating against unfair conditions). Without these weapons, unions have little power.

Fourth, public attitudes toward unions also led to the decline. When surveys ask a crosssection of Americans to say what comes to their mind when they hear the word "union," some common responses include:

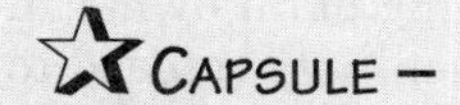

CAPSULE – EMPLOYEE BENEFITS

Percent Having Desired Employee Benefits
Source: U.S. Labor *Occupational Handbook*, 2001

- Health Insurance (25%)
- Cumulative Sick Days (15%)
- Paid Holidays, Vacations (70%)
- Personal leaves (e.g., family, funerals) (28%)
- Pension (29%)
- Income Protection from long-term disability (10%)

Note: Young people seem to think that "everyone gets benefits." These numbers tell a different story. Even among those with benefits, situations vary. For example, health insurance and pension plans vary greatly from employer to employer.

Even when the fast food franchise hires a cashier for $10.50, the cost to the employer of the benefits makes the actual employee cost $17.00. Entry level jobs at $30,000 probably cost the employer $50,000 with benefits and employment taxes that have to be paid.

"corrupt," "greedy," "incompetent ," "selfish," "inept," "decaying," and "lazy." The resulting lists are usually much more negative than positive. Some economists claim that union wages keep prices high and protect incompetence, leading to high cost, low quality goods. True or untrue, once in place, such attitudes are hard to counter.

The famous **PATCO Strike** of 1981 may have galvanized the negative attitudes about unions in recent times. The Professional Air Traffic Controllers Organization struck for shorter shifts and more rest between shifts in a very stressful profession. President Ronald Reagan ordered them back to work. Some members did return to the control towers, but approximately 12,000 strikers stayed out. Reagan declared PATCO violated a nonstrike provision of the *Taft-Hartley Act* (1947). He ordered the Department of Transportation to replace the strikers.

12,000 PATCO members were fired by President Reagan when the air traffic controllers struck in 1981. ©PhotoDisc

This mass firing affected the attitudes of other employers. Before PATCO, they would not have considered using the law to replace an entire segment of their work force because of a strike action. The downsizing in the 1990s showed many employers making wholesale job cuts without consulting unions or employee associations.

Ignoring unions is common. In 1990, the Pepsi bottling plant owner in Newburgh, NY fired more than 100 striking drivers when they refused to go back to work. Seeking public support, the drivers went to the communities serviced by this bottler and asked the people to boycott the product. Supported by other Teamster locals, the drivers sought to return to their jobs for four years. The Newburgh bottler ignored the strike, then declared it over when nonunion employees replaced the union employees. Despite a union media blitz and store demonstrations, area consumers ignored the boycott. This once strong union local crumbled under the great burden of the 4-year strike.

Another example occurred in October 1993, when members of the Newspaper Guild at the *New York Post* voted to end their strike of six days. They were embittered by the lack of support by the other nine unions at the paper when the other unions decided to cross the picket lines and help the nonunion workers get the paper out. The striking employees could not return to work until they reapplied for the jobs some of them had held for thirty years. Rupert Murdoch, the owner, was known for his "union busting."

New Directions for Unions

When a union is without power, can there be true negotiation? In the past, worker and employer saw themselves as adversaries doing battle in collective bargaining negotiations. Traditionally, they believed that what was good for one was harmful to the other. Yet, heavy competition from abroad has caused a new perspective to emerge. Many employers and employees have drawn closer as the market changed due to global competitive pressures. More awareness of the benefits of shared decision–making and profit sharing emerged.

Seeking higher productivity, many companies downsized and reduced the demand for labor. At the same time, they realized an increase in productivity had to come from better communications between labor and management. It could only be done through cooperative, not adversarial bargaining.

An example of the new perspective in labor-management relations is General Motors' creation of its new Saturn Division. The manufacturer and the United Auto Workers' union decided to create an automobile produced through a new accord. The result was a positive rapport between the employer and employee. Future collective bargaining agreements will focus more on efforts to tie workers wages to producers' profits.

Labor must deal with balancing the labor supply with the producers' demand for it. Different groups handle this balancing act in various ways. Attorneys must be licensed by the state in which they wish to practice their trade. Each state administers a bar examination. Anyone that meets a passing score gets a license to conduct their business. There is no way of calculating how many people will pass or fail this examination. Right now, in this country, there are many more licensed lawyers than there are jobs for them.

Conversely, there is the technique used by Certified Public Accountants. For them, there is no passing score on the licensing test. Only a percentage of the highest scoring candidates are licensed to replace those that are leaving the profession. This way, the supply always remains controlled and limited, keeping the market equilibrium at a higher wage level. Unions must find new and creative ways to defend the worker as employers change their demand for labor.

Government and Labor

Unions do not represent everyone. In the 20th century, government has often come to the aid of workers. Affirmative action programs, minimum wage, right-to-work, and comparable worth are significant issues in which government takes the side of workers.

Affirmative Action Programs

Government action for workers addresses discrimination. One way is to set up **affirmative action** programs. *Black's Law Dictionary* defines these programs as "employment programs required by federal statutes and regulations designed to remedy the discriminatory practices in hiring minority group members; designed to eliminate existing and continuing discrimination...; to create systems and procedures to prevent future discrimination..."

The original purpose of affirmative action was to insure the equitable recruitment of workers. The idea's backers did not consider the difficulty of being the first "outsider" to be recruited. Imagine being the first female to qualify for employment as a firefighter, or the first African American to take the oath to "serve and protect" in a small town, all-white police department? Many could not or would not put themselves at risk of the psychological and/or physical pressures that were likely to occur.

That is why "recruitment" changed to what critics called **preferential treatment**. Civil rights proponents felt that if enlistment could not increase the number of minority members in the workforce, then partiality might work. What came to be called the "quota system" became the basis of federal and state employment and government contract laws.

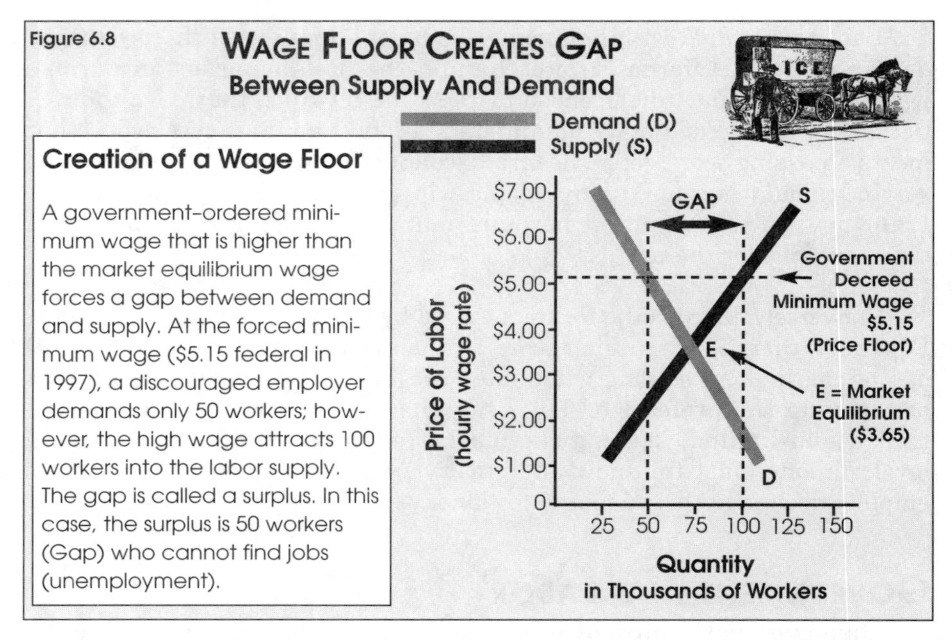

Those who support more drastic action to break discriminatory barriers claim that it is the only way to deal with traditional discrimination. Opponents of such laws believe that they can only lead to "reverse discrimination." Lawsuits initiated by individuals and governments have attempted to settle the questions in courts. After years of debate in Congress and the Judiciary, as well as in the private and business sectors, an equitable solution has not yet emerged.

Minimum Wage Laws

State and federal minimum wage laws create a wage rate that has a floor built under it. This means the hourly rate of pay in most industries cannot go any lower than the law allows. In the 1950s, it was $.75 to $1.00 per hour, and in the late 1960s it had risen to $1.60 per hour. In 1997, Congressional increases raised the federal minimum hourly wage to $5.15 per hour.

The original reasoning for such action by the United States Congress was to give low income families more purchasing power. Figure 5.7 presents the situation in graph format. Yet, some problems are evident to those who understand how our system works. If government forces employers to raise the wage rate, employers lose profit. If this loss is significant, employers diminish the losses by cutting expenses. One way is to fire employees or cut hours. Another choice is to pass the loss on to the consumer. That means higher prices and inflation. Higher prices may consume any gain in the employees' purchasing power. Minimum wage laws may place the wages for those jobs covered above the equilibrium point of supply and demand for labor. There are many factors that force employers to make decisions about laying off workers.

Right-to-Work Laws

Some unions negotiated clauses in their contracts that allow a **closed shop** (all employees must be union members). Other contracts included **union shop** clauses (nonunion employees must pay an agency fee). In 1947, the ***Taft-Hartley Act*** (*Labor Management Relations Act*) forbade closed shops but allowed union shops to continue. It also allowed states to legislate **open shops** (employment of union and nonunion workers under same contract). Twenty-one states have such **right-to-work laws**. While these laws prohibit union shops, they do allow unions to charge "agency fees" to nonunion employees to cover negotiation of contracts. What these laws establish are open shops that allow employers to hire either union or non-union workers.

Comparable Worth

Discrimination on the job hurts people in many different ways. Recently, the term "glass ceiling" has gained national attention. It refers to an unspoken bias of many companies. They allow women to rise to a particular place in the company's hierarchy and then stop the promotions, no matter how deserving the female employee is. The ***Civil Rights Act of 1964*** (amended in 1972), ***Equal Pay Act of 1963***, and ***United States Code 1963*** prohibit gender discrimination. With these as a basis and many other laws passed by the federal and state legislatures, suits for damages from sexual discrimination in the workplace now flood the courts. While there are laws protecting workers from bigotry, firms still pay women only 60-70% of what men collect for doing the "same job." Seeking **pay equity** continues to be a legal battle. Some states, including New York, Connecticut, Iowa, Minnesota, and Wisconsin, have passed laws to combat such chauvinism in the workplace.

Laws that discourage other forms of discrimination in the workplace include:

- **The *Rehabilitation Act of 1973*** prohibits employers from discriminating on the basis of handicap.

- **The *Age Discrimination In Employment Act of 1967*** (amended 1978) protects persons between the ages of forty and seventy from arbitrary age discrimination in a workplace of twenty or more people and by all levels of government.

What the future holds for workers is uncertain. Still, the Dream has not changed. Those placing their labor in the marketplace seek honest pay for honest work.

ASSESSMENT • QUESTIONS • APPLICATIONS

1 Hard work has always meant security and advancement in the workplace.
   a Is this statement as true now as it was in the past? Explain.
   b What career do you plan on training for? Analyze the supply and demand aspects of labor in this field.
   c How is your entering the job market going to be different from your parents' experience?

2 For many years, labor unions achieved their goals in the workplace.
   a Is this statement as true now as it was in the past? Explain.
   b In what ways do unions benefit even nonunion workers?
   c Why does the public seem to have a strong anti-union sentiment?
   d How must unions change to meet the changes in global economics?

3 In the United States, workers have basic rights.
   a List the employment rights to which workers are entitled.
   b Assume you thought that you were being denied one of those rights. Explain how you would remedy the situation and what obstacles you think might arise when you seek the remedy.

4 Investigate the Supreme Court decisions in *University of California v. Bakke* (1978) and *United Steel Workers of America, AFL-CIO v. Weber* (1979).
   a Summarize the facts in each case.
   b Identify the issue in each case.
   c Explain the Court's ruling in each case.
   d What impact did each decision have on labor in America?

5 In the 20th century, governments have often helped the worker at the expense of the employer.
   a Explain why you agree or disagree with this statement.
   b Is government involvement in the economy a good or bad thing?

Explain your response.

Assessment Project: Joining the Job Market

Will the job market be ready to accept you when you are ready to join it? This is a major question that many young people do not even consider before they decide to study at a college, attend a trade school, join the military, or just go out looking for a job. The intelligent way to approach your life choices is to research and investigate "the real world."

Student Task

Write a report analyzing the supply of labor and the demand for labor in a field you wish to work.

Procedure

1 Assume that you are going to college to train for a particular career. Select three schools that specialize in education for that field. Call each of them and get the following information:

a How many graduates did the school have in the area you are interested in?
b How many of them got jobs?
c What was the average starting salary for those who were placed?
d How many went on for a graduate degree in the field?
e How many were placed after achieving a graduate level degree and what was their starting salary?
f How many were not placed in their field of study, and what kind of employment did they find?

2 Locate the current U.S. Dept. of Labor *Occupational Outlook Handbook* in a library. Review the statistics given for your particular interest.

3 Compile all college and government data and make your judgments about the field.

EVALUATION

The criteria for the evaluation of this project are itemized in the grid (rubric) that follows. Choice of appropriate category terms (values) is the decision of the instructor. Selection of terms such as "minimal," "satisfactory," and "distinguished" can vary with each assessment.

Joining The Job Market Evaluation Rubric

(Refer to the teacher's supplement for suggestions of scoring descriptors for evaluation.)

Evaluation Item
Item a: (5) Does the report analyze problems and evaluate decisions about the economic effects caused by human, technological, and natural activities on societies and individuals?
Item b: (6) Does the report present ideas in writing (and orally) in clear, concise, and properly accepted fashion?
Item c: (7) Does the report employ a variety of information from written, graphic, and multimedia sources?
Item d: (8) Does the report show monitoring of, reflection upon, and improvement of work?

ISSUE **6**

MONEY AND FINANCE

How do people use money, credit, and banking?

THE COLLEGE CRUNCH: GETTING CREDIT FOR MORE THAN COURSES

Jorge Melendez' 1985 CJ-5 kicked up some dust as it turned down the Oroscos' drive. He and Felipe had been friends since grade school in Burnet. Now both were finishing their Associate degrees at Austin Community College.

Felipe shuffled down the steps as the Jeep pulled in front of the house. "Hey, lot of dust, man! Mamma's going to want that porch swept because of you," Felipe said.

Jorge shrugged and smiled, "Dry for this time of year."

They stopped at the mailbox when they got to the road. Felipe jumped back in the seat waving a letter. "This is the third offer for a credit card this week. I must be on a list."

"Me, too," said Jorge. "I really don't want to get one. You know cousin Miguel... goes to Howard Payne U. up in Brownwood? A credit card burned him. He ran up a balance and had trouble paying it off. His mother made him get rid of it. It's too easy to run up a balance, and the interest you pay is phenomenal."

"Most of the college kids I know at Austin Community have one," Felipe said. "Their parents co–sign. My parents are not very hot on the idea. They are afraid I won't manage it well, and they will wind up bailing me out. These mail offers say I can get one on my own. I don't know. I would like to get some decent clothes to go job hunting. If I move to my own place, I could charge some furniture and stuff."

"Listen, Felipe," Jorge said. "Maybe we can talk to my sister Maria. She's taking Financial Management at Baylor University up in Waco. I want to go there to see the place. I know you are taking those computer skills and going out for a job when we graduate, but I want to transfer credits to a four-year school. What do you say we make a trip to Waco?"

A few weeks later, the CJ pulled in front of a dorm at Baylor. Maria was waiting with a group of friends. After Maria put Jorge and Felipe through the "little brother" and "he's cute" introductions, the group walked around the campus, then headed for the snack bar.

"So, Maria, you're the financial genius. What can you tell me about getting a credit card?" Felipe asked.

Maria smiled at her roommate Liz Colgan. "As one of our professors always says, 'There is good news and bad news. Nothing is easy when it comes to money.'"

"The good news is credit cards can help you manage money, and they are great in emergencies," said Maria, gazing over her glasses as she settled into her accountant mood. "The bad news is, unless you know what you are doing, they get out of control very quickly."

"Maria and I have a test coming up on them next week," Liz said hastily. "It might help us if we went over our notes aloud with you tomorrow. Right now, we have a basketball game to see."

The next afternoon, the four of them were sitting on a couch in the dorm lounge.

"Hey, this is nice. You study here often?" asked Jorge sinking into the cushion.

"No," said Liz. "The place gets too noisy during the week. That is a big problem in college. The dorms are too noisy, even during exam time. When we want quiet, we head for the library.

"Anyway, I looked at my notes about credit cards. There are many ins and outs. I have a supplementary American Express charge card on my dad's account, but he told me not to use it unless I am in a bind. I've only used it once when my Toyota needed a battery last winter. I used the card, but Dad paid the bill."

"After Aunt Louisa told Mamma about Miguel's payment problems with his card at Payne, she told me to forget it," said Maria.

Jorge glanced at Felipe. "You two haven't much practical experience, do you?"

"No," said Liz, "but we do have Professor Garnsey's notes. It will help us all to go over them aloud. First, he says to check the cost of revolving credit cards versus charge cards. Different cards charge membership rates, have different APRs, and charge transaction fees."

Felipe blinked. "I thought they were all the same, and what is an APR, anyway?"

Maria held up her hand. "The offers you are getting in the mail may waive the annual fee for a year. That could save you $20 – $30, but the APR, the Annual Percentage Rate, might be high on those offers, sometimes over 20% of any balance you are running."

"There is also a difference in how each card issuer computes the interest. So you really have to do some reading," said Liz. "Hey, between the two of us we sound like we know something!"

Jorge threw his arms in the air. "Wait! You two may know something, but I'm lost. I'm not sure of the difference between a charge card and a credit card."

Liz flipped a couple of pages of her notebook. "Stores issue charge cards, so do gasoline companies, and travel / entertainment services such as Carte Blanche, Diners Club, and American Express. Most have an annual fee, but mostly you have to pay off the entire bill when it comes.

So, there is no interest rate on an outstanding balance, because there isn't any balance – OK, but there is an annual fee on most of these cards.

"Almost every bank and credit union issues international credit cards like Master Card, Visa, or Discover. Besides the bankcards, big corporations like AT&T, GM, Shell, and Ford are offering those cards. They allow you to charge purchases, get cash advances, and carry a balance from month to month if you can't pay it all at once."

Felipe blinked and with his exaggerated accentuation said, "Well, if you can stretch out payments, a CREDIT card is better than a CHARGE card."

"Maybe," said the skeptic Maria, "but Miguel got into trouble with his credit card. He ran up bills and just paid the minimum each month. Then, he charged more stuff. For pocket money, he used the card to get cash advances at the college ATM. Miguel forgot they charge a fee for that, too. Miguel wound up carrying a $2000 balance, and Aunt Louisa blew a gut! She made him cut up the card. It took him two years to pay off the balance. At 19% APR, he wound up paying the company $2697."

The boys looked stunned. Then Jorge chuckled,"Wow, almost $700 in interest! No wonder Aunt Louisa went nuts."

"There is a lot more to these things than you think," said Liz, waving her card. "People whip them in and out of their wallets all the time. They are always there. They are too convenient."

"I'll say," said Felipe. "At least with cash, you stop when your wallet's empty. Sounds to me like a wise person would avoid them completely."

Maria smiled. "Actually, Professor Garnsey says they are a good financial tool – if you know your limits. If you control your use and pay off your balance as quickly as possible, they give you a good record of spending. That can help you stay within a budget. If you don't run into problems, they can provide you with a good credit record for later, when you want bigger loans for a car or a house."

Jorge stretched. "Say, Ms. Colgan, maybe we can use your American Express to get ourselves a nice pizza?"

"Not on your life, buster. That is probably what your cousin Miguel did all the time. If you want to eat, then, we'll climb into the Jeep and head for the dining hall ready to revel in the exotic pleasures of Baylor's fine college cuisine."

* * * * * *the end* * * * * *

Money, Credit, and Banking

High school, college, or after – whether learning about credit cards or balancing a checkbook – money situations cause pleasure and pain for everyone. Avoiding the pain takes hard work. There is no easy way around dealing with money. It is a necessity. The better people understand the role money plays in the economy, the more success they will have in dealing with money.

Since money is such an important part of any economic society, keeping the right amount of it in circulation is important. In most market economies, banks circulate money. Throughout U.S. history, crises have arisen because of this arrangement. Today, the government issues the money to banks and regulates them. Following a discussion of some general ideas about money, a look at the U.S. banking system will take a substantial part of this lesson.

Money: History, Characteristics, and Functions

Money is anything generally accepted for payment in **transactions** (exchanges of goods and services). Early societies used **barter** (exchanging one good for another). Villagers spent much time trading and retrading goods until they could get what they wanted in the first place. Bartering still exists. Kids always trade comic books and baseball cards. People sometimes pay for goods by swapping for something else. Sometimes they perform some acceptable service in exchange for something of similar value. Often, this is called the "gray market" in which some people pay others "in kind" to avoid paying sales and income taxes. For the purpose of avoiding taxes, this is illegal.

As time went by, money began to serve three basic functions. First, universally acceptable **mediums of exchange** began to surface. They simplified transactions and replaced the barter process of endless trades. Salt, shells, jewels, grain, and even cows have served as money over time. The Egyptians used coins as early as 2500 B.C. The use of precious metal coins as money became widespread in early times. They met the criteria for a good medium of exchange: scarce, portable, durable, symbolic, and universal. They were also divisible. They could be minted in different sizes and shapes to denote degrees of value.

Coins from around the world. ©PhotoDisc

Second, as money evolved as a practical medium of exchange, it took on other functions. It became **standard of value**. Today we make purchases based on whether the amount asked by a merchant seems right to us. There is a general awareness of how much money will buy, and people judge what goods and wages are worth in terms of money.

Third, money also functions as a **store of wealth**. This means money is kept for future use. People stockpile it until they have enough to buy something they cannot buy immediately. People save money and safeguard it to give them security against unseen misfortune.

Paper as a symbol to represent wealth emerged in medieval times. Goldsmiths stored gold and gave out receipts for it. People traded with the receipts (or notes) as **representative money**. Accepting the paper meant one individual had faith the other had gold, silver, or some other wealth to back it. Our paper money of today and our banking system evolved from these practices.

Since medieval times, notes and paper money have been used throughout the world by most governments as legal tender and to represent wealth. ©PhotoDisc

From the days of the goldsmiths to recent times, paper money (notes) represented other tangible wealth. In the 20th century, societies moved away from this to **fiat money**. This is when a government decrees the notes it issues are "legal tender" and must be accepted for all "legal transactions." As with most modern nations, U.S. currency is fiat money. It has no gold and silver backing. (Figure 6.1 shows one of the last dollars the U.S. backed with silver.) Paper money fluctuates in value (inflation/deflation) based on the society's ability to grow and prosper and people's faith in the stability of the government. If that faith is shaken, serious economic problems begin to arise.

Figure 6.1 Silver Certificate

From 1886 to 1968 Silver Certificates were backed and redeemable for silver dollars.

MONEY SUPPLY: CURRENCY, CHECKING, AND MORE

Most young people use government currency for transactions. They find it hard to believe that only *one-tenth* of **M-1** (the basic money supply) circulating through the economy is bills and coins.

The other *nine-tenths* of **M-1** is in **demand deposits** (checking accounts) in banks (see Figure 6.2 below). A satellite view of money changing hands in U.S. businesses and daily life would show most people writing checks and depositing them in banks. Think of how most households pay big bills. The major payments for mortgages, heating, autos, and most goods and services are in the form of checks.

Checks are safe, easy to use, handwritten bank forms. They are the money used for most of the transactions inside and outside America. Banks are private businesses, but through checks, they can radically alter the money supply. To attempt to keep the right amount of money in circulation and to allow the economy to run smoothly and grow, federal and state governments regulate banks (see section on Banks: Gatekeepers of the Money Supply on page 123).

Checks represent 90% of the transactions for households and businesses. ©PhotoDisc

Figure 6.2

MONEY SUPPLY

Measuring the Money Supply

Money Supply Chart

Measure:	**Includes**:
M-1 =	currency, checking accounts, travelers checks
M-2 = M-1 +	savings and investment funds (money market funds, mutual funds, ATM accessible savings accounts) that allow investors to make easy transfers and withdrawals
M-3 = M-2 +	time deposits over $100,000 (CDs, etc.)
L = M-3 +	Everything else: Treasury bonds and other long-term securities, even cash value insurance policies.

L
$9,229.4 Billion
M-3
$7,821.6 Billion
M-2
$5,398.7 Billion
M-1
$1,194 Billion

Source: *Economic Indicators*, Sept 2001, Joint Economic Committee U.S. Congress

The actual money supply is broader than **M-1**. There is also a considerable portion of the money supply in **near money**. This includes accounts and securities involving simple formalities to be converted into currency or checks. Therefore, these accounts are very *near* to being money. Economists say they are **liquid** because they flow easily into money. Including near money in the picture gives a much broader measure of the money supply (**M-2**, **M-3**, **L**) as shown in Figure 6.2.

MONEY: CREDIT AND CREDIT CARDS

What about those credit cards that are so often used in transactions? Where do they fit in the broad money supply picture? Cards are technically near money. Each time a person charges purchases to a credit account, he/she is borrowing money. In the end, when the card company's bill comes, it has to be paid with a check or currency (**M-1**).

Young people often get frustrated when this whole question of credit arises. Most parents of today's high school and college students did not have access to credit cards. The credit cards that are so commonplace today only emerged as financial tools in the 1960s and 1970s. The nation absorbed them into its financial life rapidly. Their advantages and disadvantages were not always well understood.

Figure 6.3 shows that credit card debt grew significantly in the 1990s. According to the Federal Reserve System, in 1992 there was more money outstanding on revolving credit loans than on auto loans: $402 billion v. $390 billion (Council of Economic Advisors, *Economic Indicators*, Nov. 2000). Today, credit card debt makes up 33.3% of consumer loans. According to the President's

Figure 6.3

RISE IN CONSUMER DEBT

Consumer Use of Revolving Credit

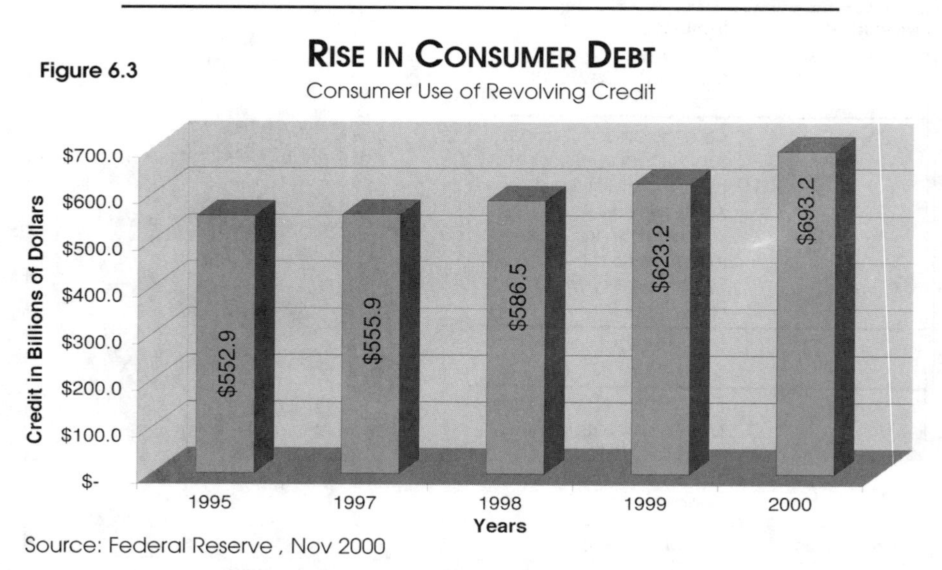

Source: Federal Reserve , Nov 2000

Council of Economic Advisors, the average consumer paid $651 in finance charges in 2000 (*Economic Indicators*, Nov. '99). It is big business, too. Credit card interest is one of the largest income generators for banks. Putting $700 billion in revolving charges on their cards, Americans pay the banks nearly $91 billion in finance charges annually (*Economic Indicators*, Nov. 2001).

Usury is the charging of illegally high interest. Congress and state governments passed many laws to regulate credit. Yet, twenty states have no interest ceilings, and for those that do, the average is 24%. Even at a 20% rate, carrying a $1,000 balance for 36 months would cost the card holder an additional $500 in interest. Saving money at 3% or 4% in a bank while carrying a $1,000 credit card loan is foolish. The small gain at the savings bank cannot offset the 20% being paid on the card. It amounts to a 15-17% net loss of money. According to financial columnist Humberto Cruz, a card holder would be better off using the savings deposits to pay off the credit card balance faster ("Credit Cards, Even Unused, Can Cost You." *Poughkeepsie Journal*. 31 January 1994, B1).

Today, society expects young people to come out of high school and college using sophisticated credit devices as a matter of course. In this issue's opening story, Jorge and Maria mentioned their cousin Miguel's problems. This is not uncommon. Choosing and using credit cards properly takes education and discipline.

For young people just starting out in life, qualifying for credit of *any* kind is very frustrating. Their applications for credit may be turned down. The problem is that young people have no credit history. Therefore, convincing a bank or other creditor that they are **credit worthy** becomes a problem. It is exasperating, but a person needs to have used credit to get credit!

☆ Capsule – Getting Started With Credit

Adapted from American Express Co., *Building a Credit Record*, NY 1993

- Open a savings account and **make regular deposits**. Deposit amounts can be small, but they should show persistence.
- Open a checking account and **do not "bounce" any checks**.

These two simple steps show a bank or other creditor that a person has care and discipline in financial affairs. In addition:

- Find a full-time job and establish a steady work record.
- Apply for a small loan from a bank or credit union, ask a relative or friend to co-sign. **Pay it off as quickly as possible without missing any payments**.
- **Pay bills promptly**.
- Apply for a store charge card on your own or as an extension of a relative's account. Pay charges **completely** each month.

☆ CAPSULE – CHOOSING A CREDIT CARD

Adapted from American Express Co., *Building a Credit Record,* NY 1993

Credit can be convenient, but it can easily become a nightmare for an individual who lets it get out of control. A credit advantage is that a monthly bill can help keep track of purchases and control expenses. A disadvantage is that it provides excess purchasing power. Temptations may lead to overspending and carrying a balance. The extra interest payments on that balance may wreck a budget. Choosing the right low cost card can avoid unpleasantness and enhance an individual's creditworthiness.

- Use a budget as a restraint. (Subtract housing expenses from monthly take home pay. Keep credit payments below 15% of this figure.)
- Check the APR. (Call Bankcard Holders of America at 1-800-845-5000. Ask for a free list of banks with low credit card rates.) The ***Federal Truth-in-Lending Act*** (1968) requires creditors to inform consumers of interest rates applications and bills.
- See if there is an annual fee charged just to carry the card. (Some companies do not charge one and others will waive the fee if asked.)
- See if there is a 25-day grace period before interest is charged.
- See if there are insurance charges.
- Check for special offers. (Shell's Master Card offers gas discounts. GM's offers discounts on the next new GM car.)

How can young persons get credit if they have never had it? The answer is to build a credit history to show *creditworthiness*. From the creditor's point of view, lending money in any amount involves risk. Good credit performance records provide some assurance the money will be repaid. The Star Capsule "Getting Started" on page 121 shows steps a young person can take to build a credit history.

Credit bureaus (local credit reporting agencies) are linked to national information networks such as TRW, Equifax, and TransUnion. They keep records and sell them to banks and other creditors. The ***Federal Fair Credit Reporting Act*** (1971) allows a person to see credit bureau records for a small fee. Errors or omissions can be corrected. A good credit history record is important when it comes time for the bigger loans people need such as mortgages.

☆ Capsule – Handling a Credit Card

Adapted from American Express Co., *Building a Credit Record*, NY 1993

- Have no more than two or three cards. Too many open accounts scare many bank loan officers. (Just one is plenty for college students.)
- Keep a list of card numbers in a safe place.
- Beware of "Minimum Payment Syndrome." Pay card balance in full when possible to avoid interest charges.
- Grace periods only count when you have no outstanding balance.
- Keep track of charges to avoid exceeding the card's limit.
- Cash advances at banks, ATMs, or by telegraph are very costly.
- Save receipts and compare them to your card statement.
- Be careful in stores. (Get the card back from clerks. Ask for and destroy carbons after the transaction.)
- Inform card company of loss and of change of address.
- Never give card number to an unknown caller.
- Work out a repayment plan if you get in trouble.
- Don't be afraid to switch to cards that offer lower rates or no annual fees. (Remember, this is a consumer service, not a doctor-patient relationship.)

Banks: Gatekeepers of the Money Supply

In the aggregate sense, credit and savings do help the economy grow. Money stored by consumers and businesses provides financial institutions with the funds to lend to others.

Many categories of borrowers spend the money, expanding economic activity. Consumers borrow to buy more goods and services. Businesses borrow to buy capital resources and expand production. Government borrows to provide more services. Therefore, the elements of economic growth depend on money being stored (savings) and made available (credit) to borrowers.

Because the money supply changes with conditions in the economy, it is important to keep watch over it. This is the realm of financial institutions. In particular, regulation of the banking system is the realm of the central bank of the United States, the **Federal Reserve System**, or "the **FED**."

Financial institutions include commercial banks, savings and loan associations, and credit unions (see Figure 6.4 on next page). Although they vary, this discussion refers to them generally as "banks." Banks are private businesses that make profits by lending money. Because loans create new money, banks have enormous power to alter the money supply and economic life in general. Most are habitually careful to make judicious loans.

Figure 6.4

FINANCIAL INSTITUTIONS

Types of Financial Institutions and Characteristics

Type	Characteristics
Commercial Bank	• Business banks. • Chartered by state and federal government (latter have "National" in their name). • Cater to large-scale businesses activities with short-term, high risk loans. • Handle approximately 65% of loans in the country. • Offer full range of services (consumer loans, savings and checking accounts).
Savings and Loan Association	• Primarily consumer banks. • Began as consumer mortgage banks. • Still make more than half the country's private home mortgages. • 1980s deregulation allowed S&Ls to enter commercial markets with checking, short-term business loans and other investments.
Mutual Savings Bank	• Primarily small consumer banks (most on east coast). • Make about 10% of nation's mortgages and some installment loans.
Credit Union	• Employee-owned banks within corporations and labor unions that work from payroll deduction deposits. • 1980s deregulation allowed CU's to enter commercial markets with checking, short-term business loans, and other investments plus offer services such as insurance and financial planning. • Through recent growth and collapse of many S&Ls, CU's now exceed all other banks in number.

Yet, 19th and 20th century history shows examples of widespread bank misjudgments, causing the economy to crumble. In 1913, Congress created the independent Federal Reserve System to regulate the supply of money and act as a general supervisor of banks. Before looking at the mechanics of the FED, some groundwork on banking in general is necessary.

Lending rarely takes place in currency. Remember that nearly 90% of the M-1 money supply is in demand deposits or checkbook money. (In 2000, M-1 = $1,194 billion.) When a bank gives a loan, it credits the borrower's checking account. The borrower begins writing more checks. Those who receive these new checks deposit them in their banks. Their banks' assets grow, and they can lend more. This scenario takes place in thousands of places, thousands of times in a business day, and it expands the money supply.

"How Banks Expand Money" (Figure 6.5 on page 125) offers another example. If Jane Olsen, owner of Olsen's Figures & Fitness, arrived at the Sparta National Bank wishing to borrow $14,000 and the bank agreed, this amount would be transferred into Olsen's account. Suppose Jane buys 10 exercycles for the $14,000 from Argonaut Enterprises. Then Argonaut deposits the $14,000 in its accounts at the Athens bank.

Figure 6.5

HOW BANKS EXPAND MONEY

See example of Olsen Figures & Fitness, Argonaut enterprises and Athens Bank.

Deposits		Less 10% Reserve		Loan Money Available	
A&P Supermarket	$8,000	minus	$800	results in	$7,200
Wendy's Restaurant	$6,000	minus	$600	results in	$5,400
Exxon Service Station	$1,000	minus	$100	results in	$900
Cotillion Hair Salon	$750	minus	$75	results in	$675
Total	$15,750	minus	$ 1,575	results in	$14,175

The money supply would continue to expand. The Athens Bank would keep 10% of the deposits on reserve and lend the balance of $12,600 to other customers. The loans and deposits would keep flowing through the system as new money. Each bank would reduce the deposited amounts by 10% for reserves and make the rest available for loans. Eventually, the flow trickles out. Still, this procedure repeats itself thousands of times a day at banks all over the country – and the globe.

Monetary expansion works, but without limits, it can get out of hand. Like all businesses, banks want to make profits. The more loans, the more profit from borrowers paying back the principal with interest. This all takes place with the stroke of a banker's pen – or actually, a keystroke on the computer. It seems too fragile, too exposed to human error. It is. Some control is needed. In the U.S. economy, the control comes from the FED and other government agencies.

Laws require banks to keep 10-15% of deposits on **reserve** (cannot be lent) as a safety margin. This is to avoid over lending and to have money on hand for depositors' routine withdrawals. The balance is available for loans.

Historically, without some enforceable system of fractional reserve control, banks have been known to lend more than they have in deposits. Banks claim they can manage very well with only 2% on reserve. Isolated cases of reckless lending have local repercussions, but widespread imprudence can wreck the economy. An oversupply of money can cause inflation and confusion. An under supply of money can slow economic activity to a halt. Both have happened frequently (see "S&L Crisis" on page 132).

The Federal Reserve controls the flow of money in the U.S. banking system through regulations and the adjustment of the interest rate the FED charges to member banks. ©PhotoDisc

Figure 6.6

12 Districts of the Federal Reserve System

Federal Reserve Bank Cities

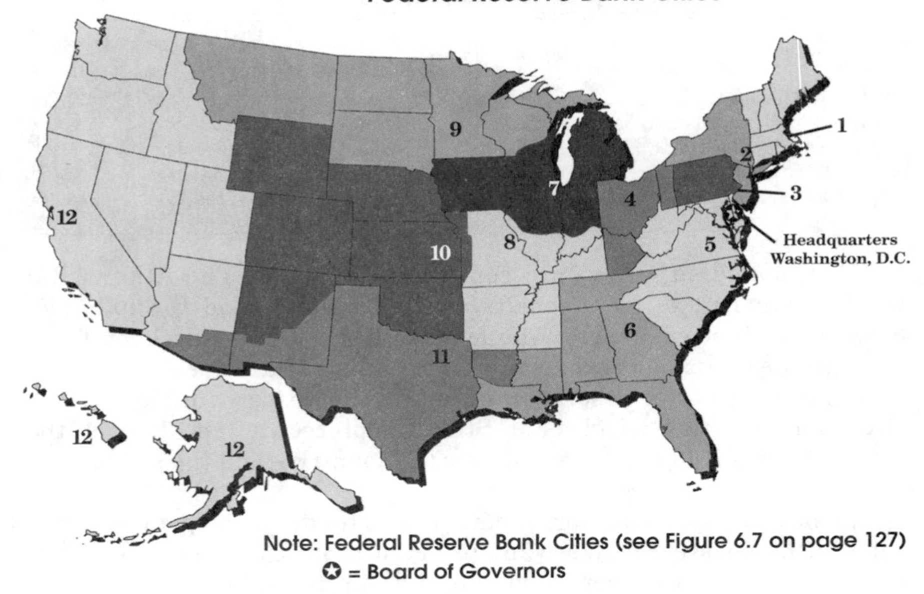

Note: Federal Reserve Bank Cities (see Figure 6.7 on page 127)
✪ = Board of Governors

U.S. Banking Regulation: The Federal Reserve

Controlling the amount and flow of money is crucial to economic life. Checkbook money flows rapidly through the country and the world. If the economy falters in a one place and one bank fails, many others are placed in jeopardy. There is much isolated judgment involved, but banks are linked with others in far-off places. Worldwide, they are vulnerable to the unevenness of economic activity, misjudgments, and even the corruption of others.

It is easy to see the important role bank deposits play in the national and global economy. Throughout history, bank failures and financial panics caused the money supply to shrink, hurting thousands of people. After a terrible panic in 1907 that nearly wrecked the national economy, Congress made significant changes in banking law. In 1913, Congress moved to bring some central control to the banking industry. It created the Federal Reserve Bank System, "... to furnish an elastic currency [and] more effective supervision of banking."

The FED, or Federal Reserve, is a "central bank." It is where the funds of the government are deposited, and where large commercial banks can borrow and deposit funds. As a major source of funds for member banks, the FED exerts a strong (but not absolute) control over the nation's money supply. It is an independent alliance of nearly one-third (6,000) of the national and state chartered commercial banks in the U.S. Membership is voluntary – except for federally chartered "national banks."

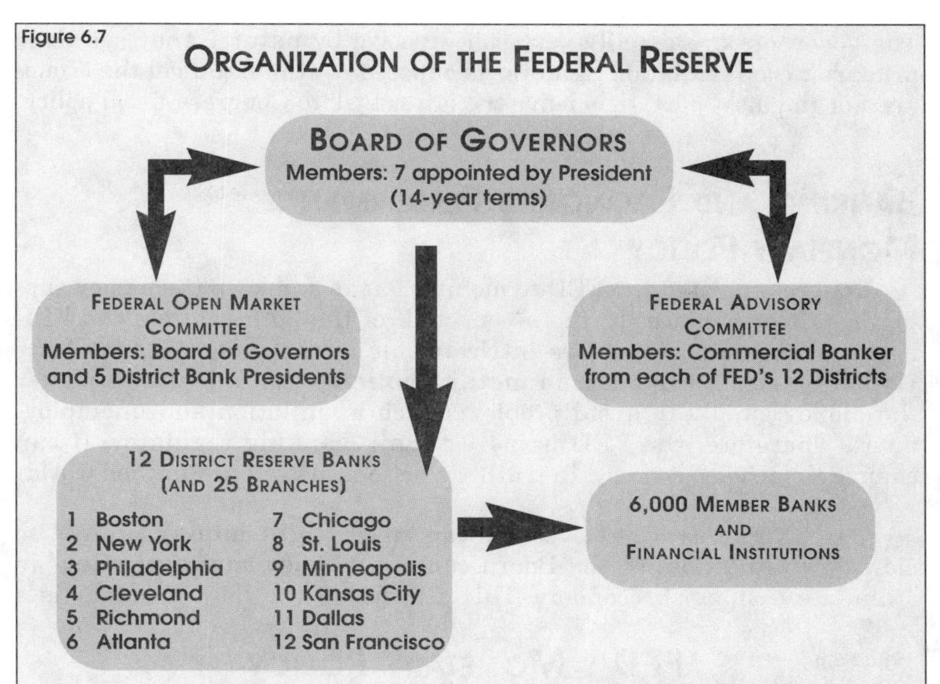

Figure 6.7 Organization of the Federal Reserve

The Board of Governors in Washington consults with the presidents of the FED's 12 district banks and supervises banking operations, regulates the money supply, and establishes credit rules for the nation. The 12 district banks are nonprofit "bankers' banks" owned by the member banks. They perform many services for the banking community:

- Make low interest loans to member banks to keep proper reserves.
- Hold reserves on account for member banks.
- Modify and administer the policies set by the FED's Board of Governors to meet the needs of banks in their district.
- Computer process (credit/debit) the 40 billion checks written in the country.
- Transfer funds among the 12 districts.
- Make loans to the government, especially for disaster aid (floods, earthquakes, hurricanes, etc.).
- Disburse new U.S. currency (and destroy old, worn currency).
- Regulate the money supply rules set by the Board of Governors.

The 12 district banks "customize and fine-tune" the basic regulations set down by the Board of Governors to the particular circumstances in their region of the country.

Member banks join by buying stock in one of the 12 district banks of the system (see Figure 6.6).

Every two years the President appoints, and Congress confirms, one of 7 individuals for a 14-year term on the FED's Board of Governors (see Figure 6.7). However, that is the only official connection the FED has to the government. It is an independent agency that operates out of the realm of politics. In this sense, it is like a "Supreme Court of Banking."

The governors are usually very conservative by nature. They see their primary task as inflation fighters, as opposed to stimulators of the economy. For the most part, they leave the latter task to Congress' fiscal policy.

Banking and Economic Performance: Monetary Policy

Congress created the FED to monitor banks and keep the money supply in proper balance. In the second half of the 20th century, the FED began playing an even more intricate role in the economic life of the United States. It can enact **monetary policies** that *intentionally* alter the money supply to avoid problems such as inflation and unemployment. Therefore, the FED is more than a banking regulator. It can change the whole economy. In truth, its actions are felt around the world.

The FED's Board of Governors can enact "**tight money policy**" to slow down inflation, or the Board can enact "**easy money policy**" to stimulate a sluggish economy. This altering of the flow of money is a

Figure 6.8 **FED's Monetary Policy**
How the FED Controls the Money Supply

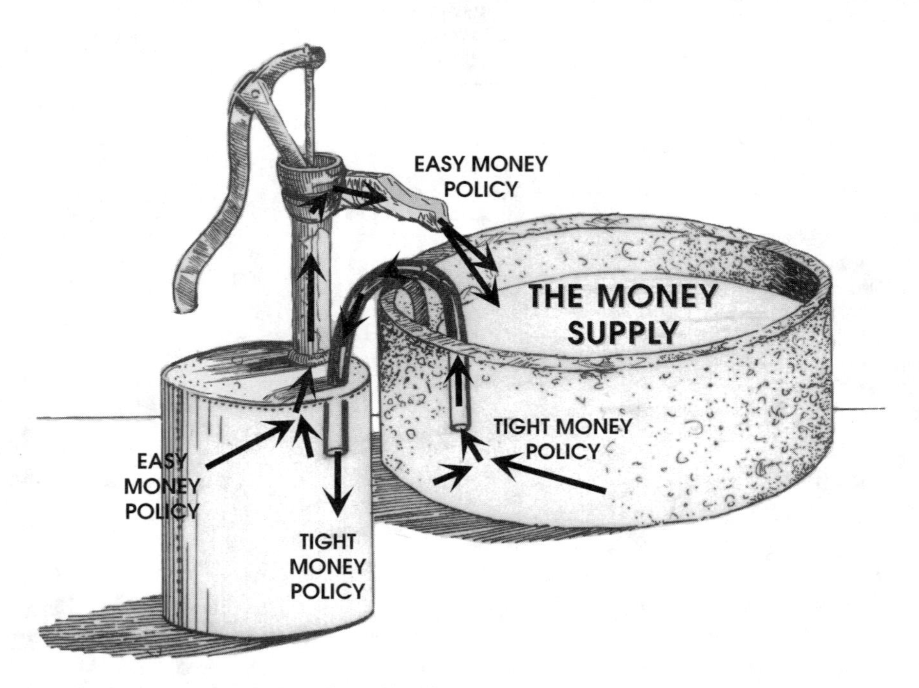

FED Monetary Policies

broad and controversial power not always popular with the public or politicians. The Board uses its basic tools to regulate banking activities. However, when the Board senses a problem, it can intensify its use of these same tools to change the flow of money through the country – and the world (see Figure 6.8). In order of frequency of use, the three basic tools available to the FED are: open market operations, adjustment of the discount rate, and adjustment of the reserve requirement.

Open Market Operations

Open Market Operations is the most frequently used of the tools. The **FOMC** (Federal Open Market Committee) meets often and authorizes the buying and selling of government securities (Treasury bills, notes, and bonds) to registered bond dealers. If the FOMC decides more money is needed in the economy, it puts in an order for the dealers to buy bonds at a price higher than the current market price. Bondholders seize the opportunity to make profits and sell. The FED gets bonds and, in exchange, pumps money to the sellers. The money supply expands, and the economy is stimulated.

If inflation threatens, FOMC sells bonds at high interest. Since they are a solid investment, dealers grab the opportunity. In this way, the FED siphons money out of the economy. FOMC activities allow the FED to make constant adjustments to the money supply over short time periods.

Discount Rate Adjustment

Discount Rate Adjustment is a stronger tool but less frequently used. It has a deeper and more longer-lasting effect than FOMC's Open Market Operations. The **discount rate** is the rate of interest that the FED district banks charge member banks for loans. Member banks borrow money from the FED's 12 district banks to keep their reserves at the proper level. At different times in the year, such as planting time in agricultural regions, commercial banks have to lend large amounts. Reserves go down and the banks borrow to keep their reserves at legal levels.

- *Lowering* the discount rate encourages banks to borrow more for loans, and money gets pumped into the economy.

- *Raising* the discount rate means banks have to pay more for FED loans. This discourages banks from borrowing, and they will have less to lend customers. Raising the discount rate siphons money out of the economy.

Changing the discount rate has broad implications. The FED's discount rate is a financial benchmark. Banks can only make a profit if they charge customers a higher rate than they themselves are paying for loans. If the FED raises the discount rate, big banks raise the **prime**

☆ Capsule – Economic Profile: Economist Alan Greenspan

Alan Greenspan, Chairman of the FED's Board of Governors, is one of the most prominent economists in the country, Greenspan was born in New York City on 6 March 1926. He was educated at New York University, where he was awarded three degrees with high honors in economics. Greenspan worked and prospered on Wall Street before being named to President Ford's Council of Economic Advisors (1974-1977). In 1987, he was appointed to head the Federal Reserve System by President Reagan and was reappointed by Presidents Bush and Clinton.

As a conservative economist, Alan Greenspan continued the strong anti-inflationary policies of his predecessor, Paul Volcker. Greenspan's policy is simple: growth is necessary, but it must be a slow, steady, managed growth. If the economy begins to expand too quickly, he feared the "boom" would be followed by a "bust." Greenspan believed that an overactive economy quickly dissolves into serious recession.

Over the years, Chairman Greenspan testified frequently before Congressional committees. Each time he appeared, his message was clear and concise: the economy must be controlled, avoiding rapid growth, inflation, and recession. William Greider, author of *Secrets of the Temple,* made an analogy of the FED as "...a supervising engineer who has the power to alter the flows inside the plumbing. Its policies could stimulate the flow of lending, choke it off, or nudge it to different channels. The Fed accomplishes this by injecting more fluid into the system or withdrawing it-that is by creating or destroying money." (John Hauchette, "Nation Asks: What Recovery? Fed Hits Brakes," *Poughkeepsie Journal* 19 February 1995, 1)

Greenspan's leadership experienced strong criticism. Many economists believed that there were areas of this country that never really recovered from the 1990-91 recession. They suffered from high unemployment and needed the stimulation that "cheap money" gave to the job market. These people blamed Greenspan's cautious fear of inflation for never having had a "real recovery." Many economic professionals and nonprofessionals alike asked: "Is the FED too preoccupied with inflation? Were people forced into part-time employment without benefits, because the Federal Reserve Board of Governors was unjustifiably afraid of inflation? Could it be that the Fed misread the economy all along? Were the Governors' forecasting antennae out of alignment?"

At the center of the controversy was Greenspan, a man that possessed political power, media access, and control of his colleagues. He was a master of understatement who always appeared frail and slightly bent. Yet, armed with strong conviction and potent ties to Wall Street, this conservative Republican – a strong free trade advocate – continued his fight for what he believed was proper policy. Alan Greenspan survived several presidential administrations and attacks by both Congress and the national press. Greenspan's vision and strategies brought the FED into the 21st century.

rate. "The Prime" is the rate the big banks charge big customers on large, short-term business loans (see Figure 6.9 on page 131). It is usually about 3% higher than the FED's discount rate. Just about all other interest rates in the country are linked to the Prime. For example, banks figure most credit card interest rates at 5-9% over the prime. If the FED alters the discount rate, big banks alter the Prime. The availability of money either increases or decreases.

Figure 6.9

LARGEST BANKS IN THE U.S. IN 2001

with combined assets exceeding $3.6 trillion

Source: *American Banker*, 2002

1- Citigroup (NY)
2 - J.P. Morgan Chase and Co. (NY)
3 - BankAmerica Corp. (NC)
4 - Wells Fargo Co. (CA)
5 - Bank One Corp. (IL)
6 - First Union Corp. (NC)
7 - Taunus Corp (NY)
8 - Fleet Boston Financial Corp. (MA)
9 - Suntrust Banks, Inc. (GA)
10 - National City Corp. (OH)

RESERVE REQUIREMENT ADJUSTMENT

Reserve Requirement Adjustment is rarely used. Altering bank reserves (currently around 12%) is an extremely powerful action. Lowering requirements – even slightly – pumps billions in loan money into bankers' hands. Raising reserve requirements siphons it away. It is so massive and unpredictable a force that using it precisely is very difficult.

LIMITS ON THE FED'S POWER

Judicious use of monetary policy by the FED can do much to keep the economy growing and stable. While this is true, there are limits to the FED's effectiveness. It is easier to withdraw money in the face of inflation than to push money through the banks in a recession. This is because in recessions business is very slow. Demand for loans declines. Banks themselves become very cautious about lending in an unstable economy, even to highly rated corporations and individuals.

Monetary policy is also limited because it is **discretionary**. First, members of the Board of Governors and FOMC must use their judgment about what to do, how much to do, and when to do it. While they are experts, they are still human beings, and their judgments can be flawed. Second, time also passes while the banks respond to FED orders. The result may be too little, too late. Lastly, other government actions can offset FED actions. For example, Reagan's tax cuts of the early 1980s pushed money into the economy and worked against FED efforts to stop inflation. It is also worth repeating that the FED Governors are notoriously conservative and see themselves as currency auditors rather than fiscal manipulators. They traditionally prefer to move slowly, in response to events, rather than take preemptive action.

Banking Reform: The Great Depression

The creation of the Federal Reserve in 1913 was one of the most significant economic actions in U.S. history, but it did not solve all the nation's banking problems. The FED was nearly powerless when banks began collapsing in the Great Depression. People were frightened. "Runs" on banks wiped out reserves quickly. Banks had few alternatives. They foreclosed on bad loans and auctioned repossessed property. This did little to meet the panicking public's demand for money.

When Franklin D. Roosevelt became President in March 1933, he called time out and ordered all banks to close. President Roosevelt went on the radio to calm people's fears. He told the public that after federal examiners gave their approval to reopen a bank, it was solvent.

This "Bank Holiday" psychology worked. People went along. Congress then passed an ***Emergency Banking Act*** (***Glass-Steagall Act, 1933***). It forbade banks to invest in stocks and began insuring savings accounts through the **FDIC** (Federal Deposit Insurance Corporation). The combination of these unprecedented federal actions stopped the runs on the banks. Later, Congress made the FDIC permanent and created federal deposit insurance programs for savings banks (FSLIC) and other financial institutions.

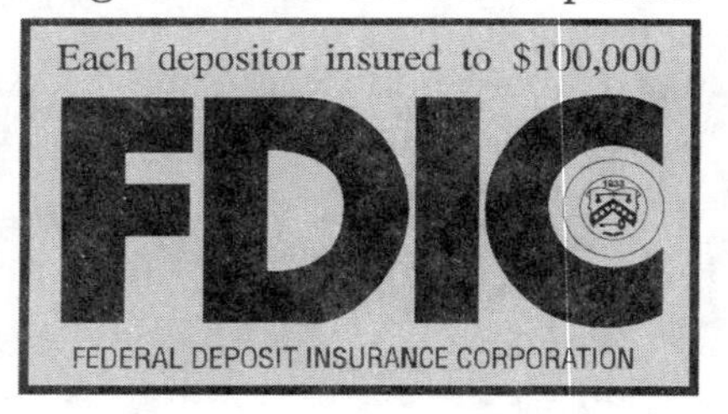

Banking Deregulation: S&Ls in Crisis

The population explosion and the rapid pace of change in people's lives after World War II led to many changes in banking. In 1980, Congress passed the ***Depository Institutions' Deregulation and Monetary Act***. Its reforms allowed savings banks and credit unions to offer nearly all the services of commercial banks, especially checking accounts. The act also placed many more financial institutions under the FED's reserve regulations. Also, it allowed banks to pay interest on checking accounts. The *Depository Act* broadened banking activities and services for the nation. States changed laws too. Small banks merged with others to become regional banks. The *Depository Act* deregulated consumer interest rates making the whole banking industry a more dynamic market.

However, there were unforeseen repercussions of this deregulation. Federal bank examiners could not keep up with inspections and some banks took advantage of the lax atmosphere. The confusion of technological changes, legal changes, and wide-open competition led to mismanagement and even corruption.

A large number of banks failed in the wake of the 1980s deregulation. Bad crop years and dropping oil prices in the middle 1980s put pressure on banks in the Midwest and the Southwest. The recession of 1981-1983 led to failures too. New, inexperienced S&Ls (Savings and Loan Associations) made too many risky loans, particularly in real estate (especially in the South and Southwest).

Some S&L operators were corrupt and manipulated the new laws and depositors' money to finance personal empires. An example was Charles Keating of Lincoln Savings and Loan of California. Keating's fraudulent activities included attempting to bribe U.S. Senators to avoid pressure from federal examiners. Resolving the problems of his bank alone cost taxpayers an estimated $2.6 billion.

Between 1985 and 1993, an average of 175 banks per year closed or were taken over by federal regulators. The Federal Farm Credit System and the FSLIC (Federal Savings and Loan Insurance Corporation) both collapsed trying to pay all the depositors of the failed savings institutions. Congress tried to stop the financial hemorrhaging. It bolstered the FDIC and created the Resolution Trust Corporation to manage failed banks affairs. The cost to taxpayers of bailing out insured depositors and liquidating assets of failed banks exceeded $600 billion.

Planning for Savings and Investment

When creating a savings plan an important aspect to consider is the amount of **risk** that is comfortable for an individual. The more security an investment presents usually means less of a return. The higher the risk, the greater the possibility of high returns. The higher the possibility of gain is tied to a greater possibility of loss.

Another aspect of investment is **liquidity**. How important is it to the investor to have assets available on demand? With a regular savings account, there is no penalty assessed on money. All or a portion of it can be withdrawn at any time without any penalty – but the interest received (return or gain) is low. Putting money into a **Certificate of Deposit** (CD), promises a higher rate of return for leaving the money untouched for a specific amount of time. However, with a CD, if the money is withdrawn before maturity, a penalty is levied. With a CD arrangement, the investor exchanges liquidity for greater gain.

The last issue to consider is **return.** The money invested should make a difference in current standard of life, future plans and general-well-being. The purpose of investing is to generate additional assets by earning income or profit. In most situations, in order to accomplish this goal working with some sort of financial intermediary such as a bank, a stockbroker, a financial advisor, or a mutual fund manager is necessary.

In order to make the best choices in a savings plan, an investor must collect information – lots of information. The investor must look to co-workers as well as family, friends, investment guides in book shops, periodicals, newspapers, television, and internet services. This information should helps to determine the three major considerations of investment: risk, liquidity, and return. Of course, an investor must remember the most basic economic concept of scarcity is at play here. Investing scarce financial resources involves choices and there are opportunity costs and trade offs to be considered.

Common Investment Choices: Bonds

Basically, a **bond** is a loan. It represents a debt created by a company or a government (local, state, or federal) that must be repaid to an investor. As is the case whenever a loan is made, the principal and interest is repaid (total return). This type of investment usually has a low risk of loss. As a result, the interest rate is generally not very high (but there are some exceptions to this).

The best known example of this kind of investment is the United States Savings Bond. Many people receive this investment as a gift on a special occasion. Some investors have a payroll deduction account that automatically purchases bonds periodically.

Local municipalities also issue bonds – when given permission to do so from local residents. Such a bond issue is often brought to the voters in order to pay for a large cost need. A town may want to build a sewer system, a school board may want to build a new school, a city may need to add more public transportation, while a state may need funds to build such things as prisons, highways, or bridges. When issued, these municipal bonds have an additional advantage: they grant the owner tax free status on the interest that the bond earns. (On most other investments, interest and dividends are considered income and add to your taxable income).

Another government issue is the United States Treasury Bond. Like municipal bonds these, are exempt from local and state taxes but not from federal income tax.

Government bonds appear to be a very safe investment since people would have a difficult time thinking that a government, at any level, could claim bankruptcy. However, such things do happen (Orange County California in the 1990s). This is why all bonds are subject to an appraisal system that rates a bond from the highest rating of triple A, to the lowest rating of D (usually in default). These grades are given to issued bonds by companies such as Moody's or Standard and Poor's.

There are three important considerations that an investor must examine and appraise when thinking of putting money into bonds: **maturity** (length of time you must wait for repayment), **coupon rate** (the amount of interest you will be paid for making the loan), and **par value** (the principal amount you must give to the borrower).

☆ Capsule – Bond Investing

Suppose a person lives in a town that has approved the construction of a sewer system and wants to invest in the project. She learns that each bond sold is in ten thousand dollar denominations. This is the par value and the town is willing to pay six percent interest (coupon rate) on the loan while the time of maturity is ten years. This means that she will have to have $10,000 to invest, which will earn her $600 a year in income for ten years leading to a **yield** (return) of $6,000.

Besides government bonds, there are other types of bonds that may be considered for your savings plan. **Corporate bonds** are loans to private businesses. Firms issue them periodically to raise money. They are available in many denominations, usually ranging from $1,000 to $10,000. Of course, the interest an investor collects is liable to income tax, so she/he must be concerned with how much income the investor will be able to keep when considering corporate bonds for her/his savings plan. Investors must also consider the risk involved - companies do go bankrupt. All payments on such corporate loans depend on the profitability of the firm.

The rule of thumb in investing is simple – the higher the promised return, the higher the risk of loss. **Junk bonds** are high yield investments. As such, they carry a high risk of loss with their purchase. New companies issue high yield junk bonds in order to generate demand in the marketplace by having a positive aspect of the investment offsetting the negative. During the 1980s, these bonds were an extremely popular type of financing corporate takeovers (mergers). More recently, junk bonds have been used by companies to expand in ways they would not otherwise be able.

Like everything else in a marketplace, the value of any bond depends on supply and demand. Supply is determined by the borrower who decides how much more money is needed than they have available. They then issue bonds for that amount. The demand is determined by the lender (those who purchase the bonds). Their motivation is simple – the income that can be earned by lending their money. The higher the return, the more people will want to buy. For example, if the federal government offers an issue of bonds at 3% and they are not bought, the government will increase the interest (coupon rate) paid until the bonds do sell.

As is the case in many markets, there is a primary and secondary purchase of a product. In the case of bonds, the **primary market** is between the government agency or company that issues the bond and the buyer. The **secondary market** is between any buyer of a bond and anyone else who wants to purchase it. Interest rates are also constantly changing and may go up or down – all of which will affect the plans of any investor.

☆ Capsule – The Junk Bond King

In the 1980s, financier Michael R. Milken made millions for the Wall Street firm of Drexel Burnham Lambert. Junk bonds are high yield securities that most companies and investors shun because traditional rating services consider them too risky. The bonds allowed rapid corporate growth and job-creation. MCI Communications and Turner Broadcasting were two firms that realized phenomenal growth by employing them.

In 1986, federal prosecutor Rudolph Guiliani indicted Milken for fraud and insider-trading on evidence from co-conspirator financier Ivan Boesky. Milken pleaded guilty and Drexel Burnham collapsed. Milken served a two-year jail sentence and was fined over $1 billion.

Common Investment Choices: Stocks

The stock market used to be a consideration for only the wealthy in our society, but in recent times things changed drastically. As employment benefits such pensions diminished, planning for retirement income has become the responsibility of the individual. Because savings kept in banks yielded low returns (1%-3%), more and more middle income workers placed money they earmarked for retirement into stock investment.

Shares of a corporation's ownership are first sold by the company in what is known as an **IPO** (initial public offering). This provides the corporation with the money it needs or wants. This primary sale is followed by many sales and purchases of the stock certificates in the secondary market (people buying from other people). With these secondary sales, the corporation itself gets no financial help, but based on supply and demand the value of the stock will increase or decrease in the stock market.

For the investor, there are two basic means of making money by including stock in a financial plan. The first is to buy shares of stock at a low price and hope that the demand for that stock increases so that it can sell at a higher price. When a company continually reinvests profits back into itself (not paying dividends) it creates growth and increases the value of the corporation. This increases the value of its stock. This practice creates what is known as **growth stock**.

The second way to earn income from the purchase of stock is to collect **dividends** (the distribution of a portion of the firm's profits among its shareholders). This type of financial practice creates an **income stock**. When the board of directors of a corporation decides not to pay a dividend to stockholders, they reward the shareholders support of the new growth by splitting the stock. The board may also decide to **split** stock because they assume that potential buyers would be discouraged from adding the stock to their investment portfolios because the price per share is too high.

A split is determined when the directors agree on a formula that allows for additional stock to be given to shareholders. It can be an even 1:1, or 1:3, or 2:5. Whatever the result, a shareholder's stock portfolio increases. The price of the stock is reflected in the split. If the stock was selling for $100 before the split and then the price becomes $50/share, the shareholder has more shares and the hope is that the value of those shares will increase as the corporation continues to grow.

There are very few situations in which an individual is allowed to purchase shares of stock. One is if you are an employee of a corporation which allows you to have a payroll deduction account for the purpose of buying shares of stock. A second opportunity given to individuals may come when a utility that the investor uses – an electric utility for instance – may allow for the purchase of stock during a specified period of time.

Usually, in order to purchase a bond or stock, a consumer must contact a third person, a broker. The broker earns a living from commissions – fees garnered from buying and selling these financial products. These agents make a bid to buy or offer to sell a person's stock for a particular price in the market. If the price is accepted by sellers or buyers, a deal is made.

The place where these actions take place is known as a **stock** or **bond exchange**. An exchange is nothing more than an actual marketplace where these certificates are bought and sold. Most major cities host such exchanges, but the best known are found in New York City. The New York Stock Exchange (NYSE), and the American Stock Exchange (Amex) / National Association of Securities Dealers Automated Quotation (NASDAQ) are the largest in this country.

The NYSE began trading in 1792 outdoors in the area which is now the financial district in Lower Manhattan. As it grew, it limited the number of members who could buy a "seat" (permission to trade on the exchange). The NYSE handles the sale and purchase of only the largest and most established companies. It lists companies that meet its criteria by value and size. It includes the best known corporations (generally known as **Blue Chip Stocks**). The stocks of these firms are generally in high demand because they are considered by investors to be stable and able to continue to do business with good profitability.

NASDAQ-AMEX was created in 1998 when the American Stock Exchange, then the second largest in the country, merged with the National Association of Securities Dealers Automated Quotation system which traded a large number of technology and energy stocks. NASDAQ-AMEX trades in lesser known and riskier stocks than does the NYSE.

Another way that stock is traded is known as the OTC (Over-the-Counter) market. This is where stock of companies not listed on an organized exchange are traded. These companies do not meet the criteria established by the major exchanges or are new and unknown. Generally, this means that they do not pay dividends, but instead take any profit they earn and reinvest it in growth. They will be listed in newspapers but will be traded electronically by brokers.

The environment in which stocks are traded changes. The majority can be very active with values going up, or they can fall and become inactive. In general, when stocks are doing well, it is termed a **Bull Market** and the opposite situation is known as a **Bear Market**. A group of indexes tell the investors what the market is doing. The best known of these indexes is the **Dow Jones Industrial Average** ("The Dow") (see Figure 6.10). Dow Jones & Company has other listings that show what the stocks in particular industries are doing such as in agriculture, transportation. "The Dow" tells investors what is happening to the value of a group of specific stocks (chosen by Dow Jones). "The Dow" indicates the value of a select portfolio of thirty different stocks on a day-to-day basis.

Figure 6.10

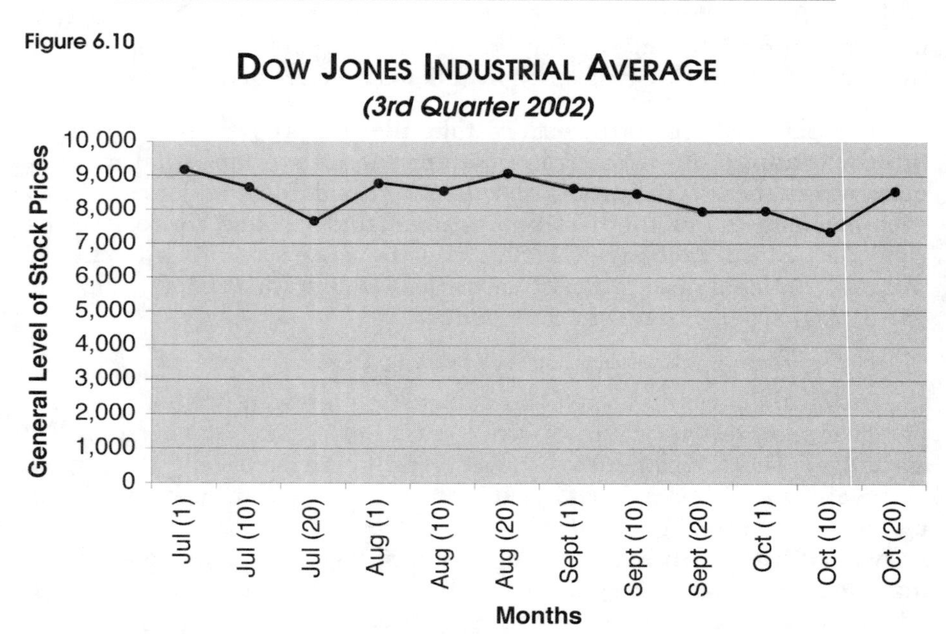

During 2002, the value of "The Dow" went from above 11,000 to just around 8,000. This happened while investors purchased fewer and fewer stocks – indicative of a Bear Market.

As opposed to "The Dow", the **Standard and Poor's 500** is a broader index of what is happening in the stock market. It tracks 500 different stocks that run the entire breadth of types and kinds of stock. The stocks found in this collection are found on the major exchanges as well as the OTC market.

Common Investment Choices: Mutual Funds

When an investor is uncertain about the stock and bond markets, or does not have the time or inclination to research all the possibilities, she/he can decide to invest indirectly through a **mutual fund**. This is a professional investment company that continually offers investors shares in its investment ventures. Mutual fund managers use a fund's capital to invest in diversified securities. In such a situation, the savings of many investors are pooled. The money is invested for them by a professional fund manager in a variety of stocks and bonds to create a diversified (broad) portfolio. Investors do not own stock outright, they own shares in the fund company which, in turn, owns the stocks.

The Educated Investor: Market Reports

Keeping track of investments can be exciting, but it can also be unsettling. It is pleasing to watch the value of a stock portfolio, bond investment, or mutual fund go up steadily. But if investments keep plunging in value, emotions seem to follow in the same direction. Some investors continually check on how their finances are doing, while others may be unable or unwilling to keep track.

Usually, an investor turns to reading the stock reports in the newspaper, watching the electronic ticker tape broadcast on television, or using the internet for specific quotes, charts, and relevant articles in magazines. Also, bond and mutual fund reports are available from these three sources.

☆ Capsule – How to Read the Stock Tables

Most newspapers report daily NYSE and Nasdaq/AMEX activities in a list format. Most papers have a general key to their particular listing format. They vary somewhat, but most reflect the general items that follows:

Name: Stocks are listed alphabetically by the firm's assigned abbreviation on the exchange.
Last: Stock's closing price for that day.
Chge: Loss or gain for the day
DIV: Current annual dividend
E/S: 12-month % change in earnings per share
P/E: price-earnings ratio over the last 4 quarters
YTD%: Percent change in price since Dec. 31

Summary

Understanding money, credit, and banking are important to everyone. Young people must know how to manage money and credit. As consumers, they must learn to select accounts and credit arrangements that meet their needs and help their earnings grow. The choices are many and often complex. Yet, they are crucial to achieving the American Dream.

Assessment • Questions • Applications

1 It is fact that maney is used as a convenient medium of exchange. However, most people do not even think about the other two important functions of money.
   a How hard would it be to function without money as a standard of value?
   b How hard would it be to function without money as a store of wealth?
   c Barter was once a way of life. Could we go back to it? Explain, why or why not.

2 This chapter begins with a story about credit cards. Credit is a an essential part of modern American life.
   a Can a person function without credit? Explain why or why not.
   b What are the advantages of having credit?
   c What are the disadvantages of using credit?

3 Suppose banks have to keep 10% of deposits on reserve. Now, suppose you borrow $10,000 for a car loan. Your bank credits your checking account with $10,000 and you write a check for that amount to Mr. Mobilo, the used car dealer. Mr. Mobilo deposits the $10,000 in his bank.
   a How much of Mr. Mobilo's deposit can his bank lend?
   b If the original $10,000 loan kept rolling through banks this way, it could create $100,000 in new money. Explain how this happens.

4 The Federal Reserve has great power to control the money supply through banking. Suppose you were a member of the FED's Board of Governors. Explain what policy you would recommend if:
   a researchers say the economy is going into a period of serious inflation.
   b researchers say the economy is going into a period of serious recession.
   c Explain which of these policies has the best chance for success.

5 "The *Depository Institutions' Deregulation and Monetary Act of 1980* caused more problems than it solved." Examine this statement from two points of view:
   a the *Act* increased competition in the banking industry and benefited consumers with more choices and services.
   b the *Act* led to instability and the worst rash of bank closings in history.
   c Explain which point of view you favor.

Assessment Project: Managing Credit Cards

Student Task

In this project, research various credit cards, choose one, and write a report on how that credit card fits into your household management program.

Procedure

1 Review the financial status (Household Financial Profile) of the household you created in the Introduction.

2 Research various credit card services. Assume one charge or credit card would be useful to handle financial matters. Decide which type of card is best for your household. In other words, for which one would you apply? Contact the National Foundation for Credit Counseling (www.nfcc.org or Springboard). Request the "Low Rate List" of card issuers.

3 Design a chart comparing at least three credit and/or charge cards (e.g., VISA, MasterCard, Discover, American Express, a department store card). List items such as annual fee, credit limits (cash and purchases), annual and monthly interest rates, number of days of "grace period" (if any), and additional benefits of card (e.g., travel or buying club, insurance, bonuses and premiums, purchase warranty).

4 Write a brief report on which card you have chosen for your household management. Include:
   - Which card and card issuer chosen and why.
   - Financial data for the card (e.g., APR, annual fee, grace period).
   - Why and how you expect the card to help or hinder the look of your Household Financial Profile.
   - "Pitfalls" to avoid with use of this card.
   - How you intend to use the features of the card.
   - How this card will help establish credit for other forms of credit (e.g., mortgage, personal and collateral loans).

Evaluation

The criteria for the evaluation of this project are itemized in the grid (rubric) that follows. Choice of appropriate category terms (values) is the decision of the instructor. Selection of terms such as "minimal," "satisfactory," and "distinguished" can vary with each assessment.

Managing Credit Cards Evaluation Rubric

(Refer to the teacher's supplement for suggestions of scoring descriptors for evaluation.)

Evaluation Item
Item a: (1) Does the report show understanding that while different socioeconomic (as well as national, ethnic, religious, racial, and gender) groups have varied perspectives, values, and diverse practices and traditions, they face the same global economic challenges?
Item b: (5) Does the report analyze problems and evaluate decisions about the economic effects caused by human, technological, and natural activities on societies and individuals?
Item c: (6) Does the report present ideas in writing (and orally) in clear, concise, and properly accepted fashion?
Item d: (7) Does the report employ a variety of information from written, graphic, and multimedia sources?
Item e: (8) Does the report show monitoring of, reflection upon, and improvement of work?
Item f: (9) Does the report show cooperative work and respect for the rights of others to think, act, and speak differently?

ISSUE 7

MAKING FISCAL AND MONETARY POLICY I

What are the economic roles of government?

RIDING THE MERRY-GO-ROUND

The managing editor looked harried; that was normal. "Gene," he said, "I know you're the cartoonist for the Op-Ed page, but I don't have a reporter to cover the school board fracas out at Granville tonight. You live out there; could you do me a favor?"

"Jim, I haven't reported on anything in almost twenty years!"

"Come on, Gene. You never lose those skills. We have to get coverage out there. And, you know you owe me about 4,000 favors. Besides, the weather is fantastic."

I had to admit, it was a beautiful spring evening as I sat in the Granville H.S. auditorium. The warm breeze was blowing through the windows, and the sunset was coating all the trees outside in a bright yellow-orange haze. I was feeling wonderful and believed that nothing could upset this fantastic feeling of "spring fever." I thought of a balmy spring night years ago at Oceanside Park with Cindy, the woman who became my wife. We strode the boardwalk and rode the carousel…

A bang of the gavel brought me back to reality. Being at this school board meeting was strange. Both of my children were attending college and I had lost touch with the issues that stirred controversy in the local public school. At a picnic last week, some neighbors voiced concern about the overcrowding of students into elementary classes, but lots of people were moving into the area. Growing pains, I thought.

While I daydreamed, people packed the auditorium. Now they began to yell and scream at one another. When the public comment segment

opened, it was easy to see the audience was divided into factions. I was trying to scribble notes on each group's position. Listening to them attack each other for being an "interest group" brought a cynical smile to my face. I was wondering how naive could they be not to realize that everyone seeks out what is best for themselves. Don't we all belong to special interest groups – both, formally and informally, perhaps intentionally or unintentionally?

One group supported smaller class sizes. That meant more teachers and classrooms and more money. Others wanted to increase class size so that teaching positions would be eliminated, and costs brought down.

There was the parent group with banners trying to influence the Granville Board of Education with their presence. There was a taxpayer group waving charts and graphs. Each had perceptions of what was best for them – and everyone else. One group wanted what was best for their children's future. The other group wanted to protect their lifestyle and finances.

Speeches poured forth, some with impressive statistics and figures, others with personal anecdotes. A senior citizen spoke about the possibility of losing her home of 47 years if taxes increased. A group of young parents spoke about the problems their children faced in large classes that would handicap them for life.

There I was, caught in the middle. I was not just a reporter, I was a taxpayer, too. Of course, the final decision had to be made by the elected officials on the school board. They had to read the sense of the community, but they had to weigh all the local, state, and even federal regulations controlling the finances of education.

The gavel banged again. I sat there as the crowd exited. I got the story, but my head was spinning. I thought back to that lovely spring evening at Oceanside. It was like getting off a merry-go-round… Hey, maybe there is an editorial cartoon in all this!

***** *the end* *****

Introduction

Nothing stirs more controversy than mentioning the role of government in the economy. It is an issue that has existed since the founding of this nation. The American Revolution (1776-1783) was a struggle against the tyranny of unfair taxation and economic restriction. Soon after, a struggle over government's economic power began in President Washington's Cabinet (1790s) between Thomas Jefferson and Alexander Hamilton. Jefferson insisted on a small role for the federal government. Hamilton insisted on a strong, active government as a force for economic development. This sounds somewhat similar to the controversies that flow daily from the national and state capitals in the 1990s.

Alexander Hamilton
First Secretary of the Treasury

CONSTITUTIONAL BATTLES OVER THE ROLES

What does the ***United States Constitution*** have to say about the role of government in the economy? The authors offered some definition of the role of government in this area, delegating to Congress specific economic powers:

Thomas Jefferson
First Secretary of the State

- to impose and collect taxes
- to provide for the common defense and general welfare of the people
- to borrow money on the credit of the United States
- to regulate commerce with foreign nations and among the states
- to coin money and regulate its value
- to establish a post office and roads
- to raise and support military forces
- to make all laws which shall be necessary and proper for carrying into execution the foregoing powers, and all other powers vested by this *Constitution* in the government of the United States

George Washington
First President
of the United States of America

On the basis of these last words (Art. I, section 8, called the "Elastic Clause"), Secretary of the Treasury Hamilton justified his call to create the first Bank of the United States. He argued such a bank was necessary for the government to accomplish its other economic tasks. Hamilton claimed the specific powers to tax, to borrow, and to regulate money and commerce *implied* a bank was necessary. This idea of **implied power** justified a loose (elastic), stretching of the meaning of the delegated powers of Congress.

A struggle soon emerged in President Washington's Cabinet. Secretary of State Jefferson rebutted

Hamilton. In a paper, he claimed Hamilton was stretching government authority too far. Jefferson cited the **Tenth Amendment**. It seemed to contradict the Elastic Clause; it reserved for the states all powers not delegated to the federal government. In a strict approach to government power, Jefferson argued that there was no specific banking power delegated to Congress in the *Constitution*. Therefore, under the Tenth Amendment, the power to create such an institution must be reserved for the states, not the federal government.

This early struggle over strict v. loose interpretation of constitutional clauses shaped the two earliest national parties. In the 1790s, Hamilton's view was the conservative political view (Federalist Party) and Jefferson held the liberal position (Democratic – Republican Party). Over the past two centuries, the meanings of liberal and conservative have changed. Today, **liberal** refers to a loose view that calls for a strong government involvement, and the term **conservative** usually reflects a strict view that calls for as little government rule as possible.

The Supreme Court of the United States, Washington, D.C. @ Photo Disc

After much debate and compromise, President Washington sided with Hamilton. Congress passed the bill and created the first Bank of the United States in 1791. Later, when the bank's power was challenged in the Supreme Court, Chief Justice **John Marshall** upheld Washington's and Hamilton's view (***McCulloch v. Maryland***, 1819). Marshall legitimized the Hamiltonian view that the federal government did have implied powers (unwritten, but hinted at in the *Constitution*). These powers could be used to strengthen the economic role of the national government. Still, for the first 150 years of our history, the economic role of the federal government grew very slowly.

New Roles in the Great Depression

In 1929, everything changed. Prior to the Great Crash, a sense of rugged individualism characterized American thought. The Frontier, or Western Ethic of the 19th century, was a feeling that urged people to "sit tall in the saddle" and "pull yourself up by your bootstraps." The ethic held that individuals could solve their own problems. It implied there was failure, shame, and humiliation in taking charity and welfare. The popular sense was that depressions were part of the normal ups and downs of the economy, and people just had to put up with them. There was an acceptance of laissez-faire: government had to remain separated from the business cycle. Left alone, the economy would always heal itself. Meanwhile, people had to make do with what they had. As a result, Congress and Presidents felt no need to get the federal government involved in relieving economic problems.

Thus, in the early 1930s, there was no established tradition of government intervention. Yet, there had never been a depression affecting the nation so deeply. Understanding of such matters was unrefined. The common feeling was that any interference from government would worsen an economic downturn.

Franklin D. Roosevelt, 32nd President 1933-1945 FDR helped Americans regain faith in themselves.
(photograph of the President portrait, White House)

As the economic turndown worsened, President Herbert Hoover managed to follow the worst possible plan. He and Congress raised taxes. ***The Federal Revenue Act of 1932*** nearly doubled the tax rates. A depression is characterized by a very high rate of unemployment and little consumer spending in society. Taking additional taxes curtails spending even more.

What should Hoover have done? One liberal economist had some ideas. English scholar **John Maynard Keynes** believed that demand (spending) had to be increased. Keynes said increased demand triggers an increase in supply. As people spent more, more goods and services were needed. Factories would rehire people to produce the goods that consumers were demanding. Once the workers were back in the factories earning

☆ Capsule – English Economist John Maynard Keynes

The basis for demand-management or demand–side economics originated in the writings of John Maynard Keynes. The British economist was born in Cambridge, England in 1883. His father, John Neville Keynes, made sure his son was well educated at both Eaton College and Cambridge University, where the elder Keynes taught economics and logic. John Maynard Keynes' first love was mathematics. But influenced by many of his instructors, he finally chose to complete his studies in economics. Keynes distinguished himself as a businessman, as well as a scholar in his field. Right up to his death in 1946, he spent his life mixing and blending many different careers – teacher, editor, civil service, college bursar, scholar, author, and patron of the arts – while amassing a fortune by investing in the stock market.

After World War I, Keynes served his government as an advisor to the British delegation at the peace talks in Versailles. From this experience, he wrote *The Economic Consequences of the Peace*. This book was inspired by the harsh treatment of the German people by the Allies. In it, Keynes predicted the collapse of the European economy because of the severity of the conditions imposed on Germany. His analysis of the circumstances proved prophetic and precise.

Keynes writings covered a wide range of topics, but his most important and influential work was presented in *The General Theory of Employment, Interest, and Money* (1936). This book was written during the Great Depression when millions of American and European workers were unemployed. Traditional economists were unable to present a reason for such a long and painful period in which so many desperate people could not find any work. What had happened to Adam Smith's "invisible hand"? Classical economists considered unemployment an irregular and deviant condition that was only a temporary circumstance. They cautioned that if government would not interfere, the economy would right itself, making a few price and wage adjustments that would put full employment back into place.

Keynes' *General Theory* presented a different view of how the market economy operates and a new prescription for curing the terribly high unemployment rates. Left on its own, the economy may get back into balance, but Keynes demonstrated that it would not necessarily return to full employment. At the center of his theory was the message that government had to become involved and could no longer trust any invisible force to right the economy. He said there was no natural method of correction that would easily and quickly force the economy back into full employment. Keynes claimed the level of employment depended on the total demand for goods and services in the market place. In a depression, this aggregate demand diminishes, and so producers cut back on production and lay off employees. This causes a decline in demand and a downward spiral begins.

In order to increase the aggregate demand for goods and services in the marketplace, Keynes proposed that the government must provide the means to stimulate consumer spending. The increased government spending would ignite a need for increased production, and people would have to be rehired.

Since the Great Depression, capitalist governments all over the world have responded to periods of high unemployment with Keynes prescription. Governments engaged in two major activities designed to stimulate aggregate demand: lowering taxes to give people more spending money and providing jobs by increasing government contracts for public works. Eventually, this government money, spent in the marketplace, would prod private business to begin increased production and put people back to work. When this happens, taxes can be collected to pay back the government for the money it had to spend. From Roosevelt's *New Deal* through the Carter Admin., John Maynard Keynes' ideas were part of our government's economic activities.

wages, they would add to the demand. In turn, factories would have to hire more people, and so on (see sidebar on Keynes, page 149).

How would people get more money in their pockets to start this demand chain reaction? The answer came with the ***New Deal***. When the Democrats won the 1932 Presidential and congressional elections led by New York Governor **Franklin D. Roosevelt**, the nation prepared for a significant change in economic policy. The Democrats campaigned on a platform that promised a *New Deal* for the victims of the Depression, or for that matter, for all Americans.

When Roosevelt took office in 1933, more than a quarter of all workers were jobless, and he was ready to act immediately. In his inaugural address, Roosevelt said, "The nation asks for action, and action now ... We must act, and act quickly." The words were not empty. A series of extraordinary measures followed. They began the slow and painful recovery out of this horrible economic depression.

President Roosevelt's *New Deal* program is an example of government's use of **fiscal policy** (see Figure 7.1 below). This is when the government attempts to use two of its powers, taxation and spending, to stabilize the economy (maintain the level of growth).

Is this role of stabilization Constitutional? It fired up the perpetual loose v. strict battle over implied powers. The New Dealers claimed the role was implied as an evolution of the function of taxation. The Elastic

Figure 7.1

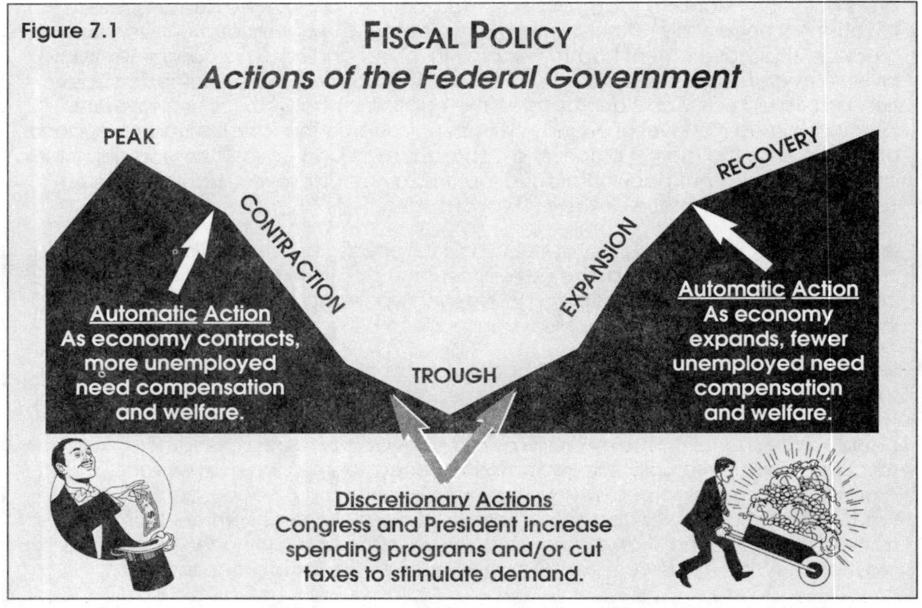

Figure 7.2

FISCAL POLICY: *THE NEW DEAL'S 3 RS*

President and Advisors Suggest Legislation.
Congress Legislates Recommended Programs.

RELIEF	RECOVERY	REFORM
Immediate Action To Halt The Economy's Deterioration	"Pump – Priming" Temporary Programs To Restart the Flow Of Consumer Demand	Permanent Programs To Avoid Situations Causing Contractions and to Provide Insurance for Citizens Against Economic Disasters
Bank Holiday	Agricultural Adjustment	Securities and Exchange Commission
Emergency Banking Act	*National Industrial Recovery Act*	Federal Deposit Insurance Corporation
Federal Emergency Relief Act	Home Owners Loan Corporation	Social Security Admin.
Civil Works Admin.	Works Progress Admin.	National Labor Relations Board

Clause allowed it, just as it did a Bank of the United States to stabilize finances. Hamilton would probably approve, whereas Jefferson and today's conservatives would oppose this new role.

When the economy suffers from recession or depression, Congress can adopt **discretionary** (intentional) **fiscal policies** that reduce taxes and increase spending. The objective is to pump more money into the society to stimulate aggregate demand. When people get a tax break, they take that "extra money" and spend it, increasing demand for goods and services.

In the Great Depression, *New Deal* leaders avoided fiscal policies related to taxes (increasing or decreasing). Taxes were already low, and raising them for revenue would take away purchasing power. Instead, *New Deal* programs centered on spending actions such as the **Civilian Conservation Corps** (**CCC**) which put young men to work on environmental projects, and the **Works Projects Administration** (**WPA**) which created public street cleaning and construction jobs for the unemployed (see Figure 7.2 above). To do this, it had to borrow and run a deficit.

ROLE OF STABILIZER: SUCCESS OR FAILURE?

Employment rises when the government increases spending. Sometimes, government spending is massive, and employment in certain industries soars. Examples include defense spending during the Cold War or increased spending in the construction industry when Congress spends for interstate highways and urban renewal. With more people employed, consumer spending (aggregate demand) rises. When used appropriately, discretionary fiscal policy can be an effective means of stabilizing the economy. During the twenty years between the end of World War II and the mid-1960s, the government's taxation and spending grew, and the economy flourished. This convinced many authorities of Keynes' wisdom. It was clear to them that fiscal policy could be used to keep the economy growing.

Besides discretionary action, government has also put into place **automatic fiscal stabilizers** (see Figure 7.1 on page 150). These are fiscal policies built into the system, and no one in Congress or the White House has to use discretion to trigger them. They provide money to needy people when the economy declines. They maintain a level of demand, softening the downward trend and easing personal loss. An example of an automatic fiscal stabilizer is the unemployment compensation system. It rises as the rate of unemployment rises. As times get better, the amount of unemployment compensation paid declines because the number unemployed declines.

On a national scale, these automatic benefit payments to unemployed workers help to maintain aggregate demand. Other automatic stabilizers include social services and some Social Security payments. They help to smooth out the ups and downs of the business cycle. Automatic stabilizers help the unfortunate survive, but they are not strong enough to cure the

Figure 7.3 **FEDERAL DEFICIT AND SURPLUS**

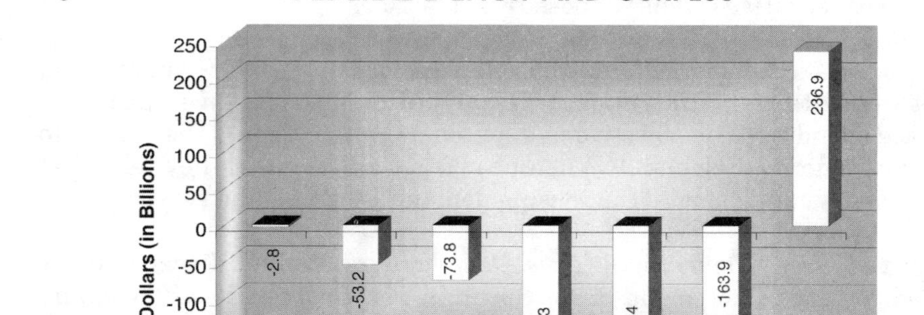

Source: Joint Council of Economic Advisors, *Economic Indicators*, July 2001

economy. To really alter the economy, Congress must use discretionary fiscal policies (see Figure 7.1 on page 150).

Today, Americans are more aware of the limitations of this policy. In order for the government to "prime the pump" (stimulate), it must have the financial resources to use. To spend more while keeping taxes low, government goes into financial markets to borrow money on a very large scale. In truth, the government begins spending what it does not have. This is called **deficit spending**. This borrowing increases the national debt, and just as in a personal credit situation, the debt can become burdensome.

When any debt is too large, prudence dictates that spending stop. It seems governments should be restricted by this same common sense rule. They are not. Uncontrolled spending created a huge **national debt** (the total amount the federal government owes to creditors). The debt is the accumulated unpaid balance of many past years' deficits (see Figure 7.3 on page 152). The 1995 debt was approximately $4.5 trillion (see graph on page 13). The United States federal government is running out of credit. Since the value of the dollar rests on peoples' confidence in the government, there is a great deal at stake in bringing the debt under control. Unfortunately, many state and local governments follow the same pattern and also have massive debts.

Role of Stabilizer: Demand-side or Supply-side?

Since the *New Deal*, most Presidents and Congresses have followed the liberal Keynesian style of fiscal policy. The ***Employment Act of 1946*** institutionalized the Keynesian approach. By this act, Congress required the President to make an annual report on the condition of the economy. To help, Congress authorized a three-person Council of Economic Advisors for the President, and its own Joint Economic Committee.

The *Employment Act* acknowledged a permanent role for government to use tax policies and spending programs to stabilize the economy. It now had a legal obligation to use discretionary fiscal policy to influence aggregate demand and make other adjustments to the economy. This Keynesian approach of government intervention to change aggregate demand is called **demand management policy**, or **demand-side economics**. By the 1980s, this policy seemed to be out of control. Deficits were mounting, and public reaction also rose (see Figure 7.4 on page 154).

In 1980, with the election of **Ronald Reagan** to the presidency, the approach to fiscal policy changed. The liberal (loose) v. conservative (strict) battle raged once again. Reagan's conservative supporters denounced most liberal demand-side policy as inefficient, short-term manipulation of demand. Conservative programs sought to generate a balanced budget and end deficit spending. They cut taxes. But, unfortu-

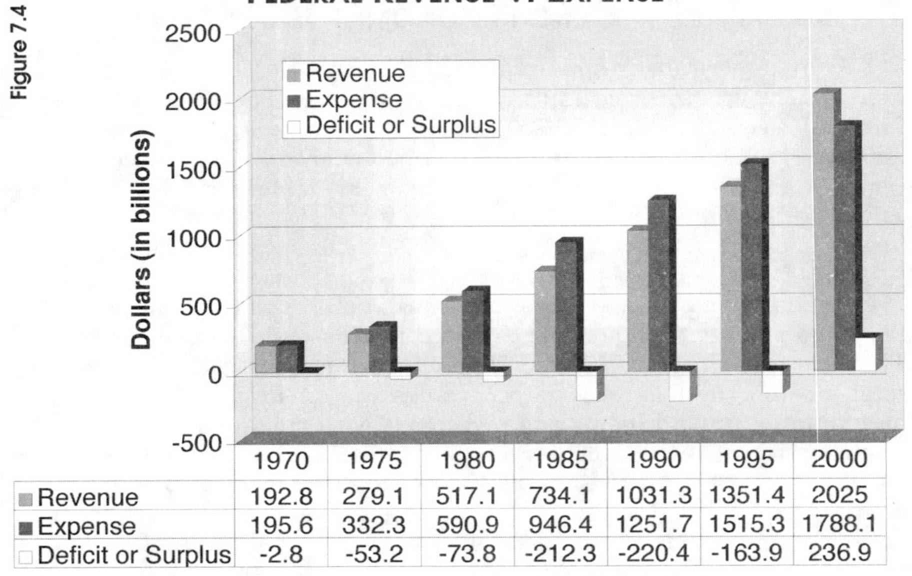

	1970	1975	1980	1985	1990	1995	2000
Revenue	192.8	279.1	517.1	734.1	1031.3	1351.4	2025
Expense	195.6	332.3	590.9	946.4	1251.7	1515.3	1788.1
Deficit or Surplus	-2.8	-53.2	-73.8	-212.3	-220.4	-163.9	236.9

Source: U.S. Department of Commerce, *Business Statistics*, 2001

nately they never managed to reduce spending. To replace (Keynesian) demand-side economics, President Reagan's advisors saw a solution in the writings of **Jean-Baptiste Say**, a 19th century French economist (see sidebar, page 155).

Say believed that most government intervention with the economy was harmful. He claimed that economic stability can be assured not by stimulating aggregate demand but by increasing aggregate supply. Say's supply-side ideas became the basis for Reagan's conservative economic programs, popularly known as "**Reaganomics**." Conservatives wanted reduction of the economic roles of government. Their program included income tax cuts for citizens and corporations, government spending cuts on social programs (but not military defense), and cuts in government regulation of the economy (deregulation).

Conservative "supply-siders" claimed these changes would provide producers with incentives to increase investment and production. They reasoned that more production would mean more jobs, and more jobs would mean more income, and more income would mean more spending, and more spending would mean growth and prosperity. Thus, supply-siders believed that stimulating supply would trigger a growth of aggregate demand. Supply-side economic policy has the same objective as demand stimulation. It is a different route for getting to the same place but with a diminished government role.

★ Capsule – French Economist Jean Baptist Say

The basis for today's Supply-Side Economics originated in the writings of the French economist Jean Baptiste Say (1767-1832). In his *Treatise on Political Economy* (1803), Say reorganized and popularized Smith's market theories in Europe. Say expounded the theory of entrepreneurship in the six volume *Cours Complet d' economie Politique Practique*, a massive discourse on political economy. In Say's interpretation of Smith's ideas, he argued that supply creates its own demand. Producers, not encumbered by government rules (laissez-faire) act in their own self-interest to realize profits, and in doing so, they stimulate growth. This became the basis for what is now known as Say's Law: Producers create demand by paying for all of the factors of production necessary to put a good or service on the market. That means every payment made by a producer is income for someone else. Once that income is obtained, it is spent, essentially becoming new demand. Thus, Say maintains the production of one good stimulates the creation and consumption of others. To supply-side economists, this means that growth is defined by an economy's ability to produce, not consume. The more the economy produces, the wealthier it is.

Jean Baptiste Say's economic theory also embraced and endorsed Smith's doctrine of laissez-faire. According to Say, any economic depression that existed was caused by trade barriers (tariffs) that government put up to prevent the free exchange of goods and services with other nations. Output must have markets in which to be sold. When government prevents producers from accessing these markets, it causes the depressions. Say claimed overproduction cannot harm the economy if trade is free. Only government interference with trade keeps goods and services from reaching world markets.

Still, there is a problem. The supply-side approach assumes business tax cuts will go wisely into investment. But what if this increased investment never occurs? Keynes claimed that putting money in consumers' hands will lead to spending. Say claimed putting money in producers' hands will lead to investing.

Congress cut business taxes with Reagan's ***Economic Recovery Act of 1981***. There was a flurry of intense investment that stimulated the economy out of the recession by 1984, but it faded quickly.

In the long run, not enough money went into product research and development or plant expansion as many supply-siders had hoped. Businesses used the extra money to increase corporate executives' salaries, raise dividends for their stockholders, invest overseas, and/or buy out competitors (mergers and acquisitions). In fact, the lower bank interest rates in the early 1990s led to more investment than did the 1980s supply-side tax incentives.

Each Congress and Presidential administration has its own perception of the proper relationship between the government and the economy. That relationship changes as time and power changes. The final response of any Congress and administration is partly made according to public opinion and the political priorities of elected representatives.

ROLE OF GOVERNMENT: THE GREAT SAFETY NET

Increasingly, the American people have become dependent on the government for economic help. The public's desire to create a smaller, less costly government has always been hindered by its dependence on government services. Consider that amid their cries for lower taxes and budget deficit reduction in the 1990s, many Americans still wanted a national government health care program in spite of the cost.

Since the Great Crash of 1929, local, state, and federal bureaucracies have been growing continually. In the 1930s Depression, the situation was desperate enough to alter the sacred doctrine of laissez-faire. In the *New Deal*, Congress frequently stretched the Elastic Clause to give the federal government more and more economic power, and the public accepted all the help it could get.

From the Great Depression's desperate experience, people came to expect help anytime they needed it. Floods in the Mid-West, earthquakes in the Far West, hurricanes on the East Coast, unemployment in the cities, bad weather freezing crops in the South – it makes no difference. People now *expect* government grants, subsidies, low interest loans, and emergency finances to rebuild, restore, replace, replenish, resurrect, repair, and recover. Today, people demand more from government, and its economic roles have grown. (For a sense of size, see government agency listings on page 157.) More people, with more problems, means more spending and bigger government.

Think of all the economic roles that people expect government to play. Government is expected to:

- provide public goods and services
- protect consumers and workers from harm in the marketplace
- furnish the needy with assistance through transfer payments
- keep jobs safe while keeping the prices stable

Figure 7.5 **FEDERAL DOLLAR**

HOW A DOLLAR IS BUDGETED

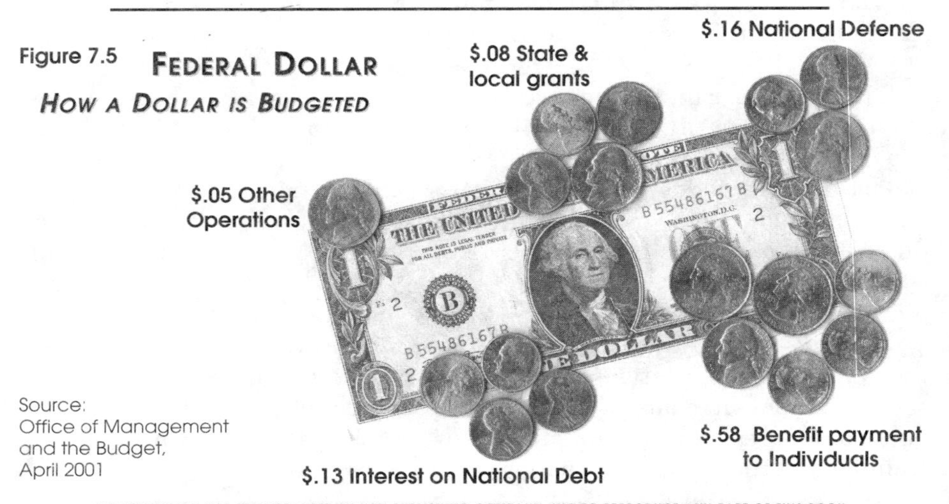

Source: Office of Management and the Budget, April 2001

☆ Capsule – Selected U.S. Government Agencies Involved with Economics

Congressional Committees
Copyright Office (Library of Congress)
H.R Agriculture Committee
H.R Committee on Interior & Insular Affairs
H.R Energy & Commerce Commit.
H.R Interior Committee
H.R Public Works & Transportation Committee
S. Agriculture, Nutrition, & Forestry Committee
Sen. Commerce, Science & Transportation Committee
Sen. Energy & Natural Resources Committee
Sen. Environment & Public Works Committee

Presidential Offices
Council of Economic Advisors
Office of Management & the Budget (OMB)

Cabinet Dept.
U.S. Dept. of Agriculture
U.S. Dept. of Commerce
U.S. Dept. of Energy
U.S. Dept. of the Health & Human Services (HHS)
U.S. Dept. of Housing & Urban Development (HUD)
U.S. Dept. of the Interior
U.S. Dept. of Justice
U.S. Dept. of Labor
U.S. Dept. of Transportation
U.S. Dept. of the Treasury
U.S. Dept. of Veterans Affairs

Departmental Agencies
Admin. for Children & Families (HHS)
Antitrust Division (Justice)
Bureau of Alcohol, Tobacco & Firearms (Treasury)
Bureau of Economic Analysis (Commerce)
Bureau of Indian Affairs (Interior)
Bureau of Labor Statistics (Labor)
Bureau of Land Mngmt. (Interior)
Bureau of Mines (Interior)
Comptroller of the Currency (Treasury)
Drug Enforcement Admin. (Justice)
Employment Standards Admin. (Labor)
Employment & Training Admin. (Labor)
Federal Aviation Admin. (Transportation)
Federal Crop Insurance Corp. (Agriculture)
Federal Energy Regulatory Commission (Energy)
Federal Housing & Equal Opportunity Office (HUD)
Federal Housing Commissioner (HUD)
Fish & Wildlife Service (Interior)
Food & Drug Admin. (HHS)
Food & Nutrition Serv.(Agriculture)
Food Safety & Inspection Service (Agriculture)
Internal Revenue Serv. (Treasury)
Labor Management Standards Admin. (Labor)
Minority Business Development Agency (Commerce)
National Highway Traffic Safety Admin. (Trans.)
National Marine Fisheries Service (Commerce)
National Institute for Occupational Safety & Health (Labor)
Occupational Safety & Health Admin. (Labor)
Occupational Safety & Health Review Commission (Labor)
Office of Consumer Affairs (HHS)
Office of Economics (Agriculture)
Office of Surface Mining Reclamation & Enforcement (Int.)
Patent & Trademark Office (Commerce)
Social Security Admin. (HHS)
Soil Conservation Services (Agriculture.)
U.S. Coast Guard (Transport.)
U.S. Customs Service (Treasury)
U.S. Forest Service (Agriculture)

Independent Agencies
AMTRAK (National Railroad Passenger Corp.)
Commodity Futures Trading Commission
Consumer Affairs Council
Consumer Information Center
Consumer Product Safety Commission
Energy Regulatory Commission
Environmental Protection Agency
Equal Employment Opportunity Commission
Export-Import Bank of the United States
Federal Communications Commission (FCC)
Federal Council on Aging
Federal Deposit Insurance Corp. (FDIC)
Federal Highway Admin.
Fed Home Loan Mortgage Corp.
Federal Labor Relations Authority
Federal Maritime Commission
Federal Mediation & Conciliation Service
Federal Mine Safety & Health Review Commission
Federal Reserve System
Federal Trade Commission
General Accounting Office
General Services Admin.
Government Printing Office
Interstate Commerce Commission
National Bureau of Standards
National Credit Union Admin.
National Economic Council
National Labor Relations Board
National Mediation Board
National Transportation Safety Board
Office of Conservation & Renewable Energy
Postal Rate Commission
Resolution Trust Corp.
Regulatory Information Service Center
Securities & Exchange Commission
Small Business Admin.
Tennessee Valley Authority (Independent)
U.S. Postal Service
U.S. Intl Trade Commission

A look at the federal budget dollar (see Figure 7.5 on page 156) shows the expense of government providing these things. While they often denounce the cost, leaders feel people want a "great safety net" to protect them from life's problems. When the government is unable to meet people's expectations, they blame its activity (or lack of action) for everything that is wrong.

The 1990s brought some re-thinking of the massive scope and cost of government. Americans began to question how much government should be expected to do. Conservative criticism led to Republican victories in the mid-1990s elections, causing legislatures to make serious attempts at budget control, cuts in spending, and deficit reduction.

ROLE OF GOVERNMENT: WHO PAYS FOR IT?

Some people feel *entitled* to all the services and protections of this great safety net as if it were a birthright. Yet, when government turns to taxpayers for **revenue** (income), they balk. **Taxes** are the obligatory fees citizens pay for government. Yet, nothing causes more reaction to government than the mere mention of taxes.

Historically, citizens rage against government collection of these revenues. Revolutions start over them. Whatever decreases personal income is viewed as evil. As purchasing power declines, anger escalates. It seems to be a great conspiracy – government changes tax laws and gets a greater portion of the hard-earned money of people and business, reducing aggregate demand (see Figure 7.6 below).

Today, the array of taxes is bewildering. Some taxes are highly visible, and some nearly invisible. Governments impose taxes on consumers, producers, wage earners, and property owners. The federal, state, and local governments levy taxes. Governments tax people on what they earn, on what they spend, on what they save, and on what they own. Industries are taxed as well as individuals. It all takes a "big chunk" out of individual wealth.

Figure 7.6

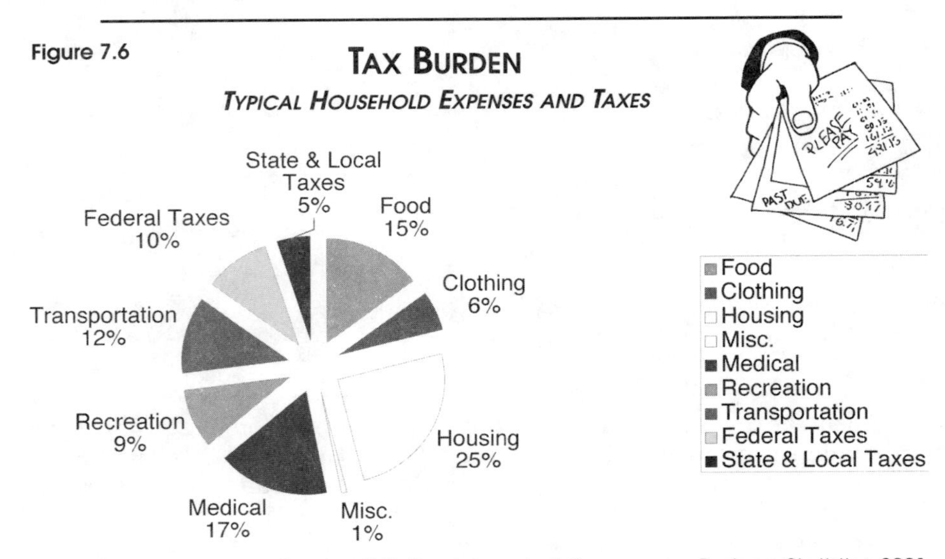

Source: U.S. Department of Commerce, *Business Statistics,* 2001

Figure 7.7

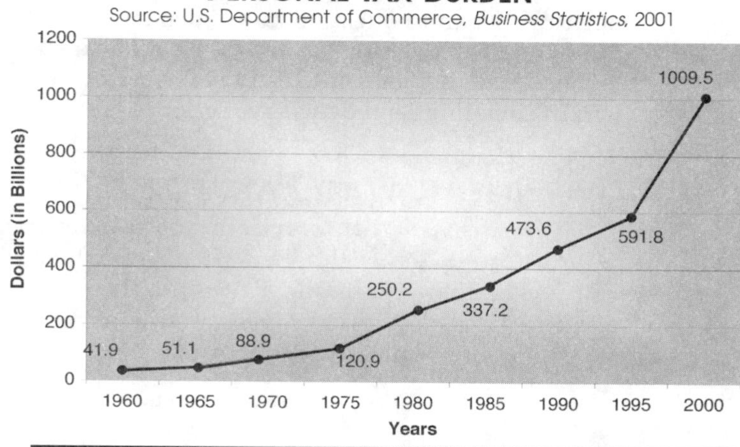

Throughout the United States, the average "**Tax Independence Day**" comes sometime in May. That means that the average taxes paid per year is an amount equalling that earned between January and May. The thought of spending five months a year working to pay your share of government bills has an agonizing effect on most people. The distress hits home every April 15th (federal/state income tax filing deadlines) or when the school or county property tax bills arrive in the mail (see Figure 7.7 above). Questions begin to whiz through citizens' minds as to why such vast amounts of money are being spent. Government has become the biggest business in this country. During the last half century, government has grown bigger and bigger trying to respond to more demands and responsibilities. As it grows, it spends greater sums of tax money.

Examining our history provides some idea of why such rapid growth took place:

- As population grew, all levels of government expanded: more teachers, police officers, fire fighters, accountants, judges, public defenders, district attorneys, public health personnel, etc. (According to the 2000 Census, there are over 20 million federal, state, local, and city employees [*Statistical Abstract of the United States*. pgs. 320].)
- With more people, the numbers of disadvantaged or poor citizens grew. Unfortunately, the number of people that need government aid has grown at a much faster pace than the general population.
- In addition, the United States plays a significant role in global affairs. Being a world leader requires responsible reaction toward global emergencies. There are wars, relief efforts, police actions, natural catastrophes, and terrorism. If the government responds to these events, it costs the taxpayers money.

★ Capsule – The *U.S. Constitution* and Taxation

The original *Constitution* (effective 1789)
Article I. Section 9, Clause 4
"**Apportionment of Direct Taxes**. No capitation or other direct tax shall be laid, unless in proportion to the census or enumeration herein before directed to be taken."

The 16th Amendment (ratified 1913)
nullifies Article 1, Section 9, Clause 4.
"**The Income Tax**. The Congress shall have power to lay and collect taxes on incomes, from whatever source derived, without apportionment among the several states, and without regard to any census or enumeration."

Note: The original *Constitution* allowed for the taxation of the individual, but only in proportion to each state's population. This provision was included to keep Congress from abolishing slavery by taxing slaves.

Role of Government: Redistributing Wealth

Government now assumes a considerable amount of responsibility for the economic well-being of people. Federal, state, and county governments engage in redistributing wealth through **transfer payments** (taxing people that have resources and transferring money to those in need). The system of transfer payments includes public assistance, social insurance, subsidies, and grants-in-aid.

Many individuals and groups devote themselves to influencing the system. There are lobbyists, **PAC**'s (Political Action Committees), factions, coalitions, confederations, unions, blocs, and leagues. All try to influence lawmakers' decisions on public economic policy. Each struggles to have government act in its best interests. It seems like a nightmare. The system is flawed and perhaps out of control. Yet, people expect government to provide a "safety net" to protect citizens.

At first glance, most people see taxation as a major roadblock to the American Dream. Yet, the government provides a wide range of protective services to help everyone achieve the American Dream. By monitoring the marketplace, agencies keep citizens from harm. Government inspects and examines food, water, air, cars, banks, etc. to protect the public.

A very important aspect of our mixed economy is the maintenance and encouragement of competition. Competition is the life blood of the economy. By promoting competition, the government protects the people from the negative side effects of business operation. It maintains the protection of the consumer from the price-fixing practices of oligopolies and monopolies.

Antitrust laws that flow from the *Sherman Antitrust Act* (1890) outlawed any contract or combination that worked toward a monopoly or any conspiracy that would restrain trade or commerce. Under the *Sherman Act*, the federal government brought a number of legal actions in the early 1900s that resulted in the breaking up of several large corporations, or "trusts" as they were then called, including Standard Oil of New Jersey (today's Exxon-Mobil), American Tobacco, and DuPont.

Despite this and other laws created to maintain the element of competition in the economy, combinations kept growing because of weaknesses in the laws. Huge corporations are a fact of modern economic life. They offer economic benefits and technical efficiencies, but ordinary people fear the abuse of corporate power. However, for the American economy to remain viable, competition must be maintained. This takes a "watchdog effort" against those corporate moves that can destroy a competitive market.

Government Revenue: Types of Taxes

The programs and protections people want cost money, and taxes have to pay for them, but taxes also can be used to modify consumer behavior. Placing an excise tax on specific goods may make prices too high for an individual to purchase. **Excise taxes** are commonly known as "sin" or "luxury" taxes. To deter the use of a product, governments add an excise tax. For example, the states of Massachusetts and New York have very high excise taxes on cigarettes in addition to that of the federal government. Economists categorize taxes by the way they affect people – progressive, proportional, and regressive.

Progressive Tax

A **progressive tax** is designed to make those most able to pay contribute more than those less able. When thinking of this type of levy, a staircase comes to mind. For example, Family *X* has a yearly income of $25,000 and four people. Family *X* may pay income tax at a rate of 15%. Family *Y*, on the other hand, has four people but an income of $100,000. Family *Y* faces a 31% rate. Family *Z*, with a $250,000 income, will pay its tax income tax at a 36% rate (Omnibus Budget Reconciliation Act of 1993). The higher up you go, the more you pay. Congressional policies often change these rates and steps.

Proportional Tax

A **proportional tax** creates the same tax rate for everyone. All people are on the same plane, paying the exact same percent. For example, with proportional taxation, all three families above would pay the same percentage. If government set the rate at 10%, Family *X* would pay $2,500, Family *Y*, $10,000, and Family *Z*, $25,000. Each would pay more not because of what the government charged but because of the difference in their earnings.

Regressive Tax

A **regressive tax** is the kind that hurts one group more than another. For example, two families live in a state with a sales tax rate of 8%. One family earns $50,000 per year, the other $100,000 per year. Both have similar needs and purchase approximately the same amount of taxable items. For this example, suppose the sales tax amounts to $5,000. For the family with an income of $50,000, this tax is equal to 10% of what it "grosses." For the other family, the tax will take only 5% of its total income. The family that makes less income ends up paying a greater percent of their total income to the government.

Government Revenue: Varieties of Federal Taxes

Government uses a combination of progressive, proportional, and regressive taxes to raise revenue for operations. It assesses taxes on citizens at each level of government (federal, state, and local). The most common and widely used taxes are: individual income tax, corporate income tax, sales tax, property tax, Social Security tax, Medicare tax, excise tax, estate tax, gift tax, utility tax, custom duties (tariffs), and capital gains tax. Figure 7.8 below gives a view of the proportions of these taxes in the revenues of state and federal governments.

For individuals, government sets an **income tax rate** by law. It is based on **gross income** (total earned and unearned) allowing certain deductions such as medical expense, mortgage interest, charity, etc. Similarly, the government places an income tax on gross corporate profits but allows certain deductions, too.

In legal terms, reporting and paying income tax is by "voluntary compliance." In most cases, wage earners really have no choice. Wages and salaries are subject to an **employer withholding system**. Employers must deduct a specified amount from an employee's gross wages. Employers decide the amount based on a form filed by the employee (W-4 form – Figure 7.9a above). At the end of each year, employers provide

Figure 7.8 **Federal and State Tax Revenues**

Source: U.S. Department of Commerce, *Statistical Abstract*, 1994

Average Federal Tax Sources (% of total revenue)	Average State Tax Sources (% of total revenue)
Social Security / Medicare Taxes (36.1%)	Property Taxes (2%)
Federal Individual Income Tax (45.6%)	Sales Taxes (49.5%)
Federal Corporate Income Tax (8.5%)	State Excise Taxes (Alcohol, Tobacco – 2.8%)
Federal Excise Taxes (Alcohol, Tobacco, Jewelry, Furs, Leather, Telephone) (4.4%)	Energy Taxes (6.7%)
Estate and Gift Taxes (0.9%)	State Individual Income Tax (31%)
Other (4.5%)	State Corporate Income Tax (6.5%)
	Other (1.5%)

Form **W-4**
Department of the Treasury
Internal Revenue Service

Employee's Withholding Allowance Certificate

► **For Privacy Act and Paperwork Reduction Act Notice, see page 2.**

OMB No. 1545-0010

2003

1 Type or print your first name and middle initial | Last name | 2 Your social security number

Home address (number and street or rural route) | 3 ☐ Single ☐ Married ☐ Married, but withhold at higher Single rate.
Note: *If married, but legally separated, or spouse is a nonresident alien, check the "Single" box.*

City or town, state, and ZIP code | 4 **If your last name differs from that shown on your social security card, check here. You must call 1-800-772-1213 for a new card.** ► ☐

5 Total number of allowances you are claiming (from line **H** above **or** from the applicable worksheet on page 2) 5

6 Additional amount, if any, you want withheld from each paycheck . . . . 6 $

7 I claim exemption from withholding for 2003, and I certify that I meet **both** of the following conditions for exemption:
- Last year I had a right to a refund of **all** Federal income tax withheld because I had **no** tax liability **and**
- This year I expect a refund of **all** Federal income tax withheld because I expect to have **no** tax liability.

If you meet both conditions, write "Exempt" here . . . . ► 7

Under penalties of perjury, I certify that I am entitled to the number of withholding allowances claimed on this certificate, or I am entitled to claim exempt status.
Employee's signature
(Form is not valid
unless you sign it.) ► **Date** ►

8 Employer's name and address (Employer: Complete lines 8 and 10 only if sending to the IRS.) | 9 Office code (optional) | 10 Employer identification number

Figure 7.9a

employees with a statement of how much they have deducted and paid to the government for the worker (W-2 form – Figure 7.9b below). With this information, the worker must file a report with the government by the April 15th deadline – using 1040 forms. The calculations determine if the employer has sent the government enough, too much, or too little from the worker's wages. Adjustments are then made: too little deducted by an employer means the employee has to pay the difference; too much means a refund must be requested. Businesses operate in a similar manner, making payments according to estimates of quarterly revenue.

Tax liability may be adjusted as the government constantly redefines deductions and exemptions ("tax breaks") in new tax laws. These incessant changes force most businesses to utilize special accountants and tax attorneys to keep up with changes in the codes, to keep them in legal compliance, and perhaps to take advantages of "loopholes."

a Control number | 22222 | Void ☐ | **For Official Use Only** ► **OMB No. 1545-0008**

b Employer identification number | 1 Wages, tips, other compensation $ | 2 Federal income tax withheld $

c Employer's name, address, and ZIP code | 3 Social security wages $ | 4 Social security tax withheld $
5 Medicare wages and tips $ | 6 Medicare tax withheld $
7 Social security tips $ | 8 Allocated tips $

d Employee's social security number | 9 Advance EIC payment $ | 10 Dependent care benefits $

e Employee's first name and initial | Last name | 11 Nonqualified plans $ | 12a See instructions for box 12 $
13 Statutory employee ☐ Retirement plan ☐ Third-party sick pay ☐ | 12b $
14 Other | 12c $
12d $

f Employee's address and ZIP code

15 State | Employer's state ID number | 16 State wages, tips, etc. $ $ | 17 State income tax $ $ | 18 Local wages, tips, etc. $ $ | 19 Local income tax $ $ | 20 Locality name

Form **W-2 Wage and Tax Statement** (99) **2003**

Department of the Treasury—Internal Revenue Service
For Privacy Act and Paperwork Reduction Act Notice, see separate instructions.

Copy A For Social Security Administration—Send this entire page with Form W-3 to the Social Security Administration; photocopies are **not** acceptable.

Cat. No. 10134D

Figure 7.9b

The federal government also collects Social Security and Medicare taxes from both the employee and employer by order of the ***Federal Insurance Contribution Act*** (**FICA**). This was a *New Deal* law that established a mandatory three-part insurance policy for contributors (retirement assistance, death benefit insurance, and disability coverage). Medicare, added in the 1960s, provides free or subsidized health insurance for senior citizens. The government computes these Social Security taxes as a percentage of income. In the 1930s, the total contribution was 2% of wages. By 1995, the FICA rate for employee and employers alike had risen to 6.2% on wages earned up to the wage base of $61,200. In addition, the federal government added a Medicare Tax of 1.45% on all wages earned with no wage base. The largest percentage of federal revenues come directly from income taxes; however, Social Security taxes are the second largest source (see Figure 7.8, page 162).

A **customs duty** is better known as a **tariff** (tax on an import). When a foreign product comes into the United States, the government levies a tariff on it. It is a payment that will eventually be figured into the sale price and passed on to the final buyer. Low revenue tariffs are simple income enhancements for the federal government. Yet, protective tariffs can be set high to protect domestic industries from low priced foreign competition (see Issue 9 for more detail on tariffs).

A **capital gains tax** is levied on profits generated by individuals and businesses. It is applied when a home, stock, or piece of art is bought and later sold for a profit. The profit is subject to the capital gains tax. Many people believe the high rate of this tax discourages individual incentive and corporate motivation to do well and make profit since so much will be taken by the federal government. Of course, it is also possible to suffer a capital loss. If an asset is sold for lower price than originally paid, a capital loss can be used as a tax deduction.

Another important element of the *New Deal* program of President Roosevelt was the **Federal Unemployment (FUTA) Taxes** introduced in 1935 as part of the Social Security Act. FUTA is paid only by the employer. The employer's contribution is 0.8% of the amount of wages per employee on a federal wage base of $7,000.

Federal excise taxes were mentioned previously as "sin taxes" or "luxury taxes." Besides raising revenue on nonessentials such as jewelry, leather, and furs, they are sometimes used to alter behavior. To some extent, excises on cigarettes, alcohol, and gambling are meant to discourage their use.

Government Revenue: The Fairness Issue

What is fair when it comes to taxes? Some people insist that there is no such thing as a fair tax. Others defend a particular type of tax as being the only kind that is fair. Fairness is a difficult term to use in economics. Many variables affect the definition of the term. Since there are different values and perceptions, some people may object to one interpretation or another. Mainstream economists have two ideas on fairness of taxes:

- The **ability-to-pay principle** is on one side of the debate. This means tax fairness is based on a progressive idea: those who have the greatest resources have a social obligation to pay more than those that have less.

- The **benefits-received principle**, on the other hand, establishes the simple rule that if you use or benefit from a particular government good or service, you should pay the tax on it. Tolls on roads and gasoline taxes are used to build and maintain roadways. Those that use the roads are responsible for paying for them. A town may borrow money to construct a sewer and water system for a section of the town that needs it. The benefits-received principle says that those residents not able to "hook-up" to the system should not be expected to pay off the loan by having taxes increased. Instead, users of the system pay off the loan and pay for the maintenance of the system through fees.

Government Revenue: State and Local Taxes

When discussing taxes, people immediately think of federal income taxes. Yet many states, counties, towns, and cities levy their own income taxes. States, counties, and municipalities have property taxes and sales taxes. Combined, they take a hefty 12% to 15% out of gross earnings (see Figure 7.6 on page 158).

Property Taxes

Property taxes are levied in most states. They are based on assets, but the assessments themselves vary. For example, in most states property tax means **real property** – land and buildings (see Figure 7.11 – a school tax bill, based on real property). In other states, it may mean **chattel** (personal possessions such as autos, boats, stocks, jewelry, etc.). Real property is evaluated by officials called *assessors*. They determine the value of a home or business property in the town or county and try to equalize the values. The towns and counties then set a *tax rate*. If a home and land are assessed at $40,000 and the tax rate is 8% per $1,000 of assessment, the tax is $3,200. If government expenses rise, it may change the rate to 10%. The owner of the $40,000 home then pays $4,000.

In some cases, fear of increasing property taxes has led owners to neglect their real estate or hesitate to improve it because changes may raise its assessed value. Another problem is that this tax does not consider the

ORANGE COUNTY - MIDDLETOWN CSD
2002-2003 SCHOOL REAL PROPERTY TAX BILL
For Fiscal Year 07/01/2002 to 06/30/2003 Warrant Date 09/12/2002

BILL No: 3746
SEQUENCE No: 2554
PAGE No: 1 of 1

MAKE CHECKS PAYABLE TO
SCHOOL TAX COLLECTOR
PO BOX 882
MIDDLETOWN NY 10940

330900 31-3-16

TO PAY IN PERSON
THE BANK OF NEW YORK
135 NORTH ST
MIDDLETOWN NY 10940

PROPERTY ADDRESS & LEGAL DESCRIPTION
SWIS: 30900 **SBL:**31-3
Address:
CITY OF:
School: 330900-MIDDLETOWN CSD
NYS Tax & Finance School District Code: 394
WAREHOUSE **Roll Sect.** 1
Parcel Dimensions: 43.00 X 222.00
Account No: 5000100 **Bank Code:**
Estimated State Aid: SCHL: 38,108,368

PROPERTY TAXPAYER'S BILL OF RIGHTS
The assessor estimates the full Market Value of this property as of January 1, 2002 was $ 205,926.00
The Assessed Value of this property as of July 1, 2002 was $ 55,600.00
The uniform Percentage of Value used to establish assessments was 27%
If you feel your assessment is too high, you have the right to seek a reduction in the future. For further information, please ask your Assessor for the booklet "How to File a complaint on Your Assessment". Please note that the period f filing complaints on the above assessment has passed. SEE REVERSE SIDE FOR ADDITIONAL INFORMATION

Exemption	Value	Tax Purpose	Exemption	Value	Tax Purpose	Exemption	Value	Tax Purpose

IF YOU HAVE AN ESCROW ACCOUNT PLEASE FORWARD THIS BILL TO YOUR BANK

PROPERTY TAXES

Taxing Purpose	Total Tax Levy	% Change From Prior Year	Taxable Assessed Value or Units	Rates per $1000 or per Unit	Tax Amount
MIDDLETOWN CSD	35,579,214	4.5	55,600.00	83.247841	4,628.58

SCH TAX PAYABLE OCT 1-OCT 31. 2% PENALTY ADDED NOV 1-NOV 30.
TAXES UNPAID DEC 1 IN CITY OF MIDDLETOWN WILL BE RETURNED
TO THE CITY FINANCE OFFICE FOR COLLECTION. IN WALLKILL,
GOSHEN AND WAWAYANDA TO COMM OF FINANCE IN GOSHEN AND WILL
BE SUBJ TO INT RATES PROVIDED BY LAW. PHONE 845-341-5325

IF PAID BY	Penalty %	Amount	Penalty	Total Due
10/31/2002	0.00%	4,628.58		4,628.58
11/30/2002	2.00%	4,628.58	92.57	4,721.15

TOTAL TAXES DUE $ 4,62
Your tax savings this year resulting from the New York State school tax relief (STAR) program is: $ .00
(Total Taxes Due already reduced by STAR savings)
TAXES PAID BY____________CA CH

Figure 7.11

ability-to-pay principle. It ignores the income of the owner. As property taxes increase, owners (especially senior citizens) may be unable to pay the increases. That may lead to the loss of the home.

Sales Taxes

Sales tax is collected by the seller of goods and services at the time of the purchase. A percentage of the total sale is added at the cash register for an item or service as a payment to city, county, and state governments (see Figure 7.12, page 167). Not every state imposes sales tax. States also have many different methods of determining what is subject to taxation. Often, what is determined as a "need" is not taxed, but that list is very small and limited (e.g., basic food, medicine and, in some states, "nonluxury" clothes).

Estate and Gift Taxes

Estate and gift taxes deal with the transfer of property and money from one person to another. An **estate tax** is a payment made to the government when an inheritance is collected. If someone dies and leaves wealth with a specific value, the person that receives it may have to pay a tax on the total amount. Each state has its own regulations. A **gift tax** is placed on the transfer of property or money from one person to another. If someone is given $10,000 or more, the federal government requires

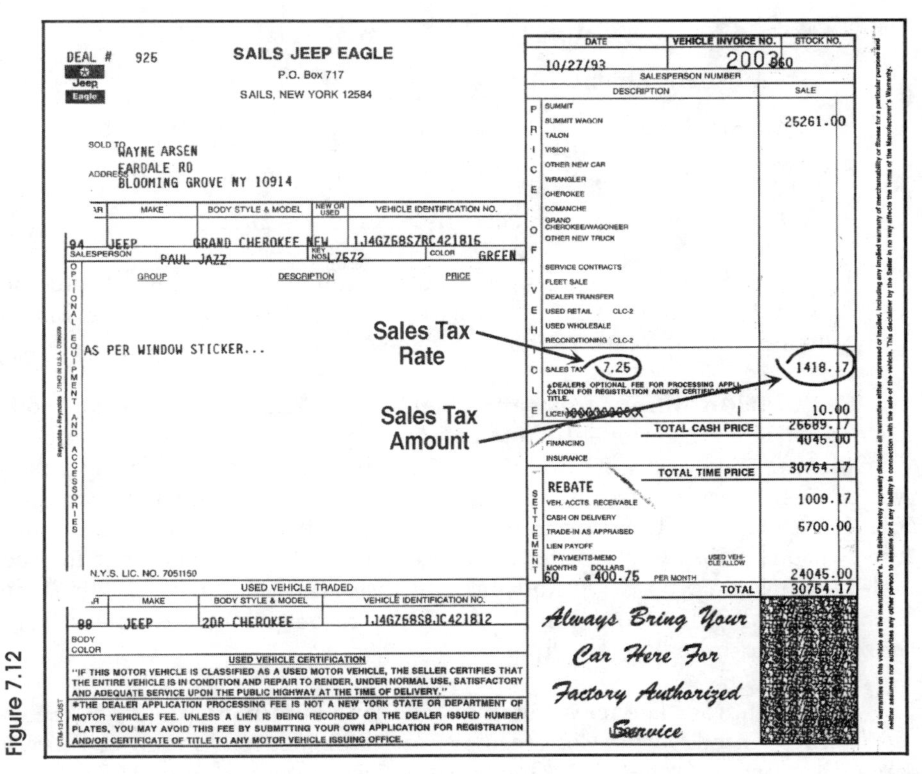
DEAL # 925

SAILS JEEP EAGLE
P.O. Box 717
SAILS, NEW YORK 12584

Jeep Eagle

SOLD TO WAYNE ARSEN
ADDRESS EARDALE RD
BLOOMING GROVE NY 10914

YEAR	MAKE	BODY STYLE & MODEL	NEW OR USED	VEHICLE IDENTIFICATION NO.
94	JEEP	GRAND CHEROKEE	NEW	1J4GZ58S7RC421816

SALESPERSON PAUL JAZZ — KEY NOS. L7672 — COLOR GREEN

OPTIONAL EQUIPMENT AND ACCESSORIES

GROUP	DESCRIPTION	PRICE
AS PER WINDOW STICKER...		

N.Y.S. LIC. NO. 7051150

USED VEHICLE TRADED

YEAR	MAKE	BODY STYLE & MODEL	VEHICLE IDENTIFICATION NO.
88	JEEP	2DR CHEROKEE	1J4GZ58S8JC421812

BODY COLOR

USED VEHICLE CERTIFICATION
"IF THIS MOTOR VEHICLE IS CLASSIFIED AS A USED MOTOR VEHICLE, THE SELLER CERTIFIES THAT THE ENTIRE VEHICLE IS IN CONDITION AND REPAIR TO RENDER, UNDER NORMAL USE, SATISFACTORY AND ADEQUATE SERVICE UPON THE PUBLIC HIGHWAY AT THE TIME OF DELIVERY."
*THE DEALER APPLICATION PROCESSING FEE IS NOT A NEW YORK STATE OR DEPARTMENT OF MOTOR VEHICLES FEE. UNLESS A LIEN IS BEING RECORDED OR THE DEALER ISSUED NUMBER PLATES, YOU MAY AVOID THIS FEE BY SUBMITTING YOUR OWN APPLICATION FOR REGISTRATION AND/OR CERTIFICATE OF TITLE TO ANY MOTOR VEHICLE ISSUING OFFICE.

DATE	VEHICLE INVOICE NO.	STOCK NO.
10/27/93	2003	60

SALESPERSON NUMBER

DESCRIPTION	SALE
SUMMIT	
SUMMIT WAGON	25261.00
TALON	
VISION	
OTHER NEW CAR	
WRANGLER	
CHEROKEE	
COMANCHE	
GRAND CHEROKEE/WAGONEER	
OTHER NEW TRUCK	
SERVICE CONTRACTS	
FLEET SALE	
DEALER TRANSFER	
USED RETAIL CLC-2	
USED WHOLESALE	
RECONDITIONING CLC-2	
SALES TAX 7.25	1418.17
*DEALERS OPTIONAL FEE FOR PROCESSING APPLICATION FOR REGISTRATION AND/OR CERTIFICATE OF TITLE	
LICENSE	10.00
TOTAL CASH PRICE	26689.17
FINANCING	4045.00
INSURANCE	
TOTAL TIME PRICE	30764.17
REBATE	
VEH. ACCTS. RECEIVABLE	1009.17
CASH ON DELIVERY	5700.00
TRADE-IN AS APPRAISED	
LIEN PAYOFF	
PAYMENTS-MEMO MONTHS 60 DOLLARS @ 400.75 PER MONTH	24045.00
TOTAL	30754.17

Always Bring Your Car Here For Factory Authorized Service

All warranties on this vehicle are the manufacturer's. The Seller hereby expressly disclaims all warranties either expressed or implied, including any implied warranty of merchantability or fitness for a particular purpose and neither assumes nor authorizes any other person to assume for it any liability in connection with the sale of the vehicle. This disclaimer by the Seller in no way affects the terms of the Manufacturer's Warranty.

Figure 7.12

that a form be filed acknowledging that the gift is taxable. Many states have similar requirements.

Utility Taxes

Utility taxes are paid on electricity, telephone, cable TV, sewer, and water services. This amounts to a user tax (sometimes called a *surcharge*) collected according to consumption. The more you use, the more you pay. Road and bridge tolls also fit into this category.

Economic Rights and Regulating Business

Government regulation influences business decision-making. Critics say it is costly to business and taxpayers, interferes with freedom, and impedes economic growth. The sheer number of regulatory agencies is staggering. On the federal level, key regulatory agencies include:

- **ICC** (Interstate Commerce Commission – 1887)
- **FDA** (Food and Drug Admin. – 1906)
- **FTC** (Federal Trade Commission – 1914)
- **SEC** (Securities and Exchange Commission – 1934)

- **FCC** (Federal Communications Commission – 1934)
- **EPA** (Environmental Protection Agency – 1970)
- **NHTSA** (National Highway and Traffic Safety Admin. – 1970)
- **OSHA** (Occupational and Safety Health Admin. – 1970)
- **CPSA** (Consumer Product Safety Admin. – 1972)

There are parallel agencies on the state and even local levels, and the number of such bodies (more than fifty on the federal level) seems to grow steadily. (See ☆CAPSULE chart on page 157.)

Regulation differs from antitrust action. Antitrust laws are concerned with the relationship between business and the level of competition in a specific market. Regulation, on the other hand, is designed to watch over specific businesses or interests in the economy. For example, the Federal Trade Commission is concerned with consumer safety, and the National Highway Traffic Safety Administration watches out for the safety of people who drive and use the interstate highway system. The Occupational Safety and Health Administration protects workers from hazardous or unhealthy workplaces.

The regulatory agencies, commissions, and administrations are created by the United States Congress or state legislatures to enforce a law's specific purpose (see *U.S. Gov't. Agencies* chart on page 157). Each agency imposes its own interpretations of rules and regulations on business. Often, the government agency negotiates with the business in question in order to reach a settlement to the "mutual" benefit of the public and the business. Should a serious violation of regulations be determined, the penalty for the violation of these rules is generally in the form of a fine. Occasionally, incarceration of the corporation officials results when a violation of a criminal nature is found or there is continued disregard of the rules. If a decision is disputed, an appeal may settle the issue of proper or improper treatment by the regulator.

Protecting the public interest is the most common justification for regulation of businesses. Some businesses (e.g., interstate commerce, television and radio broadcasting, public transportation) are so important to the well-being of the public that the government believes that it must make sure that such businesses "operate properly."

Government sometimes uses regulation to correct a situation that generates problems for a particular group. The 1980s was a decade of financial manipulation. There was glory in mergers and big stock deals – at least for a few. There was also a growing danger to the entire American securities industry. Behind the names of superstar Wall Street deal makers, Ivan Boesky and Michael Milkin, was a story of power, greed, and corruption. It shocked even the most seasoned and cynical brokers. These men with clever plans and fraudulent operations made earlier financial deceptions look like children's games.

Most of the fortunes accumulated by these men were from illegal activities known as **insider trading**. The term refers to anyone who has knowledge of information not available to the general public and who uses it to buy or sell corporate shares for profit. It is information that is illegally obtained and allows individuals or groups to have an unfair advantage in a market that depends on everyone having the same opportunity to make a profit. Obtaining insider information illegally and using it for insider trading earned huge sums of money for many unscrupulous men during the 1970s and 1980s. (Milkin made $550 million in one year from "junk bonds"). With the help of the Justice Department and the Federal Attorney General's Office, the Securities and Exchange Commission conducted investigations and found informants. Layer by complicated layer, the SEC uncovered the activities of these men and others. The probe shook the very foundation of the stock market, and it severely damaged the financial industry in this country.

Economics and Public Interest: The Influence of Lobbies

Most major organizations engage in **lobbying** – formal attempts to influence the votes of public officials on issues of concern. Group members are usually well aware of their organization's lobbying efforts. The group's methods of lobbying a decision-maker are basically the same. At the center of any lobby effort is the number of potential voters. The public officeholder responsible for policy is usually concerned with what their constituency sees as the right way to go because they want to be reelected. Board of Education members, local village, town, or city council members, or state or federal legislators can be influenced by the opinions of large numbers of voters. The more organized the voters are, the more powerful their voices.

Most major groups employ professional lobbyists who maintain direct links with influential people – committee chairs, long-time incumbents, or office candidates. Through organizations' PACs (Political Action Committees), lobbyists funnel money to help candidates friendly to the group's interest get elected and reelected (see Figure 7.13 below).

Figure 7.13

Political Action Committees (PACs) 2000

Source: *Statistical Abstract of the U.S., 2002*

Type	Number of Organizations	Disbursements (in millions)
Corporate	1,715	$26.8
Labor Unions	338	$ 7.5
Independent Associations	1,011	$17.5

Lobbyists engage such individuals in dialogue because they routinely make public statements and promises that can be used. Some public office holders are particularly sympathetic (or antagonistic) toward a certain interest. Professional lobbyists are paid to know who the most influential people are and go after them.

Professional lobbyists sometimes write bills themselves and supply them to legislators for sponsorship. Professional lobbyists in Washington, DC and state capitals are usually lawyers. Their assistants are often law school students because they are in positions to research and observe examples of model legislation. On the local level, most states require counties to maintain a law library (usually at the site of the county court house) where researchers can get help and easily gain access to law books for research.

Professional lobbyists and the organization's officers and directors monitor the bills from the offices of legislative sponsors through committee and legislative hearings. They continuously apply pressure and support. They recruit experts and make arrangements for experts to testify at every hearing level. Lobbyists also provide committee staffers with written copies of testimonies supporting the group's position on the bill.

Persuasion is continuous and unrelenting. Lobbyists use the local news channels to involve the media. Often, they turn to the group's members to write letters to newspapers to get reporters to examine what is being done. Members are mobilized to write supportive letters to editors, call in to talk radio shows, send petitions and letters directly to legislators, and make financial contributions to the lobbying efforts.

Often, lobbyists ask the organization's leaders to have members conduct "grassroots campaigns." Members are asked to act locally to marshal support for the legislation they want. Through the organization's newsletter or a special mailing, members are asked to contact other groups throughout the neighborhood, region, and state to create a constant bombardment from all over.

A less frequently used tactic is sponsorship of some kind of demonstration or protest. These mass movements are difficult and expensive to arrange and stage. Such activities must be carefully planned and supervised. Such a public tactic must have maximum participation to be effective. Legal permits must be obtained and details worked out before any announcement is made of the march, picketing, or demonstration. Such tactics are often only effective on a local basis, while marches on Washington and state capitals are usually used only for momentous causes.

Lobbyists must work on the executive branch, too. If proposed legislation is passed, an executive veto may end it all. Even after full passage, a number of things may go wrong. Lobbyists must monitor the implemen-

Figure 7.14

FEDERAL ANTITRUST LAWS

Act	Concept
Sherman Antitrust Act (1890)	Created broad foundations for government antitrust action by prohibiting all agreements and contracts "in restraint of trade" that caused monopolies.
Clayton Antitrust Act (1914)	Strengthened the *Sherman Act* by outlawing price-discrimination (charging customers different prices for the same thing if it led to monopoly or lessened competition).
Federal Trade Commission Act (1914)	Established the Federal Trade Commission to enforce the *Clayton Act* to regulate unfair methods of competition in interstate commerce by issuing cease and desist orders.
Robinson-Patman Act (1936)	Strengthened *Clayton Act* by forbidding large-scale discounts on sale of goods to large buyers unless rebate and discounts were available to all.
Celler-Kefauver Act (1950)	Bolstered *Clayton Act* by preventing mergers and buyouts to reduce competition in a market.

tation of the law. Monies may be cut, or the agency chosen to enforce the new law may be ineffective. Lobbyists have to continually monitor the laws and the programs that operate under them.

ECONOMICS AND PUBLIC INTEREST: REACTING TO MONOPOLY

By the late 1800s a reaction grew against the great industrialists' attempt to restrict competition. Their price-fixing drove up market prices and increased profits at the expense of the consumer. Support for antitrust legislation grew, resulting in the passage of the *Sherman Antitrust Act* in 1890. As dramatic as that sounds, the *Sherman Act* did not prevent much illegal activity in the 1890s. Yet, it would be a mistake to believe that the *Sherman Act* was completely ineffective. The federal government did use it – sometimes succeeding in breaking up combinations that were found to be in obvious restraint of trade. However, the *Sherman Act's* real power was felt later when it was used by the U.S. Justice Department under many Presidents to protect the economy from abuse by trusts (see Figure 7.14).

SUMMARY

Although paying taxes is not enjoyable, most taxpayers agree that life would be more difficult without the government services paid for through taxation. U.S. citizens are in the middle in comparison to some other industrialized nations, Americans pay less in taxes (review Figure 7.15 on page 172). However, it is important to not only compare the taxes, but also the services provided.

Figure 7.15

Tax Burdens in Selected Countries

Source: *Organization for Economic Cooperation and Development*, 2000

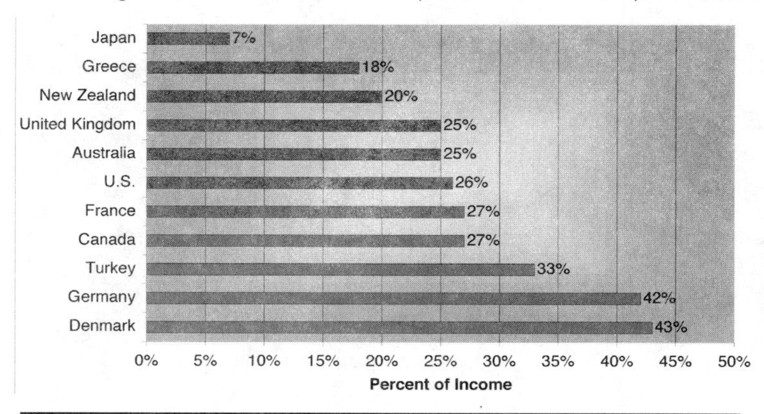

Assessment • Questions • Applications

1 The Granville story at the beginning of this chapter is about local government. The reporter/cartoonist observed, "Of course, the final decision had to be made by the elected officials on the school board. They had to read the sense of the community, but they had to weigh all the local, state, and even federal regulations controlling the finances of education."

a What does the reporter mean when he says that the school board must "read the sense of the community?"

b List the sources of revenue for schools.

c When you look at the sources of revenue, does "read the sense of the community" take on a different meaning?

d If the financial role of a school board is so complex, what does this mean about the roles of other local, state, and federal governments?

2 The *U.S. Constitution* defines several economic functions for government.

a Which functions presented in the *Constitution* affect your life now?

b Which functions presented in the *Constitution* will affect your life in the future?

c Explain which roles of government are most critical to the country's survival and security.

3 Government attempts to stabilize the economy by using fiscal policy.

a In your own words, explain how discretionary and automatic policies stabilize the economy.

b How do political issues affect the use of discretionary fiscal policy?

c Explain the difference between demand-side and supply-side economic theories?

4 The Great Depression created a major change in American economic thought.
   a Describe this change in detail.
   b Make a personal judgement whether this change has benefited or harmed the economic life of this country. Give facts to defend your judgement.

5 Opinions on taxation vary greatly.
   a Interview 5 taxpayers (at different stages of their lives – e.g., in school, working, unemployed, on public assistance, retired). Ask their opinion on the fairness of income, sales, and property taxes.
   b In a small group, discuss your findings which you have outlined in writing.
   c Choose the strongest arguments both pro and con for one of the taxes. Elect two persons from your group to present the arguments to the class.

6 With the class divided into 3 or 4 small groups, complete the following chart of Taxes identifying Categories and Principles. After reaching a consensus on all of the taxes, put the group's results on the board. The class should debate the similarities and differences among the group charts.

TAX	Category	Principle
Income Tax	________	________
Social Security	________	________
Medicare	________	________
Tariff	________	________
Capital Gains	________	________
Federal Excise	________	________
Real Property	________	________
Chattel Property	________	________
Sales Tax	________	________
Estate/Gift Tax	________	________
Utility Tax	________	________

7 Review *Tax Burdens in Selected Countries* (Figure 7.15 on page 172). Additional research will be needed to support your conclusions.
   a Classify the countries listed into economic systems according to the *Economic Systems* discussed in Issue 2 (Fig. 2.2 on page 40).
   b Analyze your answer to part *a* above. Is there a relationship between a country's economic system and its rate of taxation? Give examples and support your conclusion.
   c Compare the benefits and burdens of the taxpayers in the countries you used in part *b* with those of the American taxpayer.

ASSESSMENT PROJECT 7A: GOVERNMENT AGENCIES

STUDENT TASK

Participate in a group presentation on the operation of a government agency and its economic impact on society. The task develops an understanding and insight into the operation of government's economic responsibilities.

PROCEDURE

The class should be divided into cooperative learning groups of no more than 4 students. Each group should:

1 Choose one federal agency related to economic affairs. No two groups should choose the same agency.

2 Using the research, compose a thorough presentation that explains what the agencies do and how they do it. For example,
- protect a competitive market
- protect consumers
- redistribute wealth
- provide public goods and services
- stabilize the economy
- act in the best interest of the United States

3 Make an oral presentation to the class. Include visual support materials.

4 Contact a local village, town, city, or county government agency which mirrors the work of the federal agency in the best presentation and request a guest speaker from that local agency to speak to the class, explaining what his/her agency does on the local level.

EVALUATION

The criteria for the evaluation of this project are itemized in the grid (rubric) that follows on page 175. Choice of appropriate category terms (values) is the decision of the instructor. Selection of terms such as "minimal," "satisfactory," and "distinguished" can vary with each assessment.

Government Agency Presentation Evaluation Rubric

(Refer to the teacher's supplement for suggestions of scoring descriptors for evaluation.)

Evaluation Item

Item a: (1) Does the report show understanding that while different socioeconomic (as well as national, ethnic, religious, racial, and gender) groups have varied perspectives, values, and diverse practices and traditions, they face the same global economic challenges?

Item b: (4) Does the report show understanding that civic values and socially responsible behavior are required of members of school groups, local, state, national, and global communities?

Item c: (5) Does the report analyze problems and evaluate decisions about the economic effects caused by human, technological, and natural activities on societies and individuals?

Item d: (6) Does the report present ideas in writing (and orally) in clear, concise, and properly accepted fashion?

Item e: (7) Does the report employ a variety of information from written, graphic, and multimedia sources?

Item f: (8) Does the report show monitoring of, reflection upon, and improvement of work?

Item g: (9) Does the report show cooperative work and respect for the rights of others to think, act, and speak differently?

Assessment Project 7b: Analyzing the Impact of Taxes on a Hypothetical Household

Student Task

Compute the federal and state income taxes for all income earners in Hypothetical Household developed in the Introduction. Then, submit a report (accompanied by an IRS 1040 tax form) analyzing the fairness of these taxes and weighing their impact on your household and lifestyle.

Procedure

1 Obtain federal IRS income tax form 1040 and a state income tax form, if your state has one. (If your state doesn't, you should try to compute household tax liability for operative state property or other major taxes.)

(Note: individuals within the household may each file a 1040 or may file jointly on one 1040 as a couple.)

2 Fill in forms and use tax tables to figure taxes. Include dependents, itemize the household deductions, and add estimated interest income from savings or investments mentioned in the Introduction's *Household Financial Profile*.

(Note: if you use a computer tax calculation program, be sure to fill in the actual 1040 forms with the figures the computer produces.)

3 After determining taxes to be paid, note percentages of taxes in relation to your household income and add a statement comparing your taxes to the Figure 7.6 graph on page 158.

4 Conclude your report with a discussion analyzing the fairness of these taxes and weighing their impact on your household and lifestyle.

Evaluation

The criteria for the evaluation of this project are itemized in the grid (rubric below). Choice of appropriate category terms (values) is the decision of the instructor. Selection of terms such as "minimal," "satisfactory," and "distinguished" can vary with each assessment.

Impact of Taxes on Household Evaluation Rubric

(Refer to the teacher's supplement for suggestions of scoring descriptors for evaluation.)

Evaluation Item
Item a: (1) Does the report show understanding that while different socioeconomic (as well as national, ethnic, religious, racial, and gender) groups have varied perspectives, values, and diverse practices and traditions, they face the same global economic challenges?
Item b: (4) Does the report show understanding that civic values and socially responsible behavior are required of members of school groups, local, state, national, and global communities?
Item c: (5) Does the report analyze problems and evaluate decisions about the economic effects caused by human, technological, and natural activities on societies and individuals?
Item d: (6) Does the report present ideas in writing (and orally) in clear, concise, and properly accepted fashion?
Item e: (7) Does the report employ a variety of information from written, graphic, and multimedia sources?
Item f: (8) Does the report monitoring of, reflection upon, and improvement of work?
Item g: (9) Does the report show cooperative work and respect for the rights of others to think, act, and speak differently?

ISSUE **8**

Making Monetary and Fiscal Policy II

Can economic performance be measured?

"The Rising of the Dough" – a *Double Meaning!*

Curtis was nervous that day. He had not been himself in class. As the buzzer sounded, he rose very slowly to leave. Mrs. Cortes signaled to him. They had a good relationship, and she was concerned about his unusual lack of enthusiasm.

Reluctantly, he began to admit he was pensive about his job at the bakery in town. He had been working there for nearly three years, and each year Mr. Krug had given him a raise, praising him as a valued and productive worker. Curtis loved the job because he liked working with his hands. The 3 to 8 AM hours three days a week didn't bother him either. He arranged his college schedule around his work, making his evenings free for study.

Curtis explained that he was counting on the annual raise for some badly needed repairs on his car, but Mr. Krug had not said a word about it. Curtis told Mrs. Cortes he had good work habits, was always on time, and responded to all the requests his boss made. It was a small bakery, and Mr. Krug and the staff were all very friendly. Curtis never minded going in early or staying late, and he always worked the counter weekends so that the full-time people could have time with their families. Mr. Krug had even congratulated Curtis on the compliments customers often gave him. Curtis just couldn't figure out why he had not received the raise.

Mrs. Cortes had to get back to her office in the Faculty Tower for an appointment with the Dean of Students and asked Curtis if he would walk with her. Curtis had an hour break and was heading in the same direction.

Mrs. Cortes asked Curtis if he had begun his economics term paper yet. He chuckled, and said he was waiting for her third lecture on procrastination. She said as long as he was heading for the Thorne Library, he should check out some of the recent material on growth she had put on reserve. She said he could discover that his job performance might be the last thing to worry about. He was about to ask why, but by that time, they were at the Tower. Mrs. Cortes realized the Dean would be waiting and ducked inside.

At Thorne, Curtis checked out two articles on growth. One was from the *Wall Street Journal* on weak recovery shown by Gross Domestic Product figures and leading economic indicators. The other was from *Business Week*. It was on the slow recovery in Pennsylvania's Lehigh Valley after IBM's massive downsizing layoffs. The quiet of the library always made it a great place to think. He took a few notes and still wondered why Mrs. Cortes saw some connection between the article and his problem at Krug's. At any rate, Curtis decided to talk to his boss the next morning.

At Krug's Bakery, the 4:30 AM break came after the hard rolls and Danish were in the ovens. Curtis saw Mr. Krug doing some paper work on the counter in the back. He was still pretty discouraged. He went to the office door and hesitated.

"Hi, Curtis, dough ready on the rye?"

"Yes, sir. George is starting on it now." Curtis was not sure if this was the right time, but the frustration with his boss boiled up. "Mr. Krug, are you unhappy with me?"

"Not at all. Why?"

"Well, last month marked three years that I've been working for you, and I thought I would be getting a raise. I think I am a pretty hard worker and…"

"Hey, hold on, Curtis. Sit down, you are getting a little worked up. First of all, you are the best part-timer I have, no question about it. You are important to me and the way things work around here. Second, you are a very smart kid, but you live in an academic world. Do you ever listen to a radio newscast or read the daily paper? Take a look around. Have you noticed there are fewer customers on the weekends? Well, it is like that out at the counter all week. Things are slow because of the recession and all the cutbacks at the big firms around here. You know about those, don't you?"

"Well, yes… but people still need bread. I thought a business like this was protected from those things ”

"Don't they discuss this at your college? This is real, Curtis. My customers are upscale people. They are the ones willing to pay for quality, but some of them are losing their jobs because of the corporate downsizing and leaving this area. The others are buying cheaper stuff in the supermarkets. This store's gross income in the last six months has taken a nose dive!"

"I had no idea. Then it's not my work… it's the economy?"

"Definitely, but I guess I should have talked to you sooner. I saw you were a little down, but I thought it was a personal problem, and I didn't want to pry. Listen, I'm not sure you young people have a good grasp of how we are all linked to economic performance. Let me show you something."

Krug pulled two pies from the line in front of his work table, one large and one small.

"Look at the difference between these two. Suppose the large one represented the economic performance last year when I gave you a nice raise, and the smaller one represented this year."

"You mean what Mrs. Cortes called the GDP – Gross Domestic Product?"

"Exactly. Last year, when my slice of the pie was this big, I could share it with you. Now, look at my slice this year. What do you think?"

"Not much there to share."

"You know it! Being a good worker or a good manager can help, and the rewards are there if the total economic pie is getting bigger, but if things are shrinking, your piece shrinks. No way around it."

"OK. I guess there is not much you can do right now. I understand, Mr. Krug."

"I'll take care of you when things get better. But there is still something we can do right now, kid. Get a fork and have some of this pie I ruined – you deserve a break."

* * * * * *the end* * * * * *

Measuring Economic Performance

When asked to define the term success, people come up with varied responses. For some, it means accumulating a great deal of wealth. Others would say it means having enough to support a family. For many, it might mean the ability to help those less fortunate than themselves. For others, being a success would be nothing less than earning the recognition of being the best at what they do. Some dream of finding a new discovery or intellectual insight that adds to the encyclopedia of human knowledge. Still others want to be able to live in peace or travel when they want. For the homeless family, success may be the ability to get off of the streets into a clean, private, and warm bed every night and "three square meals" every day. No matter what the individual interpretation may be – no matter how unique or common the response – there is one necessary aspect of every reply: having enough money to do what one wants.

Whatever is identified as the American Dream, obtaining it depends not only on the individual and his/her abilities but also on the right economic conditions. Those conditions affect all people, everywhere, no matter whether they live in technologically advanced nations or underdeveloped, agricultural "Third World" countries. People everywhere gain or lose the ability to be successful because of conditions within their economic systems. The ability to make an individual choice is often determined by what happens far from one's personal world.

Knowing what these ever-present conditions are and understanding what they mean to particular situations in life helps people to act and react in their own self-interest. No matter how puzzling some data may seem, using that information gives everyone a better chance at riding the roller coaster of the "bad times" and the "good times."

At the center of any prosperous economic system is its ability to produce up to its potential. That potential must grow year after year if the scarcity problem is to be minimized and the promise of a better standard of living is to be fulfilled. This means that production of goods and services must increase. Measurement of this growth is critically important to determine an economy's success or to see if it needs stimulation.

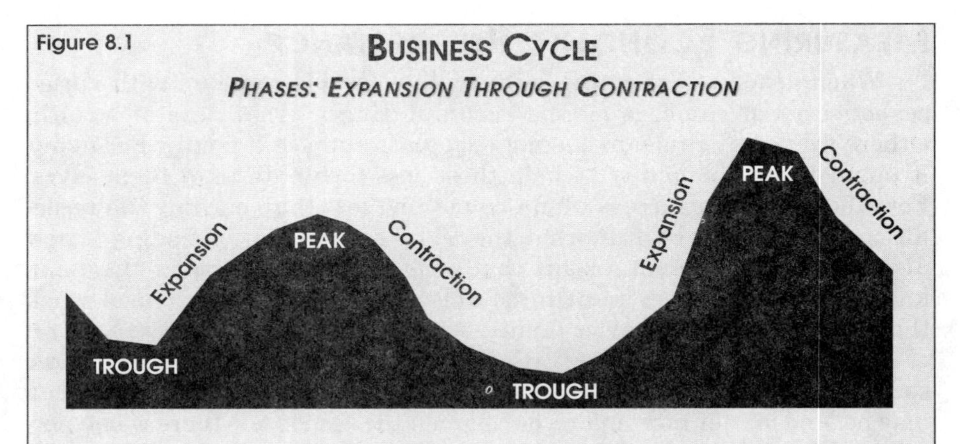

Business cycles are variations in market activities. They are measured by increases and decreases in Real Gross Domestic Product. While fluctuations occur because of the combined decisions of producers and consumers, the duration and intensity of the phases can last from a few months to a few years.

THE BUSINESS CYCLE

The economy's roller coaster ride is generally referred to as the **business cycle**. It has four key phases: **Prosperity** (the peak), **Recession** (the contraction), **Depression** (the trough) and **Recovery** (the expansion) (see Figure 8.1 above). These roller coaster ups and downs are measured according to many technical indexes. However, simply put: the "ups" are defined by high employment and high spending, while the "downs" are defined as low employment and low spending. Employment and spending are variables that are determined by **aggregate demand** (total spending). When the aggregate demand is up, and people are working and spending, the response will be a high total output of goods and services. When aggregate supply is up, the response will be more goods and services available in the marketplace.

Some economists prefer to call the business cycle the "demand cycle." As long as people have money to spend and actually use that purchasing power in the marketplace, then producers have the incentive to provide the goods and services the consumers want. Seeking increased profits, the producers will hire more people to provide what is selling. This gives more people income and greater purchasing power. As a result, economic growth moves upward.

Yet, all good things do end, and the cycle can also move downward. Judgments to not buy, to cut production, or to keep it level influence the decisions of others. Spending slows, and **aggregate economic activity** can begin to decline. Such negative signals cause producers to cut hours and eliminate jobs, causing unemployment to rise. The corporate downsizing of the early 1990s is an example. The underemployed and unemployed workers then have less purchasing power. If aggregate demand

Figure 8.2

REAL GDP IN BILLIONS

USING 1996 CONSTANT DOLLARS

Source: *U.S. Dept. of Commerce*

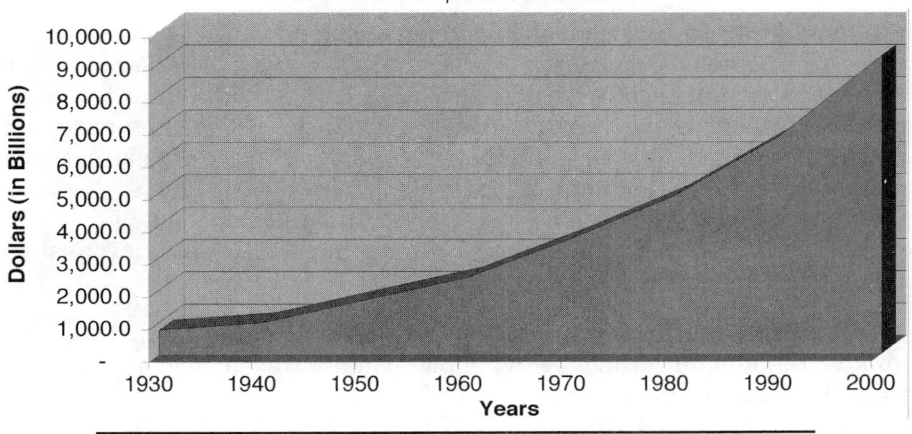

diminishes further, nervous producers' decrease aggregate supply. This means that more employees will be "laid-off," and the downward phase of the cycle gains momentum.

In the recent history of tracking this cyclical activity, the good times seem to last much longer than the bad times. At best, the peaks seem to last five years, and except for the Great Depression, the troughs last a little more than one year (see Figure 8.2 above).

There is no set rhythm or time frame to the cycle. Periods of expansion or contraction are never equal in length or intensity. While in the past, periods of growth have usually been longer than periods of decline, this may be changing.

In the past half century, government fiscal policies aimed at intervening if production or employment needed stimulation (see Issue 7). The actions were discretionary, but there are no hard and fast rules for predicting how long or strong phases of the cycle will be. Still, the public has an expectation that government can protect the society from "bad times."

VARIABLES IN THE CYCLE TODAY

Conditions today are different. The old tools of fiscal policy are less effective. The already high debt levels make new deficit spending less acceptable, and the need for revenue makes tax cutting difficult. There is less leeway to stimulate aggregate demand than during the past two generations. Without this intervention, some economists predict the contractions of the business cycle will become more painful. The recession of the early 1990s is a case in point. It lasted for considerably longer than any other recent decline, and the recovery was very uneven, with the Northeast and California experiencing prolonged suffering. With government impotence, the "bad times" may last longer than in previous history.

In addition to government impotence, another variable affecting the cycle is business consumption (how much businesses spend). The amounts that businesses spend affect aggregate demand (and the business cycle) just as much as consumer choices do. Businesses purchase new machinery, build more facilities (factories, offices, warehouses), and put capital into research and the development of new products. Business spending stimulates technology and competitive development for better products at lower costs. When these things happen, there is expansion. When they do not, there is contraction.

The **money supply** is another variable altering the cycle. The greater the amount of money available, usually the cheaper it is to borrow. The more scarce money is, the higher the cost of borrowing it. When money is cheap (interest rates are low), confident consumers and businesses borrow more and spend it. When interest rates are high, discouraged consumers and businesses borrow less and spend less. As the cost of credit changes, so do the conditions affecting supply and demand.

Expectations are variables altering the cycle, too. What people believe and predict about economic activity has a great deal to do with their behavior in the marketplace. If people expect they may be laid-off, they will spend less and save more in anticipation of being unemployed. If such negative expectations are widespread – as they were during the early 1990s – then spending diminishes everywhere, demand decreases, and the economy can go into a contraction phase.

Negative expectations have an enormous influence on consumption. They generally cause less spending on goods and services, and sometimes more saving. Businesses also have even finer tuned perspectives on what is happening in the economy, and they react dramatically to those perceptions. In the early 1990s, as a few big companies began a trend in "downsizing," medium companies laid-off workers, as many of the firms were vendors and subcontractors of big businesses. When industries believe that there are good times ahead, they invest in new growth programs. Yet, the opposite also holds true. If the view of the economic future is gloomy, then the pessimism will lead to a decrease in investment, product development, and employment.

Domestically, both consumers and producers can spur an expansion or contraction based on their expectations or visions about economic activity. Economic activity does not occur in a vacuum. What happens in the world also has a profound effect on the domestic U.S. economy, and ultimately, what goes on in our personal lives.

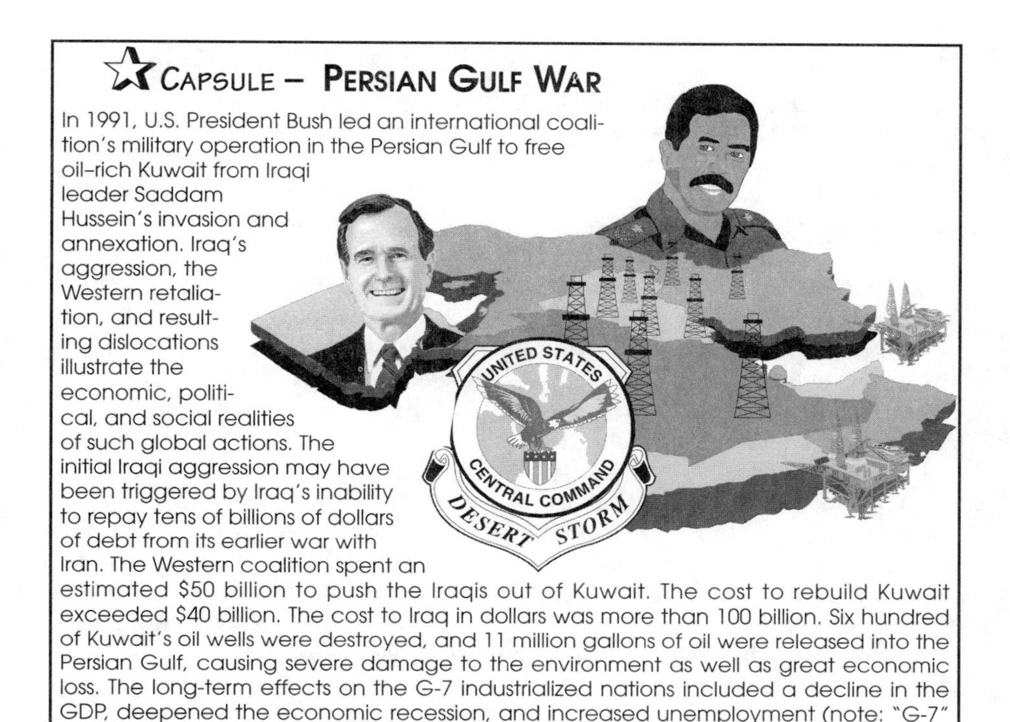

☆ Capsule – Persian Gulf War

In 1991, U.S. President Bush led an international coalition's military operation in the Persian Gulf to free oil-rich Kuwait from Iraqi leader Saddam Hussein's invasion and annexation. Iraq's aggression, the Western retaliation, and resulting dislocations illustrate the economic, political, and social realities of such global actions. The initial Iraqi aggression may have been triggered by Iraq's inability to repay tens of billions of dollars of debt from its earlier war with Iran. The Western coalition spent an estimated $50 billion to push the Iraqis out of Kuwait. The cost to rebuild Kuwait exceeded $40 billion. The cost to Iraq in dollars was more than 100 billion. Six hundred of Kuwait's oil wells were destroyed, and 11 million gallons of oil were released into the Persian Gulf, causing severe damage to the environment as well as great economic loss. The long-term effects on the G-7 industrialized nations included a decline in the GDP, deepened the economic recession, and increased unemployment (note: "G-7" became "G-8" in 1997 with the admission of Russia).

In the modern world, the linkage is astounding. Economic, political, and social events all over the globe are reflected quickly in the economic realities of other nations. For example, if **OPEC** (Organization of Petroleum Exporting Countries) could consistently enforce loyalty to the agreements made at its annual conferences, the price of oil would certainly rise, increasing OPEC profits. OPEC's political decisions to restrict oil production and exports to the Western nations in 1973 and 1980 caused inflation and hardship in the everyday lives of Americans and Europeans.

Another example is the cost of being involved in any military action. Although not beneficial to human existence, wars temporarily stimulate economic prosperity as governments spend great amounts of money on national defense contracts. However, wars also cause downturns after they end. When the massive government demand stimulating the whole economy declines, the economy declines. (Note the Desert Storm Star Capsule above.)

Panic and irrational moves can cause negative reactions and harm to the economy, too. Understanding the cycle allows knowledgeable predictions that encourage prudent activities. Being able to read economic measurements helps individuals predict direction of the cycle and act accordingly.

Performance Measurement: GNP and GDP

Measuring the performance of an economic system is not an easy task. The aim is to measure the economy as a whole, but what does this mean? What must be examined in order to measure how well or poorly the economy is doing? What data must be collected? What is included and excluded?

Not long ago, economists believed that their quandary was ended when an economist working for the National Bureau of Economic Research developed a system that would accomplish the task of measuring the economy. The *Nobel Prize in Economics* (1971) was awarded to **Simon Kuznets** for his improved methods of determining Gross National Product and National Income.

While Kuznets' is not the only method used by economists to analyze the direction in which the economy is headed, it is a popular measure of growth. The Kuznets' method depends on the production of goods and services as a benchmark of economic advancement. **Gross National Product** is the calculation of all new and finished goods produced in a one year period by American companies (domestically and everywhere in the world).

More recently, another measure has gained popularity with economists – the **Gross Domestic Product**. GDP is defined as the total output produced *within* the country (no matter what the nationality of the producer). The preferred U.S. government and U.N. measurements now use GDP figures for comparisons and general economic reporting.

GNP and GDP are calculated similarly, by adding four chief components of economic expenditure: ***C*** = all of the consumer goods (personal consumption of goods and services), **+*I*** = capital goods (investment by business into new factories, machinery, or houses), **+*G*** = government consumption of goods and services, **+*X* = net exports** (exports minus imports) (see Figure 8.3 below).

Figure 8.3

Components of Gross Domestic Product 2000

Source: Bureau of Economic Analysis - U.S. Dept. Commerce

Where:

C	=	\$6,728.4 billion – **personal consumption** expenditures
I	=	\$1,767.5 billion – gross private **investment** by business
G	=	\$1,741.0 billion – **Government** consumption
X	=	–\$364.0 billion – net **exports**

Then:

C + *I* + *G* + *X* = \$9,872.9 billion (1996 dollars) = GDP

Annual GNP and GDP figures are both gauges of economic performance. With adjustment, they also allow comparisons to other time periods. Growth is a very good thing for any economy. If the economy is like the pies at Mr. Krug's bakery, he, Curtis, and everyone else gets a piece. With growth, the pie gets bigger, and the bigger the pie, the bigger the individual's piece. Perhaps the analogy is oversimplified, but the richer the country is, the higher an individual's standard of living. Working at a job and being a cooperative employee for a productive company leads a worker like Curtis to expect to be rewarded. The reward can be a raise in salary or wages or in benefits and bonuses. If the company that employs the worker is growing and making a substantial profit, it is likely that the worker will get an increased share.

Conversely, if the company does not have a growth in profit, how can an employee expect more? The same is true for the entire economy. Growth leads to more demand and the need for more supply. Understanding this aspect of measuring the economy allows a worker to know if a raise or "pink slip" will be on the horizon.

GDP is computed either on an income base or an expenditure base. The income base adds up all the money earned by households and business firms in a given year. The expenditure base adds up the value of all the money spent for final goods and services by four sectors of the economy (***C+I+G+X***).

How the GDP (or GNP) is expressed gives a true or distorted image of the economic horizon. Growth is expressed by these two measures in dollar values, but some expressions are more accurate to use than others. Growth can be expressed as a simple **Money GDP** or a **Real GDP**. The difference is important.

Suppose a company produces luxury yachts at a rate of four per year. These products are sold at $200,000 each. In 1993, the company produced and sold four brand new yachts for a total of $800,000 (which is added to the GDP for that year). In 1994, the company produces another four, but because of an increase in the cost of stainless steel (a component used to make yachts), the price rises to $225,000. The income from the four yachts is now $900,000. When this amount is added to the raw GDP, it increases by one hundred thousand dollars. This gives the impression that there was growth.

Yet, in 1993 there were only four products built and again in 1994, only four were produced. There was no change in output – no *real* growth – only an increase in price (an indication of inflation). So the raw or **Money GDP**, reported in **current dollars**, does not always indicate if the economy actually grew in terms of production or profit.

To get a more realistic image of growth, **Real GDP** is used. This figure uses a "price deflator" formula to eliminate the inflationary value added to the total of the goods and services produced. Real GDP uses a benchmark value of the dollar called **constant dollars** to compare how much more is produced in the country this year than last (see Figure 8.4).

Figure 8.4 **GDP IN BILLIONS**

USING 1996 DOLLARS V. CURRENT DOLLARS

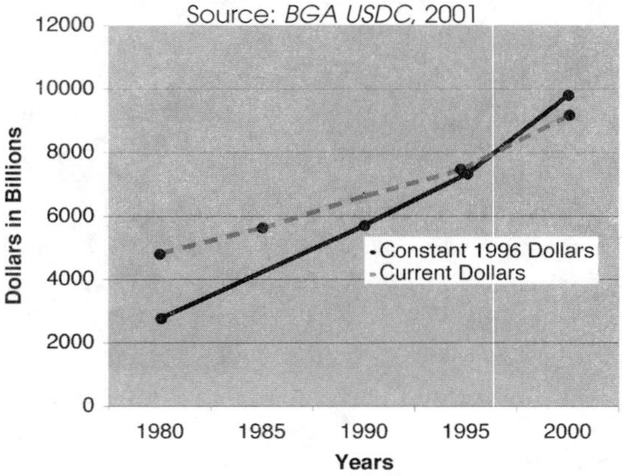

Source: *BGA USDC*, 2001

Real GDP establishes a rate of growth so one can see "how much bigger the pie is" and possibly be able to estimate what would be a reasonable increase in the size of "one's slice." In the opening story, if Curtis had understood this, he would not have been disturbed about his job at Krug's.

PERFORMANCE MEASUREMENT: NNP

There are other statistical measurements that indicate if the economy is growing. The amount of new machinery that businesses purchase every year is a significant indicator of where the economy is going. This is measured in the **Net National Product (NNP)**.

For businesses to respond to increased demand by increasing the production of goods and services that people want to purchase, they must buy more capital goods. Purchasing new facilities, machines, and tools used to put more products into the marketplace ordinarily means growth. To achieve a precise calculation of how much growth, the sale of all of this new machinery must be figured out carefully.

However, if the new capital purchases only represent expenditures for **depreciation** (replacing existing worn out, nonoperating capital goods), there is no growth. For example, if a car manufacturer orders twenty new machines that stamp sheet metal into fenders for new cars, the manufacturer's capital goods expenditures might be said to increase by the cost of the twenty machines. However, eleven of the machines were purchased to replace capital that no longer works. Only nine actually show growth in the NNP figure. Not bad, but not as good as originally thought. If each machine cost $20,000 and twenty were purchased, the total added to the NNP appears to be $400,000, but $220,000 is merely replacement value and cannot be counted into the figure showing growth. In this case, the NNP is increased by $180,000, not $400,000.

Performance Measurement: Income Levels

Income is another way of examining how much growth the economy is experiencing. Certainly the more we earn, the more we have; the more we have, the more we spend; the more we spend, the more should be produced; and the more we produce, the more we grow. The pie should be bigger.

What people earn is commonly known as **Gross Income**. This is the amount of money paid to people for their labor. When all sources of income are added together (**earned income** – for labor and **unearned income** – received from investments, rents, and all other sources), another major economic indicator is created: Personal Income.

Personal Income is the income a person has *before taxes are collected by the government*. After the taxes are taken from Personal Income, economists call what is left **Disposable Personal Income** (see Figure 8.5). Disposable income is also known as purchasing power. Disposable income

Figure 8.5

Department	Emp. No.	Name	Soc. Sec. No.	Clock No.	Filing Status		Period Ending
100	44	HABIB, CURTIS	103-88-8778		S	1	011495

Hours	Rate	Earnings	Type	Deductions Type	Year To Date	Other Pay Information
8.25	6.500	53.63	REG			

Pay Statement	This Pay	Year To Date
Total Earnings	53.63	407.89
Fica Tax	4.10	31.20
Federal Income Tax		23.71
State Tax		
Local Tax		
Other Tax		
Total Vol. Deductions		
Net Pay	49.53	

3659 P&T LOST AUTO PARTS, INC   Check Date 01/18/95   Check Number 1048

The part-time employee's paycheck stub (above) shows an hourly rate of $6.50 for a gross income of $53.63. Because the gross income is small as compared to the full-time employee's pay (below), the part-time employee has no withholding (income tax withheld) and only $4.10 deducted for FICA (Social Security) taxes – giving the employee a net pay of $49.53 (92.3% take-home). For the full-time employee with benefits, the gross income for the 2 week work period is much higher than the part-time employee at $1,314.96. However, after federal and state income taxes, FICA, and the medical insurance premiums are deducted, the full-time employee nets $967.24 (73.6% take-home).

The Hospital of North Orange   18 Montgomery St. Middletown, NY 10940   EMPLOYEE EARNINGS STATEMENT   NO. 088703

Employee Name	Employee Number	Department Expense No	Regular Rate	Social Security Number	Period End Date	Check Date	Check Number
GARSEY, JAN	37357	6166 033	21.356	114464778	03/19/95	03/24/95	088703

Current Earnings: Desc - Shift	Hours	Earnings	Deductions: Desc	Amount	YTD Amount
REG 1	40.00	854.24	INS	1.26	7.56
REG 2	20.00	457.72	SIBPOP	42.05	252.30
CHARG 1	4.00	3.00	DNTPOP	4.90	29.40

Current Year to Date Taxes and Gross

Federal	State	FICA	Gross Pay
139.14	63.37	97.00	1314.96
954.84	440.87	640.91	8659.58

Benefit Hours Available and Taken

VAC	SICK	HOLIDY	PERS
295.60	196.61	7.50	.00
.00	24.00	.00	.00

Current and Year to Date Additional Taxes

Net Pay
967.24

DETACH AND RETAIN FOR YOUR PERSONAL RECORDS: NOT NEGOTIABLE

Figure 8.6

Disposable Personal Income

Percent (%) of National Average – Per Person – 2000

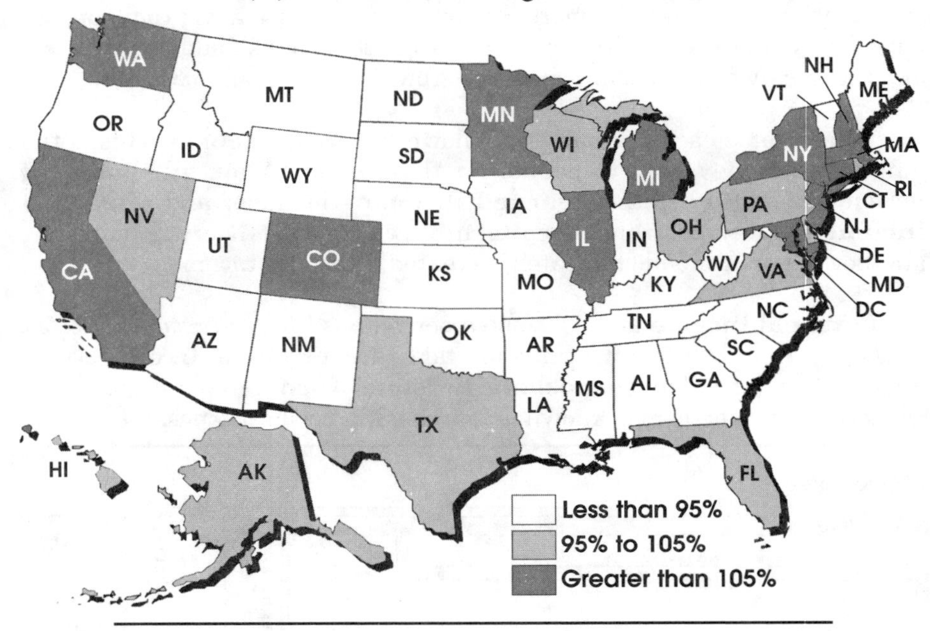

is what people have to spend, save, and invest to achieve the Dream. Of course it differs throughout the country (see Figure 8.6 above). Many economists consider disposable income the best measurement to determine if growth has been large enough to increase "one's piece of the pie."

Aggregate income, or the amount of money earned by everyone in the country (less business taxes), is known as **National Income**. Economists arrive at this total figure by adding everything paid out to people in salary, wages, and commissions, plus all of the profits earned by people that are self-employed as owners or partners in their own businesses. To this is added corporate profits, investment dividends, rental income, and interest paid to people. As National Income gets larger or smaller, it is a measure of how well or poorly the entire economy of the country is doing.

Performance Measurement: Unemployment Levels

Ever since the Great Crash of 1929, no other economic measure carries the weight of the unemployment rate. The **unemployment rate** measures the people not working but seeking employment. If after a while, an unemployed person gives up and stops seeking work, he/she is no longer considered to be part of the workforce. These people are now given another label. They are considered to be **discouraged workers** and do not show up in labor statistics.

Figure 8.7

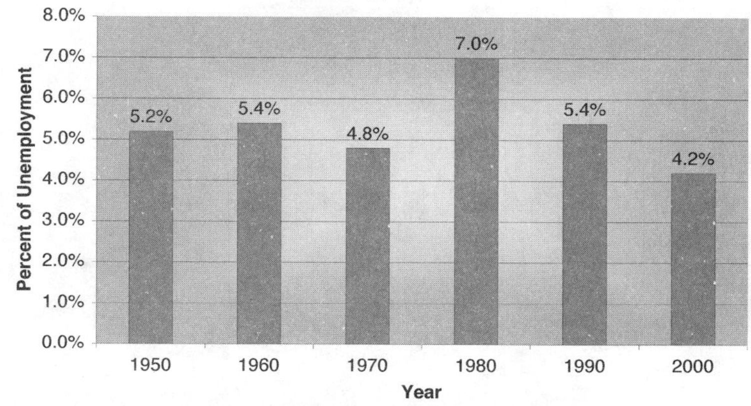

Source: *Statistical Abstract of U.S.*, Economic Indicators, 2001

Some unemployment is acceptable in a free economy. Modern economists are not disturbed by a 4 or even 5 percent unemployment rate. In fact, economists would classify such a level as near to **full employment** (the ideal that everyone wanting a job can find one) as possible. People change jobs frequently, and employers fire employees who do not meet their expectations. People take time for raising families or for travel and projects. All this is considered normal, **frictional unemployment**.

Cyclical unemployment is more serious, it results from contractions of the business cycle itself. **Structural unemployment** is also serious and may be prolonged because it results from jobs being eliminated because of technology. Structurally unemployed workers cannot easily rejoin the work force as the economy recovers, they must retrain themselves for new, more sophisticated jobs.

Whatever the cause, high unemployment is a serious problem not only for individuals and their families, but in a broader sense, for the economy on the whole. In the worst years of the Great Depression, some unemployment estimates went as high as 25%. The *Selected Unemployment Rates Since 1950* chart (Figure 8.7 above) gives averages, but in recessions in the 1970s, and 1980s, and 1990s, there were months that the numbers exceeded 10%.

When unemployment figures climb, businesses lose sales because the unemployed do not have purchasing power. The economy loses the goods and services that would have been produced by laid-off workers. The workers and businesses that are still productive are often subject to higher taxes for **public assistance** (unemployment compensation, medical subsidies, and welfare) to help support the unemployed.

Figure 8.8a **PERSONAL INCOME V. PERSONAL SAVINGS**

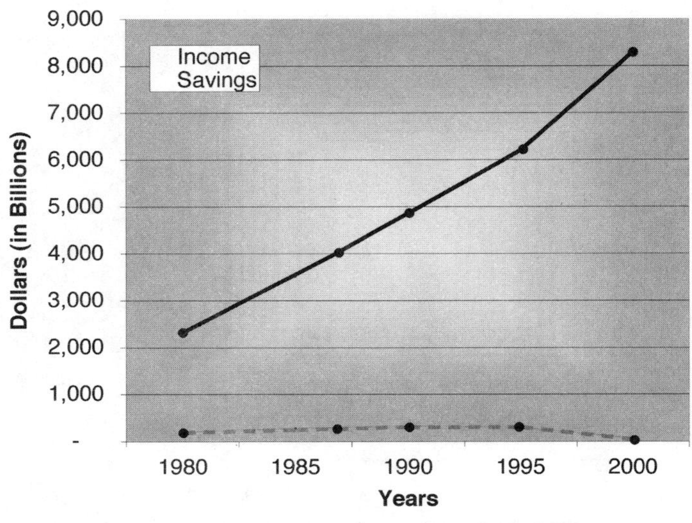

Source: *Statistical Abstract of U.S.*, 2001

A high number of unemployed workers is an indication of even further economic grief for the society. Significant unemployment also means that there are many nonproductive resources such as buildings and machinery (capital). Significant unemployment means that the entire nation will have less productivity and less income. The GDP pie gets smaller and so does each person's piece.

PERFORMANCE MEASUREMENT: SAVINGS LEVELS

Income has only two practical uses: spending and saving. Most of what the Americans earn, they spend. Still, the amount that the nation saves, called the **savings rate**, is important as an economic indicator (measurement). It shows how much we have put aside from our Disposable Personal Income into savings accounts.

The savings rate changes as income and employment change. When the income is high and people are working, the savings rate goes up. When income declines during downswings of the business cycle, people have less and use what they earn to survive. Saving becomes a luxury, and the savings rate drops. As the cycle goes into recovery or expansion, people go back to work and are able to earn more and save more. (Figure 8.8a above) shows this relationship. Note the rate changes in recent recessions.

As an economic measurement, the savings rate gives mixed signals. It can indicate the danger of inflationary trends – sometimes. Rising prices

Figure 8.8b

PERSONAL SAVINGS RATE

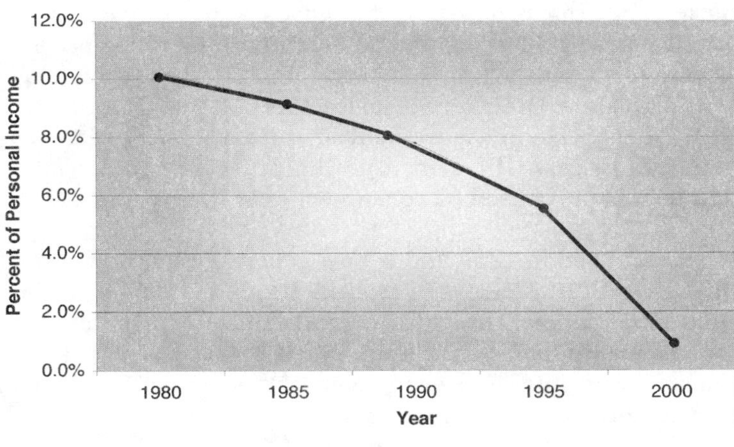

Source: *Statistical Abstract of U.S.*, 2001

mean people must spend more of their Disposable Personal Income just to maintain their standard of living. This leaves less to put into savings, and the savings rate declines. Inflation not only causes people to save less, it usually causes more withdrawals, too. Some people decide to make major purchases with their savings, fearing loss of purchasing power as their dollars decline in value.

However, there is another side to inflationary pressure on the savings rate. As inflation causes the price of limited supplies to rise, and Disposable Personal Income has less purchasing power, some consumers may actually decide not to buy, and save *more* – at least temporarily.

Because of these mixed signals, using the savings rate as an indicator on its own is vexing. However, used with other indicators, a rising savings rate can confirm expansion.

Americans seem to save less than the citizens of other industrialized nations. Part of the reason for this is cultural, stemming from our desire to achieve the American Dream. Owning a home, car, and possessions of all kinds means a great deal. Americans seem to "want it all." Traditionally, they spend much and save little. (see Figure 8.8b above) The savings rate in the 1980s and early 1990s is about 4%. Japanese and German rates in this period were 8%-12%. Examining how much Disposable Personal Income goes into saving helps indicate how the economy is performing.

Performance Measurement: Inflation Levels

Statistics showing prices paid for goods and services are another important measure of the economy. An examination of how prices change in the economy can indicate how healthy and stable the system is. The tool used to calculate the average price level is the **Consumer Price Index** (**CPI**). It is a key measurement of **inflation** – an increase in the average level of prices. CPI measures the difference in prices paid for goods and services purchased by consumers over time.

CPI was first used in 1919 and is now generated by the United States Bureau of Labor Statistics every month. Its data is given to business, government, and labor. The information leads to price changes and adjustment of wage demands. Congress alters food stamp allocations, social security payments, and even school lunch programs on CPI. The FED uses it to help in determining its monetary policies.

Figure 8.9 **Monthly CPI Market Basket Comparisons**

Year	Cost of Monthly Basket
A	$1000
B	1100
C	1300
D	1500

Year	Index
A	100
B	110
C	130
D	150

Each month, this agency prices 400 commonly purchased goods and services (known as the "market basket," see Figure 8.9) in 85 different locations throughout the country. These prices are compared to what the costs were in a "base year" which the Bureau arbitrarily chooses and assigns a reference point of 100. All other yearly prices are compared as percentages of this base year.

The Consumer Price Index (CPI) indicates that food shopping takes a larger part of the family budget. ©PhotoDisc

Assume that in Year *A*, the base year, the cost of the 400 goods and services in the "market basket" is $1,000. During the next year, the cost goes up to $1,100, then $1,300 in year *C*, and finally in Year *D*, $1,500. In Year *A*, the $1,000 is converted to 100(%) on the price index. During Year *B*, the cost went up by $100, (or 10%) of the Year *A* (base year) figure. In Year *C*, a $300 increase translates to a price index change of 30%, and so on.

What this means to the consumer is that it will cost 10%, then 20%, and then

Figure 8.10

CONSUMER PRICE INDEX

BASE VALUE OF DOLLAR IN 1982-1984

Source: *Statistical Abstract of U.S.*, 2000

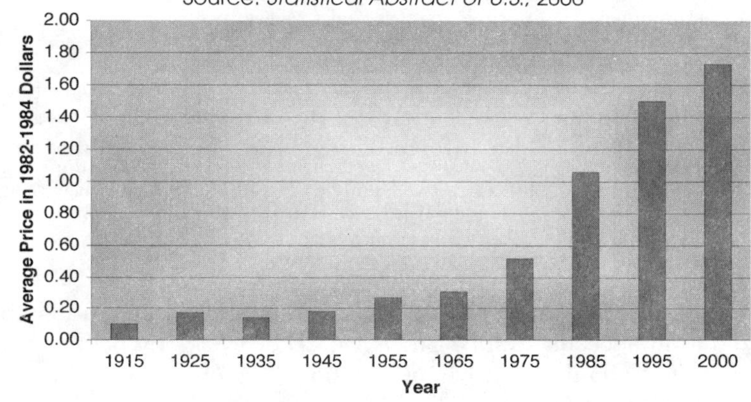

30% more to buy the same things purchased in the base year. Figure 8.10 illustrates what happens over time. As prices continually go up, a person must spend more in order to simply maintain his/her standard of living. If a person's income does not keep pace with the increased costs, purchasing power is lost, and the piece of the pie gets smaller.

PRODUCER PRICE INDEX

Consumers are not the only part of the economy that is affected by inflation. The **Producer Price Index (PPI)** indicates the changes in what producers pay to assemble their products. Just like the CPI, the Producer Price Index is calculated by the government and published monthly.

There is an important connection between the CPI and the PPI. When businesses pay more to produce their products today, consumers will pay more for them tomorrow. It seems that it is important to maintain a perspective on both of these indicators since a change in the Producer Price Index will lead to a future change in the Consumer Price Index.

WHEN PRICES RISE

Economists have a rather simple definition for a very complex economic problem: **inflation**. They call it "a period of rapidly rising prices." Of course, if prices are rising and income is not, the economy is in trouble. It means it takes more money to buy goods and services.

CAPSULE – HYPERINFLATION

The best known example of **hyperinflation** (extreme, rapid inflationary spiral) took place in Europe in the early 1920s. The devastation of World War I caused great economic disorder. In Germany, the Weimar Republic experienced the worst fate of any government – the repudiation of its money. The value of the German mark was totally destroyed. As the currency value plummeted, the prices of goods and services rose so quickly people could not believe what was happening. A loaf of bread went up in price from one mark to a million. People carted money in wheelbarrows rather than wallets. Money was used to wallpaper rooms instead of being spent in stores. People were seen running to stores to spend whatever they had to avoid increases in price in the time it normally took to walk.

More recently, Brazil and Argentina suffered through horrible double digit rises in the weekly cost of living. In 1990, these two countries risked political and social collapse because of hyperinflation. Prices increased at an alarming 70% to 195% a month.

– *New York Times* 11 March 1990

What causes prices to rise? The technical explanation sounds simple enough: demand exceeds supply. Since a market works by people making educated guesses about what, when, and how to produce, it is natural for there to be miscalculations.

Local misjudgments about supply are frequent, but they are not often too serious. Perhaps an impending snowstorm sends many more customers into the stores to buy bread and milk, rent video tapes, or buy rock salt. Normal supplies vaporize, and stores have to send out quickly for more. Perhaps stores have to pay more to get delivery from distant sources. Stores pass the added cost on to slightly panicky customers. Without much choice, the larger number of customers begin paying a little more for things they need. It is almost like an auction scenario. High demand "pulls prices up." This is **demand-pull inflation**. As the left side in Figure 8.11 on page 197 shows, when the supply is fixed and the demand for a product increases (shifts right on graph), the equilibrium price rises.

In the 1970s, U.S. auto manufacturers stopped producing convertibles. Rising thefts, poor gas mileage, air conditioning, and discomfort experienced with high speed turnpike driving in open cars made demand for convertibles decline. In the 1980s, Mazda Motors' market research showed the growing youth market might support a sporty little convertible for around town. When the Miata hit dealerships, demand exceeded supply by such a great amount that astonished dealers began letting customers bid against each other. The manufacturer's suggested price was around $12,000. Miata dealers were selling them for over $15,000. Eventually, the price came down as supply increased and the market came back into equilibrium. Similar inflationary episodes surrounded Power Ranger products and the Cabbage Patch and Tickle Me Elmo dolls.

When people are willing to spend more and more money, the may be demand-pull inflation. If there is an increase in the money or credit is too readily available, consumers compete intensely fc plies and prices escalate. To prevent this, the Federal Reserve will act to "tighten the money supply" (see material on FED in Issue 6, page 128).

On the supply side of price inflation is the influence of production costs on producer decisions. Profits (revenues – costs) drive producers' decisions. When, for example, nature causes crop failures or wars make oil hard to get or union contracts raise labor costs, production costs rise, and producers see their profits shrink. To avoid profit loss, producers pass along the added costs by raising their prices, fueling inflation.

If the situation continues, it prompts decisions which shift supply even more. Producers may convert some of their facilities to making something more profitable, or they may drop out of the market completely. Either way, the supply shrinks. With fewer goods available but demand remaining normal, prices rise. This is called **cost-push inflation**. As the graph on the right side of Figure 8.11 shows, when the demand is fixed and the supply of a product decreases (shifts left on graph), the market equilibrium price rises.

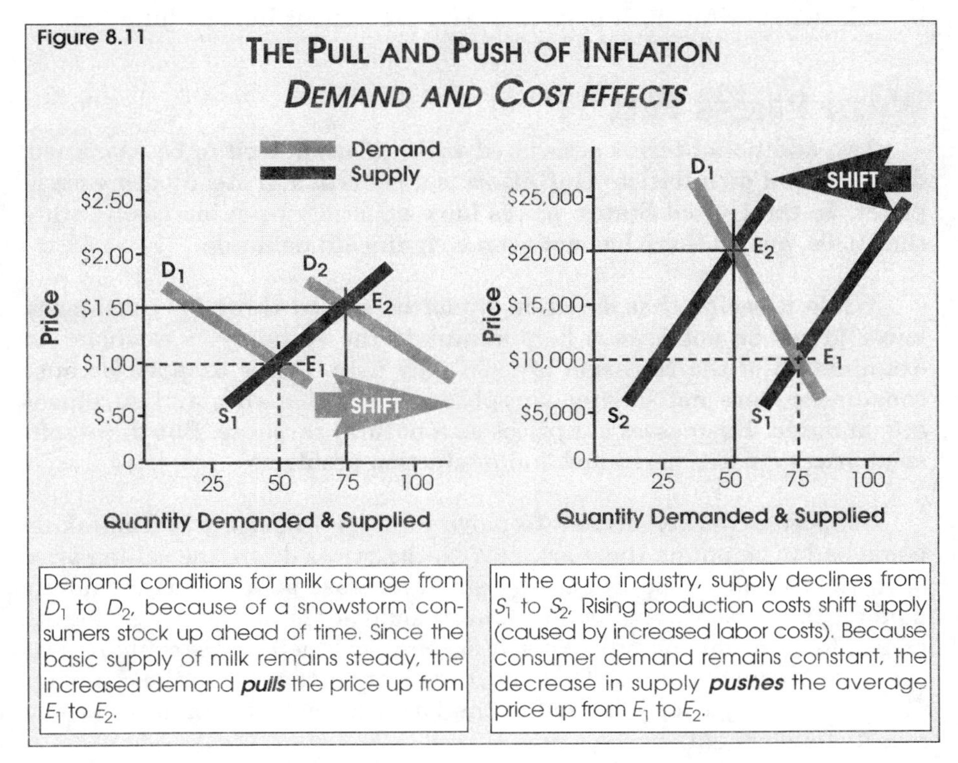

Demand conditions for milk change from D_1 to D_2, because of a snowstorm consumers stock up ahead of time. Since the basic supply of milk remains steady, the increased demand ***pulls*** the price up from E_1 to E_2.

In the auto industry, supply declines from S_1 to S_2. Rising production costs shift supply (caused by increased labor costs). Because consumer demand remains constant, the decrease in supply ***pushes*** the average price up from E_1 to E_2.

Whatever the cause, inflation can be an inconvenience for some people and devastating for others. Some employment contracts contain **Cost of Living Adjustments (COLAs)** that raise income according to some inflation index such as the Consumer Price Index. Contract COLAs are rare, however. Upper income groups find budget and expense shifts irksome, but middle and lower income groups may have to make considerable sacrifices when faced with inflation. Retirees on fixed income, unable to go out and earn more, have to juggle expenses frantically when their heating bills rise due to inflation. Often, they make up the added heating oil expense from food allocations, and malnutrition can result. Middle income groups often have to give up small luxuries and then shop for cheaper brands of food and clothing.

Everyone has to juggle finances during inflation. Yet, inflation does benefit a few individuals. Suppose a student has to borrow money for four years of college. During the four years, inflation hits. After graduation, the student begins to pay back the loan. The purchasing power of the current dollars used to pay back the loan is perhaps 3 to 10 percent less than the dollars borrowed four years before. In this case, the borrower is at an advantage and the bank loses. Banks now protect themselves with "adjustable rates" on mortgages and even short-term loans. They can raise the interest rate if necessary to make up for the losses inflicted by inflation. For the most part, however, everyone is hurt by inflation.

When Prices Fall

Two additional terms associated with inflation need to be examined: deflation and disinflation. **Deflation** is a general and steady decrease in prices. In the United States, prices have generally been increasing since the 1930s, and so there has not been a significant deflation.

While it seems that deflation would be a good thing for consumers, lower prices do not always help stimulate the economy as a whole. An examination of the recession of 1990 may help. Prices dropped because consumers were not buying. Supply exceeded demand, and surpluses accumulated. Businesses cut prices as a natural response. But these softened prices created personnel and production problems.

Suppose a worker needed to move in order to get a job. The family home had to be put on the market. With the prices down, the selling price of the house may at best be a very small increase above what the family paid for the home originally. The family could get less than it paid for the house, too. For businesses, the selling prices of their goods could be less than the production costs. This may cause, at best, a loss to the company. At worst, it may cause the end of the business, and its employees could face unemployment.

Disinflation is any reduction of the inflation rate. It does not refer to prices but to a slowdown in the rate of growth of inflation. For example, the rate of inflation dropped from approximately 13% in 1980 to 4% in 1985. Prices were still increasing, but their *rate* of increase was considerably slower. Disinflation is usually associated with actions by the Federal Reserve Board's manipulation of its monetary policy (see Issue 6, pages 127 and 130).

When Growth Stagnates

When the two negative conditions of high unemployment and high inflation occur at the same time, economists call it **stagflation**. If there is an attempt to work on curing one condition, that cure seems to make the opposite condition worsen. If the government uses tight fiscal and monetary policies to lower inflation, unemployment usually rises. If the government uses expansionary fiscal and monetary policies to lower the unemployment rate, then the action makes inflation worse.

To illustrate, suppose the economy is stagnant, but there is inflation. In the late 1960s, government spending for social programs (the Great Society) and the Vietnam War inflated the money supply, but fear of recession led firms to cut back production. Fear caused production to slow down, and jobs were cut, but the government continued its rampant spending. Congress put a surcharge on taxes to sop up some of the excess money, but that slowed growth even more, and a recession began.

The most frequent approach to controlling inflation has been for the Federal Reserve (the FED) to "tighten" the money supply. Tightening the money supply means raising FED interest rates, eventually making it more expensive to borrow money. This additional expense discourages producers and consumers and slows aggregate demand. This decrease in spending creates a surplus. To get rid of the excess supply, producers cut prices, and inflation slows.

Capsule – Difficult Tradeoffs

In order to get control of spending and reduce the rate of increase in the deficit in the 1990s, Congress reduced the federal budget. This required major cuts in defense funds. To meet these reductions, the Pentagon closed military bases. These closures helped improve the budget but produced ripple effects in the economies of the communities where the base closings were made. Due to the loss of income, unemployment increased, local businesses closed reducing the tax base for schools and services, and people moved to find jobs.

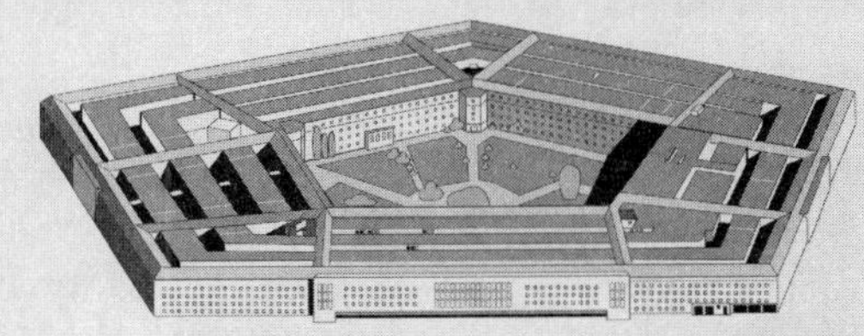

Pentagon, Arlington, VA

Such FED actions alter inflation, but they also slow down demand. This means there will be layoffs and job cuts by businesses. The only way to combat unemployment is to increase aggregate demand. In the past, Congress tried to do this with spending programs or tax reductions to flush more money into the economy. Theoretically an increase in demand would inspire producers to put more workers back to work to meet the higher demand.

The result is often what novelist Joseph Heller called "Catch-22" – an unending loop wherein solving one problem worsens the other. If unemployment is to be dealt with, more spending is required. Yet, if inflation is to be reduced, less spending is required. One treatment cancels out the other.

Treating one condition at the expense of the other is not acceptable. Government must adopt a new, coordinated outlook and attitude toward the problem, but individuals and unions must also restrain the desire for increased wages. Acting for the greater good is often a very difficult process.

Global Performance Measurement: Foreign Exchange

There are also global dimensions to measuring economic life. The United States is the world's foremost economic power. How its image is perceived by other countries has a great effect on the operation of our economy. An indicator of how the world perceives our economic well-being is how well our currency is doing in relation to the money of other countries.

If a country's economic outlook is perceived as bad in the eyes of other countries, there is reaction to the perception. In late 1994 and early 1995, the Mexican peso took a horrific drop in value on world markets. This global loss of confidence in Mexico's economy kept investors and business expansion at bay. Intervention from friends sometimes helps. U.S. government backing for loans to Mexico helped stem the peso's decline.

Everyday, billions of dollars are traded in markets where national currencies are bought and sold. The currencies of all nations are exchanged. The reasons for this swapping are: international trade, international investment, and international aid (loans and grants).

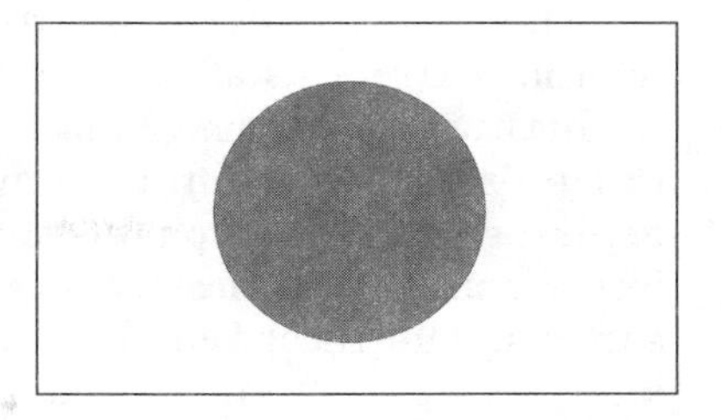

Each nation has its own money. So, what happens when an American wants to buy a Japanese-made Nikkon camera or a Japanese firm wants to buy a piece of heavy equipment from the Caterpillar Corporation of America? The Japanese manufacturer wants to be paid in yen, and the American producer wants to be paid in U.S. dollars. The practice of replacement of one currency for another at equal value is known as the **foreign exchange rate**. The price of the camera and the heavy equipment is set by each manufacturer in the amount of the country where it was produced. How the yen and dollar get to the right place and in the proper amount is established by a rate of exchange.

Banks all over the world keep currencies of all countries to finance the global exchanges of goods and services. The American corporation deposits dollars and withdraws yen and vice versa. The amount of yen received by these banks is compared to the amount of dollars they receive, and this creates a rate of exchange. What dollars are worth in comparison to all other world monies is an important measure of how well or poorly our country is doing. It is a means of measuring the financial relationship of our country to all others.

When the foreign exchange rate goes up (meaning the value of other countries' money in relation to ours goes up), our dollar is **depreciated** (loses value). It costs more to purchase the money of other nations with American dollars. When the foreign exchange goes down (meaning the value of other countries' money in relation to ours goes down), the U.S. dollar is **appreciated** (gains value). It costs less to purchase the money of other nations. Figure 8.12 below gives an idea of the variations in international currency exchange rates in relation to the United States dollar.

Figure 8.12 **CURRENCY EXCHANGE RATE**

Source: Exchange Rates.com, January 9, 2003

Currency	Exchange Rate per U.S. Dollar	Value in U.S. Dollars
Canadian dollar	1.5541	$0.643459
Denmark kroner	7.1005	0.140835
England pound	0.623636	1.6035
European Union euro	0.955384	1.0467
Japanese yen	119.57	0.0083633
Mexican new peso	10.415	0.0960154
Sweden krona	8.713	0.114771
Switzerland franc	1.3943	0.717206

This value change of our money compared to other currencies affects the business we do with those countries. This means that a nation's international economic position depends upon what payments are made for imports and what receipts are obtained from exports. The record of these transactions is known as the balance of payment accounts, and it is another indicator of the economic health of a country. Nations want to have a favorable balance of payments. This means the country has a greater flow of money into it than out of it.

The balance of payments is primarily affected by the **balance of trade**. This is the difference between the value of what a country imports and exports. A **trade deficit** means that the value of goods a country has imported is more than the value of goods it has exported (an *unfavorable* balance of trade). When the value of exports exceeds the value of imports, a **trade surplus** exists which is also known as a *favorable* balance of trade. Since the late 1970s, the United States has had a large and costly trade deficit. It has caused the depreciation of the U.S. dollar, and it has created a situation which lowers the purchasing power of our currency throughout the world. (Issue 9 explores this topic further on page 224.)

All this means that other countries are getting more of our wealth. The more they get, the less we have for ourselves. The story at the beginning of this issue noted that growth meant all of us want a bigger piece of the GDP pie. We may be producing more, but when our net exports show a deficit, our share of the pie is smaller. A trade deficit means the raises we expect from our hard work and increased efficiency trickle out to workers in other countries. It also means some loss of confidence in the U.S. economy. That can decrease the value of our currency. The way others view our strength affects our ability to get a bigger share of world markets, and that can have a negative effect on the American Dream.

Performance Measurement: Economic Indicators

When examining data about how well the economy is doing, it is customary to compare the information according to a time frame. **Economic indicators** are based on the U.S. Department of Commerce's statistics on 300 aspects of the economy (see Figure 8.13 on page 203). In a particular period, **key indicators** are reported monthly and tracked by economists to gauge the general performance of the economy. **Leading Indicators** are statistics that show a general change may occur in the

Figure 8.13

CLASSIFYING ECONOMIC INDICATORS

Source: Statistical Abstract of the U.S., 1994, pg. 556

Leading Indicators	Coincidental Indicators	Lagging Indicators
Building Permits (new private dwellings)	Industrial Production Index	Change in Labor Costs (manufacturing)
Common Stock Price Index	Employee Payrolls -nonagricultural	Ratio: Consumer Installment Credit to Personal Income
Initial Unemployment Insurance Claims	Personal Income less government transfer payments	Average Prime Rate of Banks
Producer Raw Material Prices (PPI)	Sales	Average Duration of Unemployment
Average Work Week (manufacturing industries)		Ratio: Manufacturing Inventories to Sales
Plant and Equipment Contracts and Orders		Commercial Loans Outstanding
Manufacturers' Orders for Consumer Goods		Change in CPI for Services
Money Supply (M2)		
Change in Manufacturers' Unfilled Orders		

future. **Coincidental Indicators** are statistics that show changes are in progress. **Lagging Indicators** are statistics that confirm changes have already happened.

SUMMARY

A word of caution about economic measurement is necessary. **Econometrics** (the application of mathematical and statistical methods to study economic and financial data) is still only a method of analyzing and predicting human activity in the short run. No matter which measurement is examined and analyzed, forecasts are still educated guesses as to how the economy will behave. Predicting the direction of the economy is like predicting the weather. It is an inexact science that often turns out differently than conditions indicate.

Knowing that this data exists and what it means is still a great deal better than ignoring it. Changes in all of the indicators discussed are not just studies in the academics of economics. These indicators have an important impact on decision-makers' actions which help decide the stability and growth of the economy. They also guide personal financial decisions such as how to save and invest, when to borrow, or when to buy a house. Achieving the American Dream is very difficult without a working knowledge of economic measurement.

ASSESSMENT • QUESTIONS • APPLICATIONS

1 What, in your life, determines if you are a success?
   a Why is income such a dramatic indicator of the economy in this country?
   b Explain in detail what you will be doing to achieve a sense of accomplishment in life.
   c Describe the work environment you will seek to accomplish your career goals.

2 It is normal for the the economy to go through phases of the business (demand) cycle.
   a Describe each of the four phases of the cycle.
   b What causes each of these phases?
   c What really determines prosperity?

3 Understanding measurements are critical to making business and career decisions and achieving the American Dream.
   a Explain the difference between GNP and GDP.
   b Why is the distinction important?
   c Which of the following is a better measure of the health of the economy: Real GDP or Money GDP? Why?
   d For the average person, the CPI has more meaning than the GDP or GNP. Explain why you agree or disagree with the above statement.

4 World opinion affects our economy far more than the average person perceives.
   a How is the American economy affected when one of your neighbors buys her dream car – a new – Lexus at a local dealer?
   b How may the foreign exchange rates affect your dream of a vacation in a foreign country?
   c How is international trade affected by foreign exchange rates?

5 Wars produce enormous effects on economic performance.
   a How does government demand during wars affect economic performance?
   b What happens to economic performance at the end of a war when government demand declines?
   c What kind of long-range effects do wars have on the countries involved (e.g., productive capacities, population)?

Assessment Project: Field Research Interview

Student Task

Write an individual report on field research interviews and participate in a group presentation on perceptions of success.

Procedure

Part One: (Individual Summary)

1 Based on the statement – "The meaning of the American Dream has changed during the last two generations." – prepare a list of questions to be asked during a social history survey to determine how three individuals (senior citizen, a middle-aged person, and a young adult) view the term "success."

2 Organize your interview as follows:
   a Develop a short statement of purpose to share with the interviewee.
   b Design your questions to elicit a simple "yes" or "no" – but provide the interviewee the opportunity to make a brief explanation or qualification.
   c After the last question has been asked, give the interviewee the opportunity (in light of the entire interview) to elaborate on the causes of the change.
   d When the interview is finished, thank the interviewee.

3 Compare, contrast, and analyze the three interviews. This can be done in chart or outline form.

4 Write an essay summarizing your findings.

Part Two: (Group Activity and Report)

1 Using the Part One summary, participate in a small group discussing the interview findings.

2 Produce a summary of the group's discussion of the interviews – citing differences and commonalities.

3 Present the group's findings orally for discussion by the whole class.

Evaluation

The criteria for the evaluation of this project are itemized in the grid (rubrics below) that follows. Choice of appropriate category terms (values) is the decision of the instructor. Selection of terms such as "minimal," "satisfactory," and "distinguished" can vary with each assessment.

Part One: Individual Field Interview Evaluation Rubric

(Refer to the teacher's supplement for suggestions of scoring descriptors for evaluation.)

Evaluation Item
Item a: (5) Does the essay show how three individuals view the term "success"?
Item b: (1) Does the essay show an understanding that peoples' values, practices, and traditions are diverse?
Item c: (6) Does the essay present ideas in clear, concise, and properly accepted fashion?

Part Two: Group Field Interview Evaluation Rubric

(Refer to the teacher's supplement for suggestions of scoring descriptors for evaluation.)

Evaluation Item
Item a: (9) To what extent does the group work cooperatively and show respect for the rights of others to think, act, and speak?
Item b: (7) Does the group use a variety of good sources?
Item c: (8) To what extent does the group monitor, reflect upon, and improve their members' work?
Item d: (6) Does the group's summary present ideas in clear, concise, and properly accepted fashion?
Item e: (9) How well does the group's discussion engage the whole class?

ISSUE 9

THE IMPACT OF GLOBALIZATION

What will shape the new global economy?

BEYOND THE CHAIN WALL: A NEW TRADE IS BORN

Maya pointed far across the desert floor. "There, by the rift at the edge of the cliff," she said.

Tok could barely see it – a small black dot. It must be two klicks away, but the old binoculars caught the movement. The Unsa village council had assigned the young couple to the village's outpost for two years. Their time was nearly up, and Maya and Tok had not seen anything but animals and sunrise on the east horizon. This had to be a person, judging from the slow, steady motion. Maya had taken the early morning scan along the edge of the vast, arid plateau. There were only two breaks in the far precipice. The moving dot appeared in the Arkai Pass, the one that twisted down to the TRIAD Chain Wall.

Maya and Tok were just in their twenties. In all their lives, they had not seen anyone from beyond the desert's edge. They were Inlanders. They were born in 2030, long after the Eco War. In the village school, they learned that a decade before, the old industrial nations had fallen apart trying to deal with population migrations from LDCs (less developed countries). The "Have-nots" of the Southern Hemisphere were collapsing from the HIV epidemic, starvation, and government corruption. Millions of refugees set out for the "Have" countries of the Northern Hemisphere. The northern peoples feared the waves of refugees would overburden them. They taxed their populations and raised large armies and navies to repel the refugees. After six years of trying to stop the flow, the overtaxed military economies collapsed. Nuclear weapons were useless. How could you use missiles against the small crafts of these desperate souls? The United Nations was no help. It disintegrated because no one had the money to contribute to its peacekeeping forces. Negotiations and world conferences were useless when half the nations were socially and economically bankrupt.

Only two forces remained: the three trade alliances (the TRIAD) and the MNCs (MultiNational Corporations). Amid the chaos of the mass migrations, the MNCs closed down their facilities in the LDCs. They withdrew to their headquarters in Northern Hemisphere. When it appeared the overstrained northern nations were collapsing, the MNCs threw their resources behind the trade alliances. The "TRIAD" (Europa [the European Union], AFTA [the Americas' alliance – all Western Hemisphere], and APEC [the Asia Pacific alliance driven by Japan and China]) became the great trade empires. The TRIAD merged military forces and built elaborate secure cities to protect the MNCs.

After almost a decade of negotiation, the TRIAD Empires strengthened ties among themselves and forced the refugees into the interiors of the continents. The coastal areas grew to look like overgrown medieval manors. The TRIAD Empires built successive rings of tall electrified fences for miles around the cities and their agricultural fields. Strict birth control measures kept the populations small. All supplies came by ship. Air travel ceased. There was no room for airports and no need to move people. Everyone stayed put. Hydroponic factories provided food. Desalinization plants provided water, and only armed garbage convoys ventured out beyond the Chain Walls.

Excluded, the refugees became "Inlanders." They turned to subsistence farming and herding in small, isolated communities. Fear and poverty kept Inlander communities from contact with each other.

Now, on a cool, sunlit morning in 2050, Tok and Maya watched the man trudge along the desert floor. Finally, when they were sure there were no others, they went forth to meet him. He was elderly and had a small shoulder bag and a walking staff. He halted when he saw them approach, and the old man raised his palm in friendship.

"I am Lon Gehr of Pacifica, the TRIAD city 90 klicks east. I come in peace. What is this place?"

"We are Maya and Tok of Unsa. This is our village's outpost. Come, share our fire."

Later, Lon Gher told them the Pacifica Board sent him to negotiate trade with Inlander villages for fresh meat. For fear of disease and for lack of room, no animals were allowed inside the Chain Walls of Pacifica.

The herds of closer villages were already being bought. Those villagers told Lon that Unsa had larger herds.

The next day, they escorted Lon to Unsa. Lon sat with the village's council. On the way back to the outpost, Tok told Maya this man had been a dot on the horizon at yesterday's sunrise. He might be the new dawn for the Inlanders.

***** *the end* *****

Shaping a Global Economy: The Rich and Poor Nations

The Chain Wall story presents a grim prospect for generations to come. Society degenerating into a new feudal era is possible. Yet, the world may be able to weather the problems that confront it and not dissolve into an "Eco War." History teaches that there are always options. Preserving the American Dream requires people to look beyond their local needs. People must realize that global economic performance links everyone's lives and determines if they can achieve their dreams.

It is certain that today's challenges will bring sweeping change. Understanding the issues and devising new answers will shape the future. In *Preparing for the Twenty-First Century*, historian Paul Kennedy says:

> *"Economic change and technological development, like wars or sporting tournaments, are usually not beneficial to all. Progress, welcomed by optimistic voices since the Enlightenment to our present age, benefits those groups or nations that can take advantage of the newer methods and science, just as it damages others that are less prepared technologically, culturally, and politically to respond to change."* (Kennedy 15)

Flags of NAFTA: Mexico, United States, and Canada ©PhotoDisc

The developed nations already manage technological progress. This will enable them to deal with the challenges of the 21st century. Less developed countries (LDCs) may be the ones that suffer. A look at conditions may help in predicting the future for various nations.

The Rich Nations in the 1990s

The U.S. and developed nations struggled out of a recession in the first half of the 1990s. The blistering pace of over borrowing, corporate buyouts, and mergers could not offset the lack of productivity. There were political obstacles as well. Western Europe faltered trying to reorganize after the downfall of communism in Eastern Europe and the former Soviet Union. Germany was strained trying to absorb East Germany's aged, failing industries and poorly trained workforce. Even the strong, export-driven economy of Japan felt recession when its U.S. and European customers stopped buying.

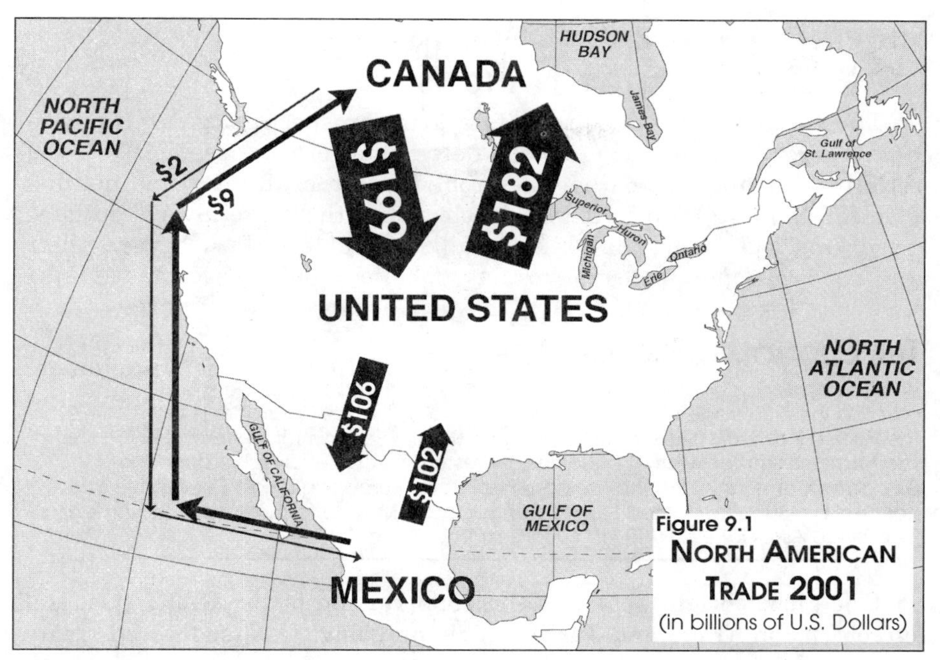

In January 1994, Canada, Mexico, and the United States created NAFTA – the world's largest "low-tariff" trading zone. It encompasses 412 million people with a combined GDP of 11 trillion dollars. In 2000, total trade exceeded 600 billion U.S. dollars.

During the global recession, the larger U.S. companies downsized and regrouped. They cut personnel and reduced debt. Some big businesses failed, but most strengthened themselves. They cut costs, especially labor costs, and they refocused on efficiency. As the United States slowly worked out of the recession, the FED became obsessed with keeping inflation in check. This slowed the pace of recovery, but revitalization drew more foreign investment – a sign of renewed world confidence. Joining with Canada and Mexico in **NAFTA** (the North American Free Trade Association) also boosted investment (see Figure 9.1). NAFTA prepared the North American nations for a global economy revolving around trade alliances such as the **European Union** (formerly called the Common Market) and **APEC** (Asian Pacific Economic Conference), a loose-knit, East Asia / Pacific Rim group. The United States also explored a free trade agreement for all of the Western Hemisphere by 2005.

On the other side of the Atlantic, European diplomats refashioned the "Common Market" into the European Union. In the 1980s and early 1990s, American and Japanese firms accelerated their investments and facilities in Europe. They wanted to beat a proposed European economic unification date in 1993 (which passed unfulfilled). Recession, disintegration of the U.S.S.R. and its communist satellites, plus the brutal civil war in the Balkans combined to slow Europe's integration plan.

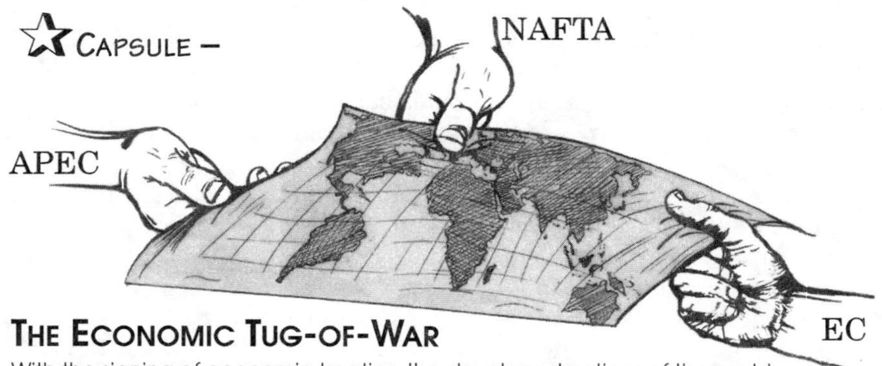

THE ECONOMIC TUG-OF-WAR

With the signing of economic treaties, the developed nations of the world created massive trade alliances. Japan, Australia, Taiwan, and other nations of the Pacific Rim tentatively formed the Asian Pacific Economic Conference (APEC). The former Common Market countries of Western Europe evolved through the European Community (EC) to the newly enlarged European Union. Feeling the international pressure, the United States, Canada, and Mexico formed the North American Free Trade Association (NAFTA), the largest trade association.

One global bright spot was the 1993 version of the **GATT** (General Agreement on Trade and Tariffs). This on-going, U.N.-sponsored treaty system tries to standardize international rules for commerce among nations recommends general tariff rates and mediates trade disagreements between members. In GATT's 1993 Uruguay Round, European nations gained some protection for agriculture and light industry. That bought some time for recovery from the recession and for building the European Union.

The export economy of Japan also slowed with the softening of the American and European markets. Yet, its business with China and other rising economies of East and Southeast Asia allowed it to stay out of the recession longer. Still, the large amounts of capital it invested abroad drew Japan into the global recession. When it did start to decline, Japan's economy went into a kind of shock.

Japan's long-term growth after World War II ultimately created a strong middle class. By the 1980s, Japan was more consumer-oriented than a generation earlier. The average saving rate (nearly 20% of the average Japanese family's income) dropped to 14% in the 1980s. The Japanese were spending more of their income. In the recession, this thinner "savings cushion" meant Japan's industries could not borrow as much to maintain normal production. Like American and European companies, Japan's corporations began downsizing, cutting operations, and laying off workers. The cuts by Japan's paternal **keiretsu** (mega corporations, formerly called zaibatsu) shook the nation's tradition of job security and steady pay raises. By 2000, only 38% of Japanese workers had job security. Irate voters unseated the long powerful Liberal Democratic Party.

While painful, the "streamlining" of companies in the United States and Japan increased competitiveness. To cut the costs of overseas trade, both countries deepened their commitments to regional trade alliances (NAFTA, APEC) and the GATT. Also, multinationals based in both countries strengthened their presence in Europe anticipating new trade barriers there.

The Europeans did not act as decisively, and the European Union struggled to admit Austria, Sweden, and Norway in the mid-1990s and prepare Eastern European states for partial membership. However, *Fortune* reporters Tom Martin and Deborah Greenwood reported that the rich nations advanced as a whole. Japan, Europe, and the United States showed GDP growth of over 4% in the mid-1990s ("The World Economy in Charts." 26 July 1993, 89). With inflation around 2%, growth was slow, but strength appeared to be returning. Except in Russia, the less tense situation after the Cold War helped developed nations meet the challenges presented by the 21st century.

The "Four Dragons"

In Asian nations other than Japan, the 1990s recession hardly slowed growth. China, Thailand, Indonesia, Philippines, and Vietnam expanded with a deluge of foreign investment capital. *Fortune*'s Martin and Greenwood showed that China's real growth was over 10%, even with 12% inflation. But, its growth was geographically uneven. It was concentrated in only the south coast cities. Yet, China's future depends on the expansion of economic freedom. Economist Kari-yiu Wong stated that if the new wealth can get to people inland, then China could remain stable (Martin and Greenwood, 94).

Asia's "Four Dragons"
Symbol of the newly industrializing economies of Hong Kong, Singapore, South Korea, and Taiwan.

Asia's "Four Dragons," the **NIEs** (newly industrializing economies) of Hong Kong, Singapore, South Korea, and Taiwan exhibited even more exceptional growth. They earned the "Dragons" nickname because of their astounding commercial growth in the late 1980s. This growth flowed from access to unrestricted Western markets and, in Taiwan and Korea, U.S. political and military aid. Low tariffs allowed these nations to sell cheaply manufactured goods in the developed countries. Their inexpensive goods are carried in many discount chains (e.g., Wal★Mart and *K*-Mart).

Figure 9.2 GROWTH OF THE FOUR DRAGONS (1999) Source: U.S. Department of Commerce, 2000		
Country	**Annual U.S. Purchases** (in U.S. dollars)	**Direct Foreign Investment** (in U.S. dollars)
Singapore	$18,191 million	$2,429 million
Hong Kong	$10,527 million	$2,084 million
Taiwan	$35,209 million	$6,860 million
South Korea	$31,178 million	$8,749 million

After World War II, grants from America helped to build new, state-of-the-art factories. Some of this industrial technology placed NIEs ahead of the older industrial bases in the United States and Europe. In the high-spending 1980s, some manufacturers in older developed nations stopped competing with cheaper Asian-made toys, electronics, and clothing. Many **low-end manufacturers** (cheaper, lesser quality goods) in older, developed nations converted to higher quality, upscale products.

Once the Four Dragons gained economic momentum, new capital from foreign investors poured into these countries. They developed more sophisticated exports. South Korea's Hyundai autos and Goldstar appliances are examples.

When the 1990s recession hit the U.S. and European markets, the Four Dragons' business accelerated. In the rich nations, consumption of expensive high-end domestic and imported goods suffered. Yet, consumers continued buying the cheaper products of the Four Dragons (see Figure 9.2 above). In addition, rising income from exports increased the spending power of Asians. The Four Dragons' domestic markets grew as their own workers bought more of their products. Trade within the Pacific region grew also. Regional consumption of goods made in the Pacific Rim rose from 31% to 43% between 1986 and 1999. The new GATT agreement insured lower global tariffs for the Dragons' major exports. Also, APEC (Asian Pacific Economic Conference) became more organized and laid the groundwork for new trade relations.

POOR NATIONS AND THE GLOBAL ECONOMY

Historian Paul Kennedy's quotation at the opening of this chapter says growth is uneven, and some nations suffer when others prosper. Gloomier forecasters point to a 21st century where they say there will be a greater gap between rich nations and poor ones. According to the World Bank, rich nations are those with an average annual per capita GDP of more than eight thousand dollars. The Bureau of Economic Analysis says the 1999 U.S. figure was $33,900 (*Statistical Abstract*. 675). Yet, LDCs such as India, Ghana, and Egypt have annual per capita figures of less than $1,000. It is obvious that the LDCs are where long-term global concerns lay (see map, Figure 9.3).

Figure 9.3

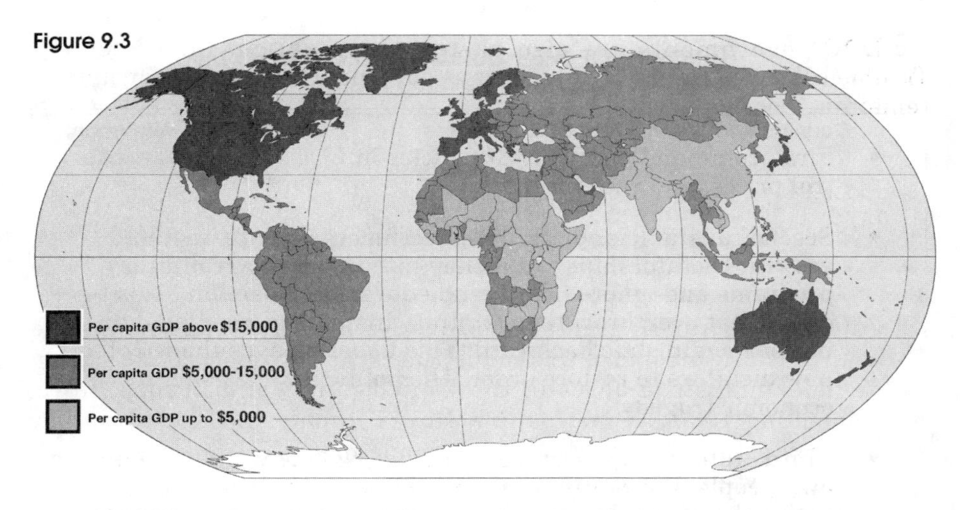

Per capita Gross Domestic Product throughout the nations of the world. In general, the lower the per capita GDP, the lower the standard of living and the poorer the country. In most cases, the low GDP countries are the "have not"nations – the Less Developed Countries or Third World nations.

Population growth is the LDCs' foremost problem. More than any other factor, it exhausts scarce economic resources. From the Amazon to the Ganges, growing populations and ignorance of conservation cause overgrazing, erosion, desertification, and deforestation. The food supply in these countries is not enough to feed the expanding population. They remain impoverished because they must sell low value **primary resources** (raw materials). Instead of using their capital for development, they must import food from developed countries.

Copyright 1992, *Time, Inc.* reprinted by permission

This TIME cover illustrates the concern for the problems of overpopulation and resulting world hunger in many LDCs such as Somalia in Africa where thousands of babies, children, and adults die from starvation annually.

Even when LDCs can buy new technology from the developed world, it causes problems. Corrupt bureaucracies pilfer funds or ineptly misallocate them. Their education systems are weak, and training people to use high tech methods is nearly impossible. Even when LDCs apply new technology, it destroys traditional occupations and raises unemployment. Simultaneously, global communications inform the people in LDCs that life should be better, and frustration grows. Many seek to migrate to other more prosperous nations, but immigration restrictions block them.

LDC governments are also part of the problem. In "Cheer Up, Troubled World," Henry S. Rowen says governments account for nations remaining poor for several reasons:

- First, command government policies in LDCs limit trade, control prices, and ruin incentives.
- Second, unstable and corrupt governments create unstable growth. Dictatorships put money into unnecessary military programs and ignore health and education. Reaction leads to coups that overthrow the dictators. Instability results, and nations again slide backward. This usually paves the way for new dictators to restore order. The political cycle generates economic tragedy.
- Third, autocratic governments actually make war on their own people. Power groups deny ethnic or religious groups political and economic freedom. Fear of risk prevents growth. (*Wall St. Journal*. 31 August 1993, 5)

Not all LDCs are weak. For security reasons, nations such as Iran, Iraq, North Korea, Bolivia, India, and even China spend large portions of their resources on weaponry. These are funds that could be devoted to education and research on productive technology. But, these priorities keep them as impoverished as Mali or Guyana.

Understanding the gap between rich and poor nations can help in seeing how life may change and how people can adjust to those changes. That kind of knowledge could help Americans be more open to altering policies and trade patterns. Also, it can help them perceive other nations' policies in a less hostile way.

Figure 9.4 **PROTECTIONIST TRADE BARRIERS AND SANCTIONS**

Source: U.S. Department of Commerce, 2000

Tariffs	High taxes on imports make imported products more expensive, give home industries temporary competitive advantages, and discourage foreign trade. (They also lead to reciprocation in which outside nations fight back with their own high tariffs.)
Quotas	Limits on import quantities also give home industries competitive advantages.
Red Tape	Complicated import applications, procedures, and paperwork.
Export Control (licenses)	Government restricts what producers send abroad. Cuts trade opportunities and prevents others from obtaining strategic resources.
Legal Currency Limits	Government restricts overseas investment and import firms' spending to keep currency stable.
Boycotts	Civilian organizations (unions, trade groups) rally public support for not buying goods of certain foreign firms or whole nations.
Embargoes	Government order banning importation of the goods of a particular country.

Figure 9.5

U.S. Tariff Rates
(1900-2000)

1897 Dingley
1910 Payne Aldrich
1913 Underwood
1930 Smoot-Hawley
1935 Reciprocal Trade Agreements
1947 GATT
1967 Kennedy Round of GATT
1980 Tokyo Round of GATT
1993 Uruguay Round of GATT

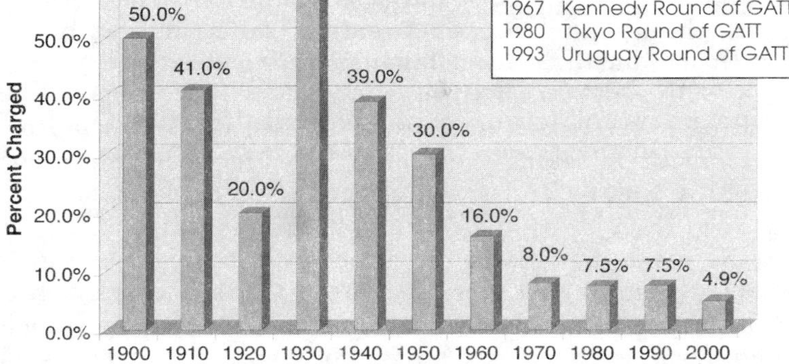

Source: U.S. Dept. of Commerce,2001

Shaping a Global Economy: Breaking Trade Barriers

Too often, nations frustrated with internal problems overreact to the trade policies of others. They don the ancient armor of **protectionism**. This often leads to raising **trade barriers** or even "trade war" sanctions (punishments) (see Figure 9.4 on page 216).

United States tariff history (see Figure 9.5) indicates that American protectionist policies have varied considerably over the years. The isolationist sentiment is especially clear in the high tariffs between the two world wars. The graph also shows the powerful effect of the GATT negotiations in the past half-century. When the economy is not performing well (as during the 1930s Great Depression), advocates of protectionism press for government action. They rely on several traditional arguments for higher tariffs and other trade barriers:

- New industries need protection from foreign competition while they get on their feet.
- Protection from foreign competition gives domestic workers job security.
- Domestic wage rates must be preserved from low wage foreign industries to keep domestic living standards high.
- Most nations use higher protections than the U.S., putting the U.S. at a disadvantage.

Normally, a free flow of trade benefits all parties. Yet, in economic contractions, when everyone is suffering, protectionists lobby for barriers. The barriers often backfire. Other nations **reciprocate** (fight back) with their own high tariffs. The high tariffs of the 1930s killed international trade when nations needed it most. The mid-1990s saw bitter negotiations with threats and counter-threats of sanctions and higher tariffs between the United States and Japan.

Avoiding overreaction and protectionism is hard when people see foreign competition taking their jobs. "Buy American" media campaigns sponsored by unions and trade councils are evidence of this. Yet, if nations keep trade open and flowing, it can revitalize ailing economies. Open trade points nations in the direction of recovery and growth, and that usually means new jobs. Increased trade enables rich and poor nations to raise standards of living and address internal problems. So, aligning international trade to a new world situation can help solve some global problems and avoid "Eco Wars."

Shaping a Global Economy: Interdependence

Scarcity forces people to trade for their needs and wants. The fact is, every nation (and every person in every nation) is part of a global economy. People routinely shrug and ignore civil wars, floods, or famines on the other side of the world, but people can no longer isolate themselves without cutting themselves off from needed resources. Americans often romanticize about self-sufficiency, and they are no longer pioneers isolated on a remote frontier. Very few of them could feed, clothe, warm, shelter, or transport themselves without the products of others. They need others to survive. They must trade their knowledge and skills to others for these things. Trade means one thing: **interdependence**.

More than ever, global relations revolve around trade. Involvement in world issues comes with trade. The list of issues is long, and it entwines environmental as well as socioeconomic issues. Among them are: population growth, depletion of natural resources, global warming, the growing gap between rich nations and LDCs, political power after the fall of the U.S.S.R., the rise of Islamic fundamentalism, automation, biotechnology, and international trade associations. Regardless of what nations want, if there is to be a viable future, people and nations must work cooperatively to address the issues.

Economist Adam Smith pointed out that self-interest drives economic interchange. Mutual profit from trade has always been a base for international relationships. If parties see advantages, they will make the effort. Of course, if a party feels cheated from an exchange, the future of the relationship is in jeopardy.

In most cases, specialization makes international trade worthwhile. The firms of one nation often specialize in trading commodities that they can produce efficiently. Colombia, Brazil, and equatorial Africa focus on coffee they can produce because of their climate. They depend on products that are **exclusive** (hard to get elsewhere). South Africa is one of the world's few sources of diamonds. It is not hard to see why Venezuela trades its petroleum on the global markets and does not compete with high tech cybernetics suppliers such as Japan. Venezuela has vast amounts of petroleum and takes aid from international firms (e.g., Exxon/Mobil, Shell, Texaco) to build technology to extract it. Venezuela has an **absolute advantage** over Japan, which has no oil. Specializing in oil production makes sense for Venezuela.

Even when a nation may have resources, it may choose not to use them fully. For example, the United States has considerable oil supplies, and it does produce approximately 48% of its own oil, but it buys from Venezuela (see Figure 9.6 below). Why pay Venezuela for oil? The answer lies in an idea economists call **comparative advantage**. The cost of U.S. labor, compared to Venezuelan labor, makes Venezuelan crude oil cheaper per barrel. U.S. refining companies import Venezuelan crude because it costs less. They can use their capital more efficiently in other pursuits. Economists would say Venezuela has a comparative advantage in this trade relationship. Again, the relationship illustrates interdependence.

Figure 9.6

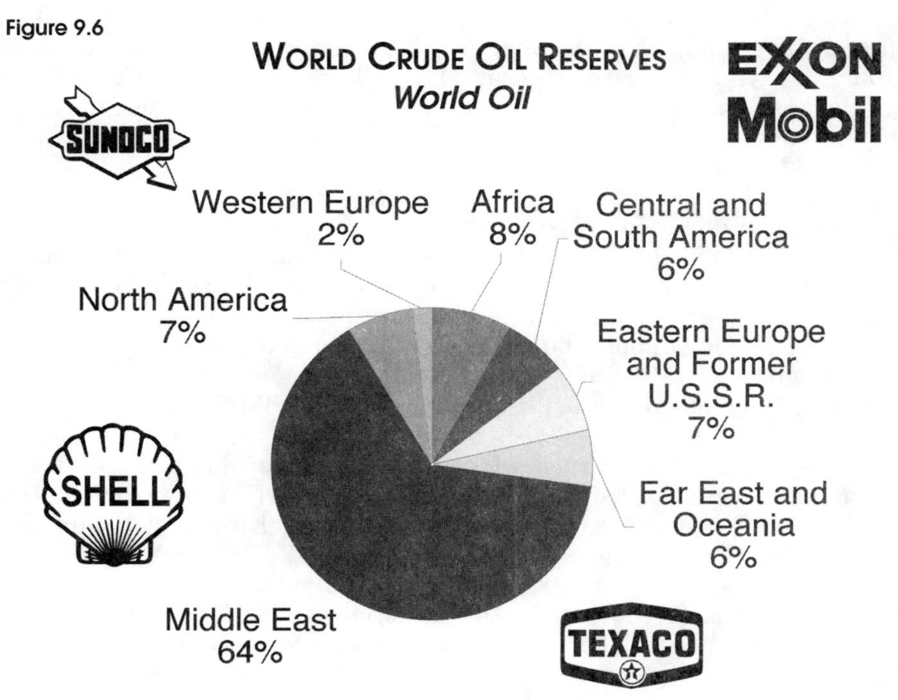

Shaping a Global Economy: Multinationals

Whatever the economic advantages in a particular place, to speak in terms of fully self-sufficient and independent nations is not as realistic as it once was. Governments do not trade much, businesses do. Yet, quite often governments make rules that get in the way of business firms engaged in international trade. (It might be well to remember protests against British trade restrictions sparked the American Revolution.)

International businesses are certainly not new. From ancient times, traders set up caravans to exchange products among empires and kingdoms. That is what brought Marco Polo to the Khan's court in the 13th century. Most European colonies in the "New World" in the 16th and 17th centuries were commercial ventures.

In the 20th century, a new form of international commercial agency emerged – the **MNC** (multinational corporation – a firm with business operations in more than one country). At first, they were just large corporations wishing to branch out for overseas markets. In the last generation, they expanded beyond looking for customers and in the process of seeking broader markets, they found advantages in **direct investments** (outright ownership of facilities in other countries). By setting up shop in other countries, MNCs lower production and resource costs, reduce patent royalty fees, and avoid tariffs and other trade barriers.

Figures on direct investment in production facilities all over the world illustrate the globalization of MNCs. In 1950, U.S. firms had $12 billion directly invested in other countries. In 1999, the U.S. Bureau of Economic Analysis says that figure stood at $1.1 trillion. Of that, MNCs invested the largest amounts in Britain, Canada, Germany, Switzerland, and Japan (BEA. *Business Statistics*. A-106). Coca Cola and Chrysler operate bustling plants in China, too.

The amount foreign MNCs invest in the United States often brings home the economic globalization idea to Americans. The 2000 BEA figure for foreign direct investment in U.S. firms and property was $1.2 trillion. Of that, Europe had $980 billion, and Japan had $163 billion (BEA. *Business Statistics*. A-107). For example, Japanese and German auto firms operate major assembly plants in Kentucky (Toyota), Ohio (Honda and Mazda), Tennessee (Nissan), Alabama (Mercedes), and South Carolina (BMW).

Today's MNCs have such widespread presence that economists see them as the foundations of a "borderless world economy." MNCs advanced the reduction of trade barriers in the European Union and NAFTA. MNCs also influence updates of the GATT. While it is a general guide for nations, it is not an ironclad set of rules. Constant pressure from MNCs has caused nations to renegotiate the GATT ten times since 1947. The most recent Uruguay Round concluded in 1993 and renamed the overseer of tariffs as the World Trade Organization.

The GATT provides only weak guidelines. National governments still negotiate **bilateral trade agreements** (two-nation mutual arrangements). The United States still designates some countries as "Most Favored Nations" (receiving lowest tariff rates and least restrictions). Still, for banking, service, and manufacturing MNCs, the GATT guidelines are vital. They want minimum standards for global stability. They also want national barriers minimized so that goods and payments flow easily in the globalized economy.

Shaping a Global Economy: Balancing Trade

Financial Exchange

People trade to get needed goods and services and to make profits. This is just as true globally as in a neighborhood shop or a suburban mall. Some businesses specialize in international trade. Their specialization and comparative advantage makes it profitable to deal with mazes of rules and regulations in many countries. Just as people in a town, international traders expect mutual satisfaction. Theoretically, the financial exchanges for imports and exports should be equal. Economists refer to this as the **balance of payments**. It measures the flow of goods and money and gives some indication of the health of an economy (see Figure 9.7).

The government calculates balance of payments in complex statements. The two major parts are the current account and the capital account. The **current account** shows the balance of imports and

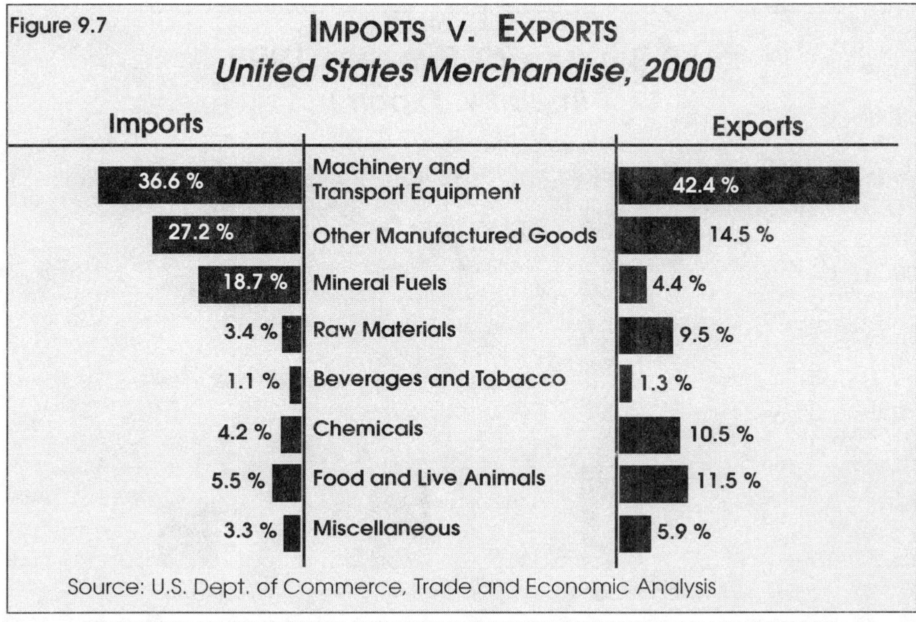

exports. It includes goods and services, shipping, insurance, short-term loans, and expenditures by tourists. The **capital account** includes long-term financial transactions such as direct and indirect overseas investments (franchise investments are among the fastest growing segments), private loans, and government foreign aid.

Seaport and airport cargo manifests, customs records, and corporate investment statements provide data for these accounts. Yet, in many cases, measuring the balance of payments is not easy. In "Exporting the Truth on Trade," Susan Dentzer said services such as lawyers fees, tourist hotel rooms, and rental car fees are hard to record (*U.S. News & World Report*. 4 April 1992, 47). Dentzer noted the government can only use surveys to estimate these "soft numbers" (*USNWR*. 47).

THE TRADE DEFICIT

The annual balance of payment statement tells a country how well it fares in trading with others. Before 1950, U.S. exports exceeded imports, and there was usually a trade surplus. Since 1950, the statements show the United States paying out more money to residents of other countries than it receives from them – a trade deficit. Causes for the U.S. trade deficit include: high amounts of foreign aid, overseas military operations, inflation devaluing the U.S. dollar, a high degree of investing abroad, and Americans buying large quantities of foreign products (see Figure 9.8). The end of the Cold War allowed reduction of overseas military expenses and foreign aid. Still, Americans' taste for imported clothes and autos kept the trade deficit high.

Figure 9.8

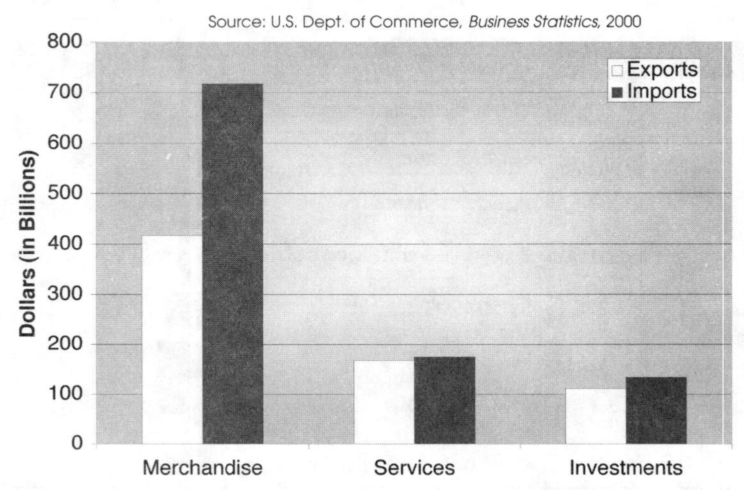

Figure 9.9

INTERNATIONAL EXCHANGE SYSTEMS

The Gold Standard	(1850s-1930s)	Trade agreements between nations specified the amount of gold a particular nation's currency was worth.
Gold Exchange Standard	(1940s-1970s)	(Bretton Woods System) International Monetary Fund created fixed exchange rates pegged to the U.S. dollar's gold conversion price of $35 per ounce.
Floating Exchange Rates	(1971-)	Supply and demand of currencies decide their exchange rates on the world's major foreign exchange markets.

EXCHANGE RATES

One of the things that complicates world trade is that each nation has its own currency. An exception is in Western Europe which in 1999 adopted a regional currency, the "euro." Economists measure currency conversions with the **foreign exchange rate**. A network of specialized import/export banks in major foreign exchange markets (Hong Kong, Tokyo, London, Paris, New York) set the rate. These banks act as financial intermediaries with other banks of other nations. They hold supplies of various national currencies for transactions.

Just as national economies vary, currencies of different nations vary in value against others. National governments backed their currencies in gold until the 20th century. This system of gold flowing among nations kept prices stable.

Yet, two world wars and the Great Depression strained national currencies and gold resources to the point of collapse. Tying money to gold was too rigid. Governments could not use monetary policy (altering their money supply) when needed. At the end of World War II, the industrial nations created the **Bretton Woods System**. It used the U.S. dollar as the basis for exchange. The dollar could be converted at $35 per ounce of gold. The **IMF** (**International Monetary Fund**) took charge of this new system. It made temporary loans to countries needing dollars for exchange. The Bretton Woods System worked until U.S. trade deficits and the inflation of the Vietnam War Era reduced the base U.S. gold supply. In 1971, President Nixon halted gold conversion of the dollar (see Figure 9.9 above).

In 1973, the major industrial nations agreed to a **Floating Exchange System**. In this system, supply and demand govern the rates of exchange in the major world finance markets. The dollar is still the leading world currency, but values of currencies change frequently. Strong governments, supporting strong economies, have strong currencies.

The international money market is volatile. Frequently, political events or fluctuations in interest rates in one country alter exchange rates. When money investors buy dollars (and other currencies) in which they have confidence, values appreciate. Buying up dollars makes them scarce and drives up their value. More expensive dollars makes U.S. goods sold abroad more expensive. It also makes weaker currencies (and their countries' products) cheaper. The strong dollar of the late 1980s and early 1990s made other countries' exports look good to Americans. However, in the mid-1990s, the U.S. dollar fell to an all time low in value on the world currency markets. This drove the value of the German mark and Japanese yen up, resulting in higher prices for foreign products sold in the United States The weakened U.S. dollar coupled with high imports and low exports deepened the trade deficit and further weakened the U.S. economic position in the global economy.

The Floating Exchange Rate created an intricate international money market system. Government moves make it even more complex. Sometimes, governments have their central banks move to alter the supply of their money on the international market. When appreciating too fast, central banks sell their currencies at lower rates to the exchange markets. This increases supplies and lowers their exchange rate. They also buy their own currencies at higher rates to slow depreciation (see Figure 9.10).

Figure 9.10 **CURRENCY EXCHANGE RATE**

Source: ExchangeRates.com, January 9, 2003

Currency	Exchange Rate per U.S. Dollar	Value in U.S. Dollars
Canadian dollar	1.5541	$0.643459
Denmark kroner	7.1005	0.140835
England pound	0.623636	1.6035
European Union euro	0.955384	1.0467
Japanese yen	119.57	0.0083633
Mexican new peso	10.415	0.0960154
Sweden krona	8.713	0.114771
Switzerland franc	1.3943	0.717206

SUMMARY

International trade is complex. There are no simple rules. Sometimes, it is a matter of governments negotiating with other countries to smooth out problems. More often, trade is companies struggling with the language barriers, currency differences, and elaborate regulations that complicate international commerce. The host of bilateral and multilateral agreements, the behavior of MNCs, the fate of LDCs and NIEs – they are all entwined in shaping the new global economy. On that new world structure rests the aspirations of all people in general and the American Dream in particular.

Assessment • Questions • Applications

1 Issue 9 begins with a story about the results of a fictional Eco War in the future. The story is based on some of the facts about LDCs, trade alliances, and MNCs in this chapter.
   a Do you agree with such a scenario? Explain why or why not.
   b Make a list of elements you think would make the story more realistic.

2 Historian Paul Kennedy says:
"Economic change and technological development, like wars or sporting tournaments, are usually not beneficial to all. Progress, welcomed by optimistic voices since the Enlightenment to our present age, benefits those groups or nations that can take advantage of the newer methods and science, just as it damages others that are less prepared technologically, culturally, and politically to respond to change."
— *Preparing for the Twenty-First Century*, 15

   a Does this quote suggest there is no future for LDCs (Less Developed Countries) that have difficulty breaking away from tradition?
   b What steps can LDCs take to enhance economic growth?
   c How will regional trade alliances such as APEC, NAFTA, and the EU affect LDCs and NIEs (Newly Industrialized Countries)?

3 Global interdependence makes the U.S. economy vulnerable to events and actions throughout the world.
   a Should the United States try to become self-sufficient? Why or why not?
   b Should the United States adopt economic isolation and stop buying from other nations? Why or why not?
   c What is the real cost of buying cheaper products from other nations?

4 Analyze this quotation from economist Henry Kaufman:
"How much are the major industrial countries willing to subordinate near-term nationalistic interests, which are often politically quite popular, to longer term benefits?"
   a What does he mean by "near-term nationalistic interests which are often quite politically popular"?
   b What does he mean by "longer-term benefits"?
   c Is choosing the long-term benefits critical to shaping the new global economy? Explain.

5 "Regional trade alliances must shape the future."
   a Take a position on this statement – agree or disagree.
   b Use library resources to validate your position on this statement.
   c Defend your position in a class debate, a learning group discussion, or a written report.

6 The dynamic nature of world trade sometimes displaces workers and companies.
   a List and explain three types of barriers to free trade.
   b Why do labor unions generally favor protective trade barriers?
   c Assume the role of a member of the United States Senate faced with voting on the North American Free Trade Agreement (NAFTA). What would be the key influences on how you would vote – in favor or opposed to the trade agreement?

Assessment Project 9A: Planning a Vacation

Student Task

Write a report which unitizes, summarizes, and analyzes all of the projects completed under the Hypothetical Household Plan.

Procedure

1 Make a list of the projects completed under the Hypothetical Household Plan and review their relationship to each other.

2 Develop an outline that takes the budget, financial statements, and related studies developed in your original hypothetical household plan and traces its evolution over the course. Show where the original plan was modified and why.

3 Write a final documented report. In your conclusion, summarize the differences between the original and current material and state what you have learned about financial management.

Evaluation

The criteria for the evaluation of this project are itemized in the grid (rubric) that follows, page 227. Choice of appropriate category terms (values) is the decision of the instructor. Selection of terms such as "minimal," "satisfactory," and "distinguished" can vary with each assessment.

Financial Management Evaluation Rubric

(Refer to the teacher's supplement for suggestions of scoring descriptors for evaluation.)

Evaluation Item
Item a: (1) Does the report show understanding that while different socioeconomic (as well as national, ethnic, religious, racial, and gender) groups have varied perspectives, values, and diverse practices and traditions, they face the same global economic challenges?
Item b: (5) Does the report analyze problems and evaluate decisions about the economic effects caused by human, technological, and natural activities?
Item c: (6) Does the report present ideas in writing (and orally) in clear, concise, and properly accepted fashion?
Item d: (7) Does the report employ a variety of information from written, graphic, and multimedia sources?
Item e: (8) Does the report show monitoring of, reflection upon, and improvement of work?
Item f: (9) Does the report show cooperative work and respect for the rights of others to think, act, and speak differently?

Assessment Project 9b: Personal Financial Tool

Student Task

After consultation with parents, conduct field research at financial institutions to select and set up an account (checking, share draft, etc.) for personal financial management. Write a 3-5 page report on needs, goals, surveying the financial institutions, and rationale for decisions on type of account and financial institution chosen.

Procedure

1 Review the advisory material on post-graduation personal financial management needs on the previous pages. Decide (with parental guidance) on type of account needed and location needs.

2 Choose 3 to 5 financial institutions in your area. Arrange interviews with the new account officer at each. (It is best to inform those individuals of your school project in advance and set up a convenient appointment.)

3 After meeting with the new account officers and reviewing notes and literature collected, decide on an account and institution. A comparison chart would be most useful in facilitating your decision–making process.

4 Write a 3-5 page report summarizing your goals, shopping experience, and the rationale for your decision to pick a particular type of account and a specific institution.

5 As a courtesy, thank the new account officers for their assistance with the project and perhaps share your summary report with them.

Evaluation

The criteria for the evaluation of this project are itemized in the grid (rubric) that follows (below). Choice of appropriate category terms (values) is the decision of the instructor. Selection of terms such as "minimal," "satisfactory," and "distinguished" can vary with each assessment.

Personal Financial Tool Evaluation Rubric

(Refer to the teacher's supplement for suggestions of scoring descriptors for evaluation.)

Evaluation Item
Item a: (5) Does the report analyze problems and evaluate decisions about the economic effects on society and the individual caused by human, technological, and natural activities?
Item b: (6) Does the report illustrate ideas in writing (and orally) in clear, concise, and properly accepted fashion?
Item c: (7) Does the report employ a variety of information from written, graphic, and multimedia sources?
Item d: (8) Does the report show monitoring of, reflection upon, and improvement of work?
Item e: (9) Does the report show cooperative work and respect for the rights of others to think, act, and speak differently?

Appendix 1
Sources, References, and Credits

Introduction

Cohen, Michael Lee. *The Twenty-something American Dream: A Cross-Country Quest for a Generation*. New York: Dutton, 1993.
Moore, Martha. "They're Like Us, Only They're Rich" *USA Today*. 22 May 1987, 1.
Phillips, Kevin. *The Politics of Rich and Poor – Wealth and the American Electorate in the Reagan Aftermath*. New York: Random House, 1990.
Stewart, Thomas A. "The New American Century." *Fortune*. 1991.
Terkel, Studs. *American Dreams – Lost and Found*. New York: Pantheon, 1980.
"The Twentysomething Generation." *TIME*. 15 August 1992, 61.
Zinn, L. "Move Over Baby Boomers – Portrait of Generation X." *Business Week*. 14 Dec. 1992, 74.
Zuckerman, Mortimer B. "The Glass is Half Full." *U.S. News & World Report*, 27 Feb. 1995, 80.

Issue 1

Greene, Mark. and Dince, Robert. *Personal Financial Management*. Cincinnati: South-Western, 1987.
"IBM Cuts Global in Scope" *Poughkeepsie Journal*. 28 March 1993, 2E.

Issue 2

Beard, Charles and Mary. *Rise of American Civilization*. Place: NY: Scribners, 1927.
Brimelow, Peter. "Why the Deficit is the Wrong Number." *Forbes*. 15 March 1993, 79-82.
Cook, Peter D. *Start & Run Your Own Successful Business*. N Y: Beaufort, 1982.
Fallek, Max. *How to Set Up Your Own Business*. Minneapolis: Am. Inst. of Small Business, 1990.
Greene, Mark and Dince, Robert. *Personal Financial Management*. Cincinnati: South-Western, 1987.
Henderson, Nancy. "Personal Finances." *Kiplinger Magazine*. March 1992, 112.
"IBM Cuts Global in Scope" *Poughkeepsie Journal*. 28 March 1993, 2E.
Marx, Karl and Engles, F. *The Communist Manifesto*. Indianapolis, IN: Liberty [1986 Ed.].
Smith, Adam. *Wealth of Nations* Indianapolis, IN: Liberty [1986 Edition].

Issue 3

Bureau of Economic Analysis. *Business Statistics: 1963-91*. U.S. Department of Commerce, Washington DC 1992.
Cohen, Michael Lee. *The Twenty-something American Dream: A Cross-Country Quest for a Generation*. New York: Dutton, 1993.
Moore, Martha. "They're Like Us, Only They're Rich" *USA Today*. 22 May 1987, 1.
Terkel, Studs. *American Dreams – Lost and Found*. New York: Pantheon, 1980.

Issue 4

Cook, Peter D. *Start and Run Your Own Successful Business*. New York: Beaufort, 1982.
Fallek, Max. *How to Set Up Your Own Business*. Minneapolis: Am. Inst. of Small Business, 1990.
Greene, Mark and Dince, Robert. *Personal Financial Management*. Cincinnati: South-Western, 1987.
U.S. Bureau of the Census. *Statistical Abstract of the United States*. Dept of Commerce. Washington DC, 1992.

Issue 5

Fierman, Jaclyn. "What Happened to the Jobs?" *Fortune*. 12 July 1993.
Magnet, Myron. "Good News For The Service Economy." *Fortune*. 3 May 1993.
Malone, Michael. "Search for Jobs that No Longer Exist." *New York Times*. 5 Sept. 1993.
Quinn, Jane Bryant. "A Generation Topped Out." *Newsweek*. 20 September 1993, 42.
Rowland, Mary. "Temporary Work: The New Career." *New York Times*. 12 September 1993.
Saltzman, Amy. "1994 Career Guide: The Changing Professions." *U.S. News & World Report*. 1 Nov. 1990.
Sookdeo, Ricardo. "A Brave New Darwinian Workplace." *Fortune*. 25 January 1993.
Sullivan, Scott. "Economic Highlights" *Newsweek*. 14 June 1993, 46-47.
Zuckerman, Mortimer. "Glass is Half Full." *U.S. News & World Report*. 27 Feb. 1995, 80.

Issue 6

American Express Co. *Getting Started*. World Financial Center, New York: 1993.
American Express Co. *Women's Credit Rights*. World Financial Center, New York: 1993.
Bankcard Holders of America. *Low Rate List*, 524 Branch Drive, Salem VA .
Consumer Action. *Saving Money on Credit Cards*. Suite 233. San Francisco CA 94105: 1992.
Consumer Federation of America. *Student Consumer Knowledge*. Suite 604. 1424 Sixteenth Street NW, Washington, DC 20036: 1992.
Cruz, Humberto. "Credit Cards Can Cost You." *Poughkeepsie Journal*. 31 Jan. 1994, B1.
Steinbeck, John. *The Grapes of Wrath*. New York:Viking, 1939.

Issue 7

Bureau of the Census. *Statistical Abstract of the United States, 1992* U.S. Dept. of Commerce: Washington DC 1992
McCall, James R. *Consumer Protection: Cases, Notes, & Materials*. St. Paul MN: West, 1977, 478-486.
Smith, Adam. *The Wealth of Nations*. Indianapolis, IN: Liberty [1986 Edition].

Issue 8

Bureau of Economic Analysis. *Statistical Abstract of the United States, 1992*. Washington: U.S. Dept. of Commerce. 675.
Isaac, Katherine. *Civics For Democracy*. Washington DC: Essential Books, 1992.

Issue 9

Bureau of Economic Analysis. *Business Statistics, 1963-1993*. Washington: U.S. Dept. of Commerce. A-106, 107.
Bureau of Economic Analysis. *Statistical Abstract of the United States 1992*. Washington: U.S. Dept. of Commerce. 675.
Dentzer, Susan. "Exporting the Truth on Trade." *U.S. News & World Report*. 4 April 1992, 47.
Kennedy, Paul. *Preparing for the Twenty-First Century*. New York: Vintage, 1993.
Martin, T., and Greenwood, D. "The World Economy in Charts." *Fortune*. 26 July 1993, 82-96.
Rowen, Henry. "Cheer Up, Troubled World." *The Wall Street Journal*. 31 August 1993, 5.
Ziegler, Bart. *The Wall Street Journal*. 14 June 1994.

Appendix 2
Glossary and Index

Ability-to-pay principle 165, 166 Idea of calculating taxes (especially income taxes) on individual's income.

Absolute advantage 219 Extreme competitive edge one country has over others when it can produce something with the highest efficiency.

Affirmative action 107-108 Government sponsored programs to eliminate hiring discrimination.

AFL (or A.F. of L. or AFL-CIO) 102-103 American Federation of Labor – late 19th c. national organization of craft unions – later merged with CIO.

Age Discrimination in Employment Act 109 Federal law prohibits job discrimination against older workers (1967).

Aggregate (Supply, Demand, Income) 10, 152, 154, 158, 182, 183, 190, 198 Total or complete, as in aggregate demand in a market.

Alger, Horatio 75 U.S. novelist (1832-1899); popular success stories of the 19th c. industrial era.

Allentown 93, 95, 97 Song by Billy Joel about the eastern PA coal/steel town which went into serious economic decline in the 1950-70 period.

American Dream 5-18, 22-23, 30, 67, 81, 89, 93, 95, 98, 140, 160, 181, 190, 193, 202, 203, 210, 224 Aspiration for a successful, comfortable life with home and other property.

American Express 121, 122, 123 (see star capsules) Major U.S. charge and credit card issuer.

American Federation of Labor (AFL) 102-103 First really successful national affiliation of craft union organizations; merged in 1950's with the industrial unions Congress of Industrial Organizations to form the AFL-CIO.

American Revolution 42, 145, 220 Political break with England 1776-1783 fostered by taxation and trade regulations.

Antitrust 88, 168, 171 Underlying concept of U.S. Dept. of Justice division prosecutes violators of the Sherman and Clayton Acts' provisions (anti-monopolies).

APEC See Asian Pacific Economic Conference.

Appreciate 79, 201 Gain in value.

Asian Pacific Economic Conference (APEC) 211, 213 Ongoing attempt to eliminate trade barriers in Pacific Region, long-range goal of some sort of "Common Market" arrangement.

Assessed value 166 An official estimate of the worth of (property) for taxation purposes.

AT&T 78 American Telephone and Telegraph Corp. – major communications firm broken up by government antitrust suit in 1984.

Attorney General's Office 171 Chief law enforcement officer in federal gov't. (Dept. of Justice) and most state governments; usually in charge of consumer protection/fraud investigations.

Automatic fiscal policy 150, 152 Permanent government systems that forestall or ease serious economic declines (e.g., unemployment compensation, minimum wage).
Avon 82 Direct sale (in-home) cosmetics franchisor.

Balance of payments 202, 221, 222 Statements measuring a nation's export-import relationship (surplus/equilibrium/deficit).
Balance of Trade 202, 221 A nation's exports measured against its imports; favorable = selling more to other countries than it buys.
BancOne Corp. 142 One of the top 10 U.S. banks (OH); see Figure 6.9.
Bank 123-133 Any institution providing financial services, chief among them the receipt of money for deposit and profits from lending the deposits at interest.
BankAmerica 131 One of the top 10 U.S. banks (CA); see Figure 6.9.
Bank Holiday 35, 130, 151 Closing of banks (1933) for inspection by President Roosevelt to calm down panic runs on banks by public.
Bank of the United States 147, 151 Officially chartered independent financial clearing house for government revenues created for stability by Hamilton during the Washington Administration (1790s); lapsed during the War of 1812, recreated in 1816, veto of renewal in 1836 by Jackson caused harsh depression; no other central financial agency until the Federal Reserve System was created in 1913.
Bankruptcy 79 Legal action placing all of a debtor's assets at risk (except for home and necessary clothes). All other assets can be sold by the court in order to pay back what is owed.
Barter 117 Making transactions by direct exchange of goods or a series of indirect exchanges until the item needed is available.
Bear market 138 Stockbroker term for a market where securities are selling poorly and fortunes on the exchanges are declining.
Beard, Charles A. 42 American historian and educator (1874-1948) who explored the economic aspects of history in works such as *An Economic Interpretation of the Constitution* (1913).
Benefits See employee benefits.
Benefits-received principle 165 Persons pay this kind of tax based on their frequency of use of a service (ex. toll on highways and bridges).
Bilateral trade agreement 221 Two-sided arrangement for lower tariff rates and import quotas.
Blue Chip Stock 137 A stock that sells at a high price because of public confidence in its long record of steady earnings.
BMW 14, 220 Bavarian Motor Works; German-based automotive multinational.
Board of Governors 127-131 Central management agency of the Federal Reserve.
Boesky, Ivan 136, 168 Wall Street financier convicted of insider trading violations of SEC rules; implicated in billion-dollar bond market trading scandal in 1980s.
Bonds 80, 134-136 Interest bearing certificate; holders lend money to corporation over specified time, money is paid back with interest.
Boycott 216 Organized sanction campaign to stop buying products from a particular country or manufacturer.

Bretton Woods System 223 Gold Exchange System used from the late 1940s to the 1970s that fixed international currency exchange rates to the U.S. dollar's gold conversion price.

Bull market 138 Stockbroker term for a market where securities are selling well and profits are being made on the exchanges.

Bureau of Economic Analysis, U.S. 214, 220 Division of U.S. Commerce Dept. gathers information on international trade.

Burger-King 81 Burger-King Corp.; fast food/restaurant franchisor.

Bush, George 14, 185 41st President of U.S., 1989-93; struggled with national debt and tax reduction, recession, and Gulf War.

Bush, George W. 14 43rd President of U.S., 2001– ; tax cuts via budget surpluses.

Business consumption 184 Spending for plants, equipment, supplies, overhead, labor, etc. by commercial enterprises; see investment.

Business cycle 148, 182-185, 192 The pattern of the economy's "ups and downs," (also demand cycle) measured according to many technical indexes (primarily GDP); four key phases: Prosperity, Recession, Depression, Recovery; the "ups" are defined by high employment and high spending, while the "downs" are defined as low employment and low spending.

Capital account 221 Portion of the balance of payment statements measuring long-term financial and investment arrangements to and from other nations.

Capital formation 80-81 Methods of raising money for a business enterprise.

Capital gains tax 162, 164 Federal tax on profits from sales of assets by individuals and corporations.

Capital goods Resources such as tools, property, factories, vehicles, machines, offices, or investment money used to produce wealth.

Capitalism 41, 42, 43, 46 Market economic system in which nearly all productive resources are privately owned; see chart 41.

Carnegie, Andrew 84 Scottish-born American industrialist and philanthropist (1835-1919) who amassed a fortune in the steel industry and donated millions of dollars for the benefit of the public.

Carter, James Earl ("Jimmy") 11 39th U.S. President, 1977-1981; plagued by rapid inflation ("energy crisis") and mounting budget deficits.

CEO 12, 78 Chief Executive Officer; person chosen by a board of directors to operate and hire managerial staff of a corporation.

Certificate of deposit (CD) 133 A document from a bank testifying that the named party has a specified sum on deposit, usually for a given period of time at a fixed rate of interest.

Chadwick's 63 Catalog-direct mail clothing merchandising corp.(MA).

Charge card 121 Certificate (usually plastic) of an individual's creditworthiness issued by a creditor; allows purchase of goods to be repaid over short period; often called a "regular credit card" – terms require full payment for all transactions at end of the billing period.

Chattel 166 Personal moveable property (not real estate – autos, boats, RVs stocks, jewelry, etc.) taxed in some states.

Checking accounts 119-120 A written order to a bank to pay money out of an account to the person or firm noted on the order; see also "demand deposits."

China 213, 220
Chrysler 83, 220 Chrysler Corp.; multinational automotive firm. (MI)
CIO 103 Congress of Industrial Organizations; 1930s national federation of industrial unions, later merged with AFL.
Citigroup 78, 131 One of the top 10 U.S. banks (NY); see Figure 6.9.
Civil Rights Act of 1964 109 Congressional act (1964) prohibited gender, religious, sexual, ethnic, income, and race discrimination.
Clayton Antitrust Act 88 Congressional law (1914) strengthened the *Sherman Act*; forbid certain business combinations which restricted a market (monopolies and near monopolies).
Clinton, William J. ("Bill") 14 42nd President of U.S., 1993-; struggled with national debt reduction, Haitian democracy, and White Water scandals and personal behavior scandals led to impeachment proceedings by Congress.
Closed corporation 78 Form of corporation in which shares are privately held among a limited number of individuals.
Closed shop 109 Contractual rule for an establishment requiring only union members be hired; outlawed by the *Taft-Hartley Act*.
Coca-Cola 85, 88, 220 Coca-Cola Corp.; U.S. based (GA) beverage/foods/general merchandise multinational conglomerate.
Coincidental indicators 203 Statistical data used to measure and assess the economic conditions that reach peaks or troughs when economy is in a particular condition (Industrial Production Index, Personal Income; see Fig. 8.13).
COLAs See Cost of Living Adjustments.
Collective bargaining agreements 103, 104, 106 Contracts relating to working conditions between employer and groups of employees.
Combinations 82-85, 161 An alliance of persons or parties usually to expand or enhance business opportunity; also used to describe monopolistic activities.
Command systems 40-42 Economy in which central authority attempts to control resources and decision-making; see communism; see chart 40.
Commercial bank 124, 126-132 Establishment in which money is kept for mercantile purposes or is invested, supplied for loans, or exchanged.
Commercial Revolution 40 14th c. - 18th c. speedup and globalization of trade; led to changes in feudal system and helped capitalism develop.
Communism 44 Command economy in which central authority. attempts to control resources and decision-making. Modern communism rests on 19th c. writings of Karl Marx and Friedrich Engels; see chart 41.
Communist Manifesto 44 Marx and Engels' 1847 work which outlined the modern worker controlled socialist state from which communist systems evolved.
Comparable worth 109 Demand by women for equal pay for equal work.
Comparative advantage 219 Favorable competitive edge one country has over others when it can produce something with the higher efficiency.
Competition 85-89, 160, 161 Rival firms seek to win consumers for their products, often basis for keeping prices low.
Conglomerate merger 83-85 A business combines with another in an unrelated industry; example, chain of hamburger stands buys an insurance company.
Congress of Industrial Organizations See CIO or AFL-CIO
Conoco 83, 84 Petrochemical company acquired by DuPont in a vertical merger in the 1980s.

Conservative 46-47, 147, 154, 158 In 20th c. U.S., those who seek to reverse strong government role in economic life; seek to cut gov't. role and promote individual laissez-faire atmosphere.

Constant dollars 183, 188 Use of a standard base year to make statistical comparisons to factor out inflation and deflation results in Real GDP or Real GNP measurements; see Figures 8.2, 8.4.

Constitution, U.S. 146-147, 160, 183 (box) Economic roles of government grew from interpretations of powers assigned to Congress in Art. I, Sec. 8.

Consumer goods 27 Products made for the general public.

Consumer Price Index 194-195, 197 CPI measures the difference in prices paid for goods and services purchased by consumers over time.

Consumer Reports 73, 74, 76, 88 Non-profit, neutral publication of the Consumers' Union (NY).

Consumer Spending (C) 186 Personal consumption or spending by individuals for goods and services is the largest component of the $C+I+G+X$ calculation of GDP and GNP.

Consumption 11 The using up of goods and services by consumer purchasing or in the production of other goods.

Contraction 150, 182, 183, 184, 218 Slump, downturn, recession; phase of business cycle characterized by economic decline (low demand, rising unemployment); see Figures 7.1, 8.1.

Corporate bonds 81, 134-136 Certificates of debt issued by a corporation guaranteeing payment of the original investment plus interest by a specified future date.

Corporation 78-85 Form of business organization in which many share ownership and divide profits, but operation decisions are delegated to a few professional managers.

Correction phase 7 Change in the pattern of economic growth (slowdown or speedup) as in a change in the business cycle.

Cost of Living Adjustments 198 (COLAs) Contractual or legislative arrangements increasing wages or transfer payments to reconcile purchasing power with inflation.

Cost-push inflation 197 Increased production costs (wages, raw materials, services, etc.) force producers to raise prices in order to maintain reasonable profit margins.

Costs 60, 100 Expenditure of something, such as time, labor, materials, rent, etc. necessary to produce a product.

Coupon rate 135 Amount of interest paid to bondholder for making a loan.

Coverall Cleaning Concepts 82 Coverall North America Corp.; commercial cleaning franchisor.

Credit 113-116 (story), 120-123 Goods or money given in belief of another's ability to pay at a later time.

Credit bureau 122 Agency that keeps financial records on individuals and sells the information to lenders determining creditworthiness of borrowers.

Credit card 128-130 (story), 120-123 Certificate (usually plastic) of an individual's creditworthiness issued by a creditor; allows purchase of goods to be repaid with interest over extended period of time.

Credit union 124 Financial cooperative set up by employees or labor union members to pool savings and lend money at lower rates than commercial banks; see Figure 6.4.

Creditworthy, creditworthiness 122 Determination of ability to repay; extension of credit based on an individual's prior experience with loans; trustworthiness.

Current account 221 Portion of the balance of payment statements measuring merchandise, service, tourism, and short-term finance exports-import relationship.

Current dollars 187, 188 Reporting figures in terms of the present purchasing power of the dollar at the time (no adjustment for inflation); sometimes called raw, or money GDP; see Figure 8.4.

Customs duty/tariff 162, 164, 209-210 A tax on imports; see Figure 9.4.

Cyclical unemployment 191 Unemployment stemming from a number of people being between jobs.

Deficit spending 10, 11, 153, 183 Intentionally going into debt beyond means of income; usually government action taken to stimulate the economy.

Deflation 198 Unbalanced condition resulting from too little money in circulation allowing supply to exceed demand and causing unnatural drop in prices.

Demand 56, 61, 62, 64, 65, 98, 99, 100, 101, 102, 184 The aggregate amount of goods consumers are willing and able to buy.

Demand curve 61, 62, 64, 65, 66 A graph line showing relation between price and quantity consumers are willing and able to buy.

Demand deposits 119 Checking accounts which function as the most frequently used type of money.

Demand, Determinants of 60, 64 Underlying factors motivating consumers.

Demand, Law of 58 As P increases, Q will decrease and vice versa.

Demand schedule 59, 62 A chart or list showing relation between price and quantity consumers are willing and able to buy.

Demand-management economics 8, 153, 154 School of thought which seeks to stimulate economic growth through fiscal policy of raising spending levels, providing wages and service payments to consumers (also known as Keynesian economics or demand-side economics).

Demand-pull inflation 196 Increased demand without offsetting increasing supply pulls equilibrium prices up.

Democrats 45-46 Of, relating to, characteristic of, or belonging to the Democratic Party of the United States.

Democratic-Republican Party 147 Farming interests and followers of Jefferson's state/local power with smaller role for central government in the early history of the U.S. (1790s through 1830s); evolved into modern Democratic Party after the Civil War.

Depository Institutions Deregulation and Monetary Act 132 1980 federal reform to make banking industry more competitive; allowed savings institutions to offer checking.

Depreciation 79, 188, 201 The loss of value as equipment wears out; also the cost of replacing machines, buildings, and other productive capital.

Depression 7, 132, 148, 149, 150, 151, 156, 182 Phase of economic activity in market economies in which there is severe and prolonged aggregate decline (high unemployment, business closings, unfavorable trade, little building, very low consumption, deflation, etc.); measured by Real GDP decrease.

Deregulation 12, 133, 154 To free from regulation, especially to remove government regulations from.

Derived demand 98 Demand for labor depends on aggregate demand in a market.

Desert Storm 185 Persian Gulf conflict with Iraq (1991-1992); example of effect of even a short war on global economic affairs.

Direct investment 214, 220 Multinationals' outright purchasing of plants and productive properties in another nation; see Figure 10.2; (By contrast, an *indirect* investment would be buying stock in foreign firms.)

Direct mail merchandising 63 Selling through catalogs rather than retail or wholesale outlets; mail-order catalog sales.

Discount merchandising 63 Offering goods at lower cost to consumers usually through selling large enough volume that makes up for lower profits.

Discount rate 129,130 FED's interest rate on loans to member banks to keep proper amounts on reserve; changes can alter the money supply.

Discouraged workers 190 Persons who give up job searches but do not count in official unemployment statistics because they do not apply for compensatory programs.

Discretionary fiscal policy 131, 151, 152, 153, 183 Immediate and intentional acts by Congress to ease or avoid serious declines or inflation.

Disincentive 63 Something that prevents or discourages action; a deterrent.

Disinflation 199 A slowing down or decline in the rate of price increases during an inflationary period.

Disposable Personal Income 13, 14, 189, 190, 192, 193 Aggregate personal income less taxes; purchasing power; what people have to spend or save; see Figures 8.6, 8.8a and 8.8b.

Diversification 84 A business or investor that has assets in a number of different kinds of businesses to diminish risk.

Dividends 79, 81, 137 Stockholder's share of profits of a corporation.

Division of labor 29 Separating production into smaller, easily mastered tasks to speed the entire operation.

Dow Jones Averages 138-139 A trademark used for an index of the relative price of selected industrial, transportation, and utility stocks based on a formula developed and periodically revised by Dow Jones & Company, Inc.

Downsizing 97, 184 Late 20th c. moves by major corporations to reduce costs by reducing and consolidating operations and labor forces.

Dunkin' Donuts 82 fast food/coffee shop franchisor; see chart, Figure 4.5.

DuPont 83 E. I. DuPont Corp.; U.S.-based (DE) chemicals manufacturing multinational; see chart, Figure 5.2.

Earned income 189 Wealth gained from direct work by the individual.

Easy money policy 128-129 FED actions which expand the money supply to offset recession and increase employment; see Figure 7.8.

EU (or sometimes EC) See European Union or Community; once also called "Common Market."

Econometrics 203 Application of mathematical and statistical methods to study economic and financial data.

Economic efficiency 45 Using scarce resources so as to minimize waste, expense, or unnecessary effort.

Economic growth 45 Using scarce resources so as to increase, as in size, number, value, or strength; extension or expansion.

Economic indicators 188, 202 Statistical data used to measure and assess the economic conditions (Real GDP, money supply, installment credit debt, building starts, etc.).

Economic justice 45 Using scarce resources so as to uphold what is just, especially fair treatment and due reward in accordance with honor, standards, or law.

Economic models 26-27, 61 Controlled hypothetical small-scale plan for an economy (or portion of an economy) allowing study of interaction of basic elements.

Economic Recovery Act of 1981 155 Reagan Era legislation of 1980s; supply-side stimulation attempt that cut taxes, especially for wealthy and corporations.

Economic stability 45 Using scarce resources so as to resist change, deterioration, or displacement.

Economic values 45-47 principles, standards, or qualities considered worthwhile or desirable which guide the economic decision-making in a society.

Economics 24 Study of how people and societies use scarce resources.

Education 33, 35, 116, 297-298 Relationship to career and to the efficiency of the aggregate work force.

Efficiency 45 Economic value that calls for production which optimizes use of resources.

Elastic clause 146, 147, 150-151, 156 *Constitution*'s Art. I, sec. 8, clause 18 allows Congress the flexibility to broaden the interpretation of its powers; the Elastic Clause conflicts with 10th Amendment, reserving powers not mentioned in the *Constitution* for the states.

Elasticity, price 61 Dramatic behavior (high % of change) of *Q* demanded or supplied when there is only slight change in price.

Embargo 216 Government sanction making it illegal to trade with a particular country; see Figure 9.4.

Emergency Banking Act of 1933 35, 132, 151 *Glass-Steagall Act*; banking reform led to federal deposit insurance (FDIC) and regular examination of banking records by federal government.

Employee benefits 105 non-wage compensation (medical, dental insurance, vacation, sick days, etc.); also "fringe benefits."

Employer withholding system See tax withholding system.

Employment Act of 1946 153 Set up agencies and committees which legitimized the Keynesian role of federal government as a stabilizer of the economy's performance.

Equal Pay Act of 1963 109 Congressional act prohibited gender discrimination in employment.

Equilibrium price, equilibrium wage 56, 63, 64, 67, 100, 101, 102 Average point of balance where interaction of forces of supply and demand meet to clear the market.

Equity 45 The ideal of being just, impartial, and fair; also a synonym for common and preferred stock.

Estate and gift tax 162, 166 Government collects a percentage on inheritances.

European Union 101, 201, 211, 212, 224 Multilateral trade and economic agreements among Western European nations (formerly the European Community or the Common Market).
Excise taxes 161, 162, 165 Government levies on certain commodities often considered luxuries or nonessentials (leather, jewelry, furs).
Exclusive products 219 Belonging to a small and select group, produced in few places and not having ready substitutes.
Expansion 150, 182, 193 The recovery stage in the pattern of the economy's "ups and downs" that is characterized by aggregate expansion, growing employment and increased spending as measured by Real GDP increase.
Expectations 184-185 Taking actions (raising prices, making purchases) which alter supply and demand based on hunches and beliefs of what may occur.
Export 186 To send or transport a commodity abroad; "*X*" = smallest component *C+I+G+X* calculation (of GDP and GNP) in which gross imports are subtracted from gross exports; trade surplus (positive yield) contributes to aggregate growth; a negative yield indicates a trade deficit.
Exxon-Mobil 78, 161, 219 Petroleum products; see chart, Figure 4.2.

Factor markets 26 In the Circular Flow Model of economic activity, the action of exchange of productive resources.
Fair Credit Reporting Act 122 Congressional law (1971) outlining consumer rights in relation to access and correction in credit records; see Figure 12.8.
Fair Deal 9 Late 1940s economic program of President Harry S Truman; reinforced large number of *New Deal* programs; stimulated consumption and expanded security for workers.
FDIC 8, 9, 132-133 Federal Deposit Insurance Corporation – 1930s federal agency insures bank deposits and inspects banks; (FSLIC, also created by Congress to oversee Savings & Loan institutions collapsed in 1987 during the S&L Crisis.)
FED, The See Federal Reserve System – popular name used by economists and media for the Federal Reserve Bank and its management agencies, most commonly, the Board of Governors.
Federal Budget 156 Federal government expenses; see Figure 7.5.
Federal Insurance Contribution Act (FICA) 164 Congressional act (1935) created a three-part payroll deduction to fund retirement, disability, death benefits under the Social Security system.
Federalist Party 147 Commercial interests and followers of Hamilton's strong government role in the early history of the U.S. (1790s through War of 1812).
Federal Reserve System 9, 11, 12, 13, 14, 120, 123, 124, 125, 126-132 194, 197, 199, 200, 211 (The FED); independent central bank of the U.S. – controls money supply.
Federal Revenue Act of 1932 148 Doubled taxes in the early years of the Great Depression to balance federal budget; curtailed demand and worsened conditions.
Federal Trade Commission 88, 167 (FTC) Investigative body created by Congress in 1914 to ensure fair competition in markets prone to monopolistic growth and regulate activities of firms in relation to fair treatment of consumers and marketplace ethics.

Federal Unemployment Taxes 164 (FUTA) Employer-paid taxes per employee for protection of workers against layoffs and other reasons for losing jobs.

Feudalism 40 An economic system of Europe from the 9th to about the 15th century, based on the holding of all land in fief or fee and the resulting relation of lord to vassal and characterized by homage, legal and military service of tenants, and forfeiture.

Fiat money 118 Money which a government decrees must be accepted as payment for goods and services; also legal tender.

FICA See *Federal Insurance Contribution Act.*

Financial institution 123 An intermediary such as a bank or credit union which functions as a depository for, and lender of, money and other fiscal services.

Fiscal policy 8, 10, 150-155, 183, 199 Actions by Congress to alter (stimulate or slow down) economic growth usually through adjusting spending levels or tax rates.

Fixed exchange rate See Bretton Woods System.

Floating exchange system 223-224 Value relationships among national currencies set by interaction of supply and demand in foreign exchange markets.

FOMC 129, 131 Federal Open Market Committee of the Federal Reserve System decides FED actions in buying and selling of government securities to maintain proper level for the money supply.

Food and Drug Administration 167 Federal agency (1906) tests and approves drugs, cosmetics, food additives and inspects preparation.

Ford, Gerald R. 10 38th President of the United States (1974-1977)

Ford Motors 6, 78, 85 U.S. based (MI) automotive multinational.

Foreign exchange rate 201, 224 Value of a national currency in relation to others; set in world exchange markets such as London, Tokyo, N Y.

Four Dragons, The 213-214 Hong Kong, Singapore, South Korea, and Taiwan make up the aggressive, surging NIEs of the Pacific Rim.

Franchise 81-82, 221 License to market and earn profits on products produced by another business as if an independently owned outlet for another company.

Franchisee 81-82 Licensee allowed to market and earn profits on products produced by another business.

Franchisor 81-82 A company which sells licenses to proprietor, partners, or corporations to market and earn profits on products it produces.

Freedom 44 In the economic sense, the value that leads to the capacity to exercise personal choice as to the resources at one's disposal (private property.

Frictional unemployment 191 Unemployment stemming from a number of people being between jobs.

Frontier (Work) Ethic 148 Strong 19th c. attitude of self-reliance and independence in sustaining oneself and family with no help from outside sources when problems arose.

FSLIC 133 Federal Savings and Loan Insurance Corporation; 1930s federal agency insured savings institutions' deposits and inspected banks; collapsed in 1987 during the S&L Crisis.

Full employment 191 Ideal economic conditions allowing everyone who wants a job to find one.

Functions of money 117-118 Money's primary uses as medium of exchange, standard of value, store of wealth.

G-8 nations 185 (picture) Called "G-7" prior to admission of Russia in 1997; major global industrial powers (Britain, Canada, France, Japan, Germany, Italy, U.S.); involvement in Desert Storm; G-8 nations meet frequently on common economic and currency matters.

Gain 133 To secure as profit or reward; earning.

GATT See General Agreement on Trade and Tariffs.

GDP See Gross Domestic Product.

G.E. See General Electric.

General Agreement on Trade and Tariffs (GATT) 211, 212, 213, 217, 220, 221 U.N.-sponsored treaty organization (1947) to minimize trade barriers.

General Electric (GE) 15, 78, 97 U.S.-based (NY) consumer and industrial electronics, appliance manufacturing multinational conglomerate; see chart, Figure 4.2.

General Foods 83, 84 Food industry giant acquired by Philip Morris in a conglomerate merger in the 1980s.

General Motors 78, 122 General Motors Corp.; U.S. based (MI) diversified multinational automotive firm; see chart, Figure 4.2.

General partner 77 One of several business owners actively involved in operations and decisions of a partnership.

G.I. Bill 9 The *Servicemen's Readjustment Act of 1944* was a Congressional program to aid military personnel and economy as a whole in making transition to post-WW II economy; gov't. mortgages, business loans, education grants.

Gift tax 166 Government collects a percentage on transfer of property or money to another individual.

Global economy 210-224 Growth of free trade (GATT), regional trade agreements (EU, NAFTA), and multinational corporations in late 20th c. changed world economic structure.

GM See General Motors.

GNC 82 Nutritional supplement center franchisor.

GNP See Gross National Product.

Gold standard 221 Monetary system (up to mid 20th c.) in which value relationships among national currencies were locked into the supply of gold (as opposed to today's free floating currency markets); see Figure 9.9.

Goldstar 214 South Korean electronics/home appliance multinational – high imports to U.S.

Gompers, Samuel 102 Founded American Federation of Labor (1886).

Government bonds 134-136 Interest bearing certificate; holders lend money to government over specified time, money is paid back with interest; interest earnings are usually tax-free.

Government Expenditures (*G*) 186-187 Spending by government for goods and services is the third largest component of the $C+I+G+X$ calculation of GDP and GNP. The government spending which is added to consumer, business, and net export spending.

Great Crash 7, 148, 156, 190 Wall Street collapse of October 1929, signalled the beginning of the Great Depression of the 1930s in the U.S.

Great Depression 8-9, 132, 148-151, 156, 183, 191, 217, 223 Collapse and protracted period of economic decline and paralysis in U.S. (and global) economy from 1929-1940.

Great Safety Net 156, 157, 160 Controversial idea that government's major role is to create a base of security for citizens; that tax revenues should be devoted to a massive welfare structure to insure citizens against economic hardship.

Great Society 10, 46, 199 President Lyndon B. Johnson's 1960s expansion of Kennedy economic program; large number of gov't. programs to stimulate consumption and render greater security.

Gross Income 162, 189 Total amount of wages, salaries, and other financial gains from investment (earned and unearned) in the nation.

Gross Domestic Product (GDP) 7, 15, 79, 183, 186-188, 192, 202, 215 Statistical measurement of value of all goods and services produced inside a country in a given year; real GDP is adjusted for inflation and reported in constant dollars; see Figures 8.3, 8.4.

Gross National Product (GNP) 7, 15, 79, 183, 186-188 Statistical measurement of value of all goods and services produced by a country – inside and outside its borders – in a given year. Real GDP is adjusted for inflation and reported in constant dollars; see Figures 8.3, 8.4.

Growth 14, 45, 82-85 Net increase in production, jobs, standards of living.

Guild 102 An association of persons of the same trade or pursuits, formed to protect mutual interests and maintain standards.

Hamilton, Alexander 145, 146, 147, 151 President Washington's first Secretary of Treasury; believed in active gov't. role in promoting business and industry; founder of Federalist Party which sought broader economic power for central government.

Haymarket Riots 102 Chicago labor in 1886 protests led to the downfall of the Knights of Labor.

Honda 220 Honda Corp.; Japan-based automotive multinational.

Hoover, Herbert 7, 8, 148 31st U.S. President (1929-1933) retained laissez-faire approach to government role in early part of the Great Depression.

Horizontal merger 82-84 A business combines with another in the same industry. (e.g., a chain of hamburger stands buys another chain of hamburger stands.)

Human resources 23 Essential factor of production that entails processes done by people; most commonly called "labor."

Hyperinflation 10, 196 Extremely rapid increase in prices, usually in double digits (rate above 10% per annum) devastating incomes and making growth unpredictable; also called "galloping inflation."

Hyundai 214 South Korean automobile multinational.

IBM 19-22, 23, 30, 78, 89 International Business Machines Corp. (NY) – major multinational computer manufacturer.

ILGWU 103 "The I.L.G." – International Ladies' Garment Workers Union – most powerful of the U.S. textile industry unions.

IMF See International Monetary Fund.

Imperfect competition 85-87 Market structure with many buyers and sellers, with similar products, some nonprice competition, usually intensely price competitive.

Implied powers 146 Idea that Congress can expand the scope of government by using the elastic clause to broadly interpret its enumerated (specified) constitutional powers.

Income tax 162 A levy on net personal or business income.

Indicators 193, 196 Statistical data used to measure and assess the economic conditions (real GDP, money supply, installment credit, building starts, etc.).

Industrial Revolution 97, 98 Conversion from hand and animal power to machine power; late 18th c. in Europe; later 19th c. in U.S.

Inelasticity, price 61 Sluggish behavior (low % of change) of Q demanded or supplied even with dramatic changes in price.

Inflation 10, 13, 14, 192-193, 194-195 Unbalanced condition resulting from too much money in circulation allowing demand to exceed supply and causing unnatural rise in prices.

Insider trading 136, 168-169 Violation of Federal Securities and Exchange Commission's rules against brokers or corporate financial officers seeking to profit by making transactions on information not yet made public.

Interdependence 218, 219 Reliance of nations and people on each other for goods and services.

International Brotherhood of Teamsters 103 Truckers and chauffeurs union.

International Monetary Fund (IMF) 223 U.N.-managed post-WWII fixed currency exchange system; now oversees international loans to nations with currency difficulties.

Interstate Commerce Commission 167 Federal agency regulates activities of firms in interstate transportation markets (1887).

Investment Expenditures (I) 186 Second largest component of the $C+I+G+X$ calculation of GDP and GNP in which business spending is added to consumer, government, and net export spending.

IPO 136 Initial public offering; a company's first stock offering designed to raise needed operational cash.

Jackson Hewett 82 Tax preparation service franchisor.

Jani King 82 Fitness center franchisor; see Figure 4.5.

Japan 14, 193, 201, 211, 212-213, 219, 220, 224.

Jazzercise 82 Tax preparation service franchisor.

J.P. Morgan and Co. 131 One of the top ten U.S. banks (NY); see Figure 6.9.

Jeep-Eagle 83, 84 Vehicle brands by Chrysler acquired from American Motors in a horizontal merger in the 1980s.

Jefferson, Thomas 145-147, 151 George Washington's Secretary of State; opposed Hamilton's view of active gov't. role in promoting business and industry; also 3rd President of the U.S. (1801-1809), embargo on European trade to avoid being drawn into Napoleonic Wars.

Jiffy Lube 82 Auto oil change service franchisor.

Junk bond 135, 136, 169 A corporate bond having a high yield and high risk.

Justice, economic 45 Basic economic value seeks to insure fairness and equal opportunity.

K-Mart 63, 213 U.S.-based (MI) clothing, general merchandising corp. (Waldenbooks, Payless Drugs); multinational chain store.

Keiretsu 212 Large, powerful corporations in Japan – usually multinationals.

Kennedy, John F. 10 35th President of the United States (1961-1963); *New Frontier* program became model and emotional foundation for President Lyndon Johnson's *Great Society*.

Key indicators 202-203 Economic statistics which give insight as to the aggregate condition of the economy.

Keynes, John Maynard 148, 149, 152, 153, 154, 155 Demand-side management British economist (1883-1946) who proposed that high unemployment, being a result of insufficient consumer spending, could be relieved by government-sponsored programs; advocated deficit spending by governments to stimulate ecomomic activity.

Keynesian economics 148-150, 153 School of thought championed by John Maynard Keynes c. Great Depression; seeks to stimulate economic growth through fiscal policy of raising spending levels, providing wages and service payments to consumers; (also, demand-side economics).

KFC 82 Kentucky Fried Chicken; fast food franchisor subsidiary of Pepsico.

Knights of Labor 102 Mid-19th c. nationwide labor union.

Kraft Foods 83, 84 Food industry giant acquired by Philip Morris in a conglomerate merger in the 1980s.

Kuznets, Simon 186 Awarded Nobel Prize in Economics (1971) for his method of determining Gross National Product and National Income.

L. L. Bean 63 Catalog-direct mail clothing merchandising corp. (ME).

Labor force 100 All the people over 16 years of age who have employment or are seeking it; also work force.

Labor productivity 99 How much profit a worker creates for an employer.

Labor union 102-109 Organization of workers for purpose of collective bargaining with employers.

Lagging indicators 203 Statistical data used to measure and assess the economic conditions that reach peaks or troughs later than others, but confirm conditions (Av. Prime Rate, Change in CPI, Change in Business Loans, etc.).

Laissez-faire 7, 9, 42, 43 46, 148, 155, 156 Economic concept in which government minimizes its economic activity.

Lands' End 63 Catalog- direct mail clothing merchandising corp. (WI).

Law of demand 58 Market economy behavior occurs when a product's market price rises, consumers will desire less; there is an opposite effect: if prices decline, consumers will demand more.

Law of supply 58 Market economy behavior occurs when a product's market price rises, producers will produce more; there is an opposite effect: if prices decline, producers will supply less or even drop out of the market.

LDCs 181, 210, 214, 215, 216, 218 Less Developed Nations (also "Third World"); poor nations of Asia, Africa, Middle America (especially Caribbean) troubled by overpopulation, food shortages, and weak industrial development.

Leading indicators 202-203 Statistical data used to measure and assess the economic conditions that reach peaks or troughs earlier than others, indicating business cycle trends (building permits, common stock price index, initial unemployment claims, etc.).

Lewis, John L. 103 American labor leader (1880-1969) who was president of the United Mine Workers of America (1920-1960) and the Congress of Industrial Organizations (1935-1940).

Liability 79, 80 Having legal or financial responsibility for something.

Liberal 46-47, 147, 148 In 20th c. U.S., those who endorse strong government role in economic life; seeks programs to stimulate consumption, render greater security, monitor competition.

Limited partner 77 One of several business owners passively involved a partnership; share profits but are basically financial backers; also "silent partners."

Liquid (liquidity) 120, 133 Ease with which a financial asset can be converted into money.

Liquidate 79 Dispose of; sell assets to pay debts or obtain capital.

Lobbying 169-170 Formal attempts to influence public policy; usually by organized groups with professional agents.

Low-end manufacturers 214 Producers of cheaper, lesser quality goods.

M-*1*, *M-2*, *M-3*, *L* 119-120, 124 Various measurements of the money supply, from narrowest *M-1* (currency and checks) to the *L* (broadest inclusion of all possible types of money and near money); see Figure 6.2.

Margin 58 Percentage of income or profit to make a venture worthwhile; lowest acceptable level of performance.

Market 56 A place where goods are offered for sale.

Market clearing price 62 Same as equilibrium price.

Market price 55, 62 Same as market clearing price.

Market system 40, 41, 42 Buyers and sellers come together to make transactions and determine prices; also private enterprise system.

Marshall Plan 10 Formally called the *European Recovery Act* (1947); Congress authorized massive aid to Western European nations to aid in rebuilding after WWII; named after U.S. Sec'y of State George C. Marshall; also stimulated U.S. economic growth after WWII because most of supplies for Europe were manufactured by U.S. corporations.

Marshall, John 147 Chief Justice of U.S. Supreme Court (1801-1835); landmark decisions interpreted the *U.S. Constitution* in broad sense to allow more federal power in economic questions.

Maturity 133 The time at which a note or bond is due.

Marxist 44 One that believes in or follows the ideas of Marx and Engels, especially a militant communist.

MasterCard 122 Major issuer of international bank credit cards.

Mazda 220 Mazda Automotive Corp.; Japanese based automotive multinational.

McCulloch v. Maryland 147 One of Chief Justice Marshall's landmark decisions (1819) allowed broad interpretation of Congress' implied power (setting up the Bank of the United States); other decisions (e.g., *Gibbons v. Ogden*, 1824) laid groundwork for more federal power in interstate economic questions.

McDonald's 82 McDonald's Corp.; fast food/restaurant franchisor.

Medicare 10, 162, 164 Extension of Social Security system which taxes workers to pay for health care of the elderly.

Medium of exchange 117 Money's use as a simple, neutral instrument for making transactions (as opposed to barter).

Mercedes 14, 220 Mercedes-Benz Corp.; German-based automotive multinational.

Merger 12, 82-84 The union of two or more commercial interests or corporations.

Microsoft 89 Microsoft Corp. (WA); major multinational computer software manufacturer.

Military expenditures 199 Extensive purchase of war matériel can have an effect on economic growth patterns, often overstimulation and causing distribution problems during the action, and withdrawal at end can trigger recession as plants close and jobs disappear.

Milkin, Michael 136, 168-169 Wall Street financier convicted of insider trading violations of SEC rules in 1980s.

Miller Brewing 82-83 One of the top three U.S. brewers; part of a Philip Morris tobacco-food conglomerate merger in the 1980s.

Mixed economy 41, 42-47, 160 Economic system combining elements of tradition, market, and command; see chart 4.1.

MNCs See multinational corporations.

Monetary policy 128-129, 131, 199 FED actions that intentionally change the money supply to deal with unfavorable economic conditions.

Money 117-140 Objects commonly accepted for transactions in markets; medium for exchange.

Money GNP or GDP 187-188 Raw GNP or GDP figures in current dollars without any adjustment for inflation.

Money supply 132-133, 184 Aggregate amount of money available in the nation (see *M-1*).

Monopoly 85, 87, 88, 160, 171 Only one seller in a market (absence of competition).

Moody's 135 Independent firm that rates municipal bonds and other financial arrangements.

Most favored nations 221 U.S. trade agreements which minimize legal restrictions and tariffs for trading partners.

Multinational corporation (MNC) 220, 221 Firm owning and operating substantial business facilities and having direct investments in many countries.

Municipal bond 134-135 An often tax-exempt bond issued by a city, county, state, or other government for the financing of public projects.

Mutual fund 139 An investment company that continually offers new shares and buys existing shares back on demand and uses its capital to invest in diversified securities of other companies.

Mutual savings bank 124 Financial institution for small consumer savings and loan services (especially home mortgages) not originally available in commercial banks; see chart, Figure 6.4.

NAFTA 101, 210, 211, 213, 220 North American Free Trade Association; 1993 Canadian-Mexican-U.S. trade agreement unifies their markets into a single unit; phases out tariffs, other barriers.

NASDAQ 138 National Association of Securities Dealers Automated Quotation System a trading exchange specializing in high tech stocks and bonds merged in 1998 with the AMEX - American Stock Exchange, NYC.

National debt 13, 153 Total of all unpaid financial obligations of the federal government.

National Income 186, 190 Total amount of wages, salaries, and other financial gains from investment (earned and unearned) in the nation less business taxes (but *including* personal taxes).

NEA 103 National Education Association; largest U.S. employee/labor organization.

Net Exports (X) 186 Smallest component $C+I+G+X$ calculation (of GDP and GNP) in which gross imports are subtracted from gross exports; trade surplus (positive yield) contributes to aggregate growth; a negative yield indicates a trade deficit.

Net National Product 188 Refined statistical measurement of national economic production which discounts cost of replacing worn out productive equipment by subtracting depreciation from the Gross National Product.

New Deal 9-10, 46, 150-151, 156, 164 Economic program of President F.D. Roosevelt (1930s); initiated large number of gov't. programs to stimulate consumption and render security.

New Frontier 10, 46 Economic program of President Kennedy (1960s); number of gov't. programs to stimulate consumption and render greater security.

Newly Industrializing Economies (NIEs) 213, 214 Nations such as Singapore, South Korea, and Taiwan that are breaking out of the less developed stages.

NIEs See Newly Industrializing Economies.

Nissan 220 Nissan Automotive Corp.; Japanese based automotive multinational.

Nixon, Richard M. 10 37th President of the U.S. (1969-1974) Vietnam War inflation, oil crises, imposed wage-price freeze, 1973.

Nonprice Competition 85-88 Rival firms seek to win consumers for their products by advertising, promotions, packaging, event, team, and media program sponsorship, etc.

Occupational Safety and Health Administration (OSHA) 168 federal agency regulates activities of firms in relation to working conditions and consumer products safety.

Oligopoly 85, 86-88, 161 Market structure characterized by limited competition; only a few sellers in a market; usually national or international corporations; see chart, Figure 5.7.

OPEC 10, 185 Organization of Petroleum Exporting Countries; a cartel of Middle East, African, Asian, and Latin American oil countries which attempts to fix crude prices and production levels on global scale.

Open market operations 129, 131 Federal Reserve's FOMC (Federal Open Market Committee) actions that change the money supply through government security transactions.

Open shop 109 Employment of both union and nonunion members.
Opportunity cost 24-26 Value of resources expended in making a choice.
Organizing 102 Inducing employees of a business or an industry to form or join a union.

Pacific Rim 14, 211 Rising economies of the region around the Pacific Ocean, especially East and Southeast Asia and Oceania (Taiwan, S. Korea, Hong Kong, Singapore, Australia, New Zealand).
PACs 160, 169 Political Action Committees subgroups formed by industrial and private interest groups and lobbies to influence election of individuals sympathetic to their cause.
Par value 135 The principal amount a bond purchaser gives to the borrower.
Partnerships 76, 77, 79, 80, 81, 82 Form of business organization in which several owners operate and divide profits.
PATCO Strike 105 Organized job action in 1981 by federal air traffic controllers, shut down airports; President Reagan dismissed participants and broke the strike.
Pay equity 109 Compensation without discrimination.
Peak 150, 182 Phase of business cycle characterized by economic growth and prosperity (high demand, low unemployment); see Figures 7.1, 8.1.
PepsiCo 85, 88 PepsiCo Corp.; beverage/foods/restaurant/general merchandise U.S.-based (NY) multinational conglomerate.
Perfect competition 85, 86, 87 Market structure with many buyers and sellers, with identical products; completely price competitive; little advertising, very sensitive to supply and demand (e.g., farm products); also called monopolistic competition.
Persian Gulf War 185 conflict with Iraq (1991-1992); example of effect of even a short war on global economic affairs.
Personal consumption (*C*) 186 "*C*" is the largest component of the $C+I+G+X$ calculation in which consumer spending is added to business, government, and net export spending to determine GDP and GNP.
Personal Income 189-190 Aggregate amount of spending power before business and personal taxes are deducted from wages, salaries, and other financial gains from investment in the nation; gross (earned + unearned) income.
Philip Morris 78, 83, 84 Diversified tobacco, food processing, brewing conglomerate; U.S.-based (NY) multinational; see charts, Figures 5.2 and 5.6.
Picket line 104 Organized line of workers to publicize a disagreement with employer. Sometimes used to stop substitute workers or customers from entering a business firm.
Pink slip 187 Jargon for notice of termination of employment.
Pizza Hut 82 Fast food franchisor subsidiary of Pepsico.
PM See Philip Morris Corp.
Portfolio 139 A collection of investments.
Preferential treatment 107 Relating to giving advantage; manifesting or originating from partiality.
Price ceiling 66-67 Maximum price sellers can charge by government decree; see graph, Figure 3.7.

Price Elasticity / Inelasticity 61 The degree of change in quantity (Q) demanded or supplied in relation to changes in price (P); high degree of change = elastic; small degree of change (little or no change in Q)= inelastic; see Figure 3.3.

Price floor 66-67, 108 Minimum price sellers can charge, or the minimum wage employers can pay, by government decree.

Primary Resources 215 Raw materials – ores, minerals; most basic natural substances used to manufacture goods.

Prime rate 129-130 Benchmark interest rate for big banks offering large commercial loans; usually 3-4% above FED's discount rate; influences almost every kind of bank and credit transaction.

Proctor and Gamble 96 U.S.-based (OH) personal care, household cleaning multinational conglomerate; major layoffs and downsizing in early 1990s.

Producer Price Index 195 PPI measures the difference in prices paid for goods and services purchased by producers over time.

Production possibilities curve 28-29 Graph representing the array of choices for using resources in an economic situation.

Productivity 28, 52, 96, 99 Measurement of the output resulting from applying economic resources in a certain situation; sometimes a synonym for efficiency.

Profit 42, 44, 57, 60, 62, 100, 134, 137, 197, 218 The amount by which revenue (sales income) exceeds production cost. (Revenue minus costs of production equals profits.)

Progressive tax 161 Tax that has escalating rates; rising with income levels (ability-to-pay principle).

Property tax 165-166 State, municipal, and school taxes on real estate and sometimes personal possessions.

Proportional tax 161 Tax that has same rate for all.

Proprietorship 76, 77, 79, 80, 81 Form of business organization in which one owner operates and receives all profits.

Prosperity 150, 182 The "peak" in the pattern of the economy's "ups and downs," characterized by aggregate expansion, high employment and high spending; measured by Real GDP increase.

Protectionism 217-218 National policy uses rules and regulations to shield domestic market from foreign competition.

Psychological (or "Psychic") rewards 81-82 Psychological benefits derived from owning and operating a business (independence, satisfaction, ego gratification).

Public assistance 191 tax-supported government social programs to help the unfortunate (unemployment compensation, medical subsidies, and welfare).

Public corporation 78 Form of corporation in which shares are publicly bought and sold on open stock markets.

"Pump-Priming" 8, 151, 153 Approach to governmental aggregate economic stimulation of consumption through governmental demand through projects that provide jobs which, in turn, should increase consumer demand and ignite business consumption and production.

Purchasing power 189 Extent of consumer's ability to buy goods and services.

QVC Network 63 Chain of television broadcasting stations organized for direct merchandising to consuming public.

Rationing system 66 Sharing or distributing goods in equal quantities; government controlled certain strategic products (e.g., tires, meats, dairy products, gasoline) in WWII by an elaborate coupon system over and above price.

Raw GDP See Money GDP.

Reagan, Ronald 11-14, 105, 131, 153-155 40th U.S. President (1981-1989) adopted "supply-side" stimulation policies; cut taxes but failed to reduce gov't. deficits.

Reaganomics 11-14, 154 1980s supply-side stimulation policies; cut taxes and reduce gov't. spending.

Real GNP, Real GDP 187-188 Statistical measurement of value of all goods and services produced that is adjusted for inflation and reported in constant dollars of an official base year; used to make statistical comparisons to factor out inflation and deflation results in Real GDP or Real GNP measurements; see Figures 8.2 and 8.4.

Real growth 13 Net increase (adjusted for inflation) in economic activity over previous period; increased jobs, higher productivity.

Real property 166 Land or buildings that are subject to property tax.

Real wages Net increase in pay over a previous period, adjusted for inflation; changes in real wages indicate growth or decline in standard of living and purchasing power; see Disposable Personal Income.

Recession 10, 11, 14, 133, 155, 182, 192, 199, 211, 212 Phase of economic activity in market economies in which there is aggregate decline for three consecutive months or more (unemployment, less factory activity, unfavorable trade, little building, low consumption, etc.); measured by Real GDP decrease.

Reciprocation 218 One government raises or lowers tariffs and trade policies in response to another's similar actions.

Recovery 150, 182 The point in the pattern of the economy's "ups and downs" after a recession or depression characterized by improving business activity, growing employment and increased spending; measured by Real GDP increase; see Figures 7.1 and 8.1.

Regressive tax 161 A tax that takes a larger percentage of poorer persons' income than from richer persons' income.

Rehabilitation Act 109 Federal law prohibits job discrimination against the handicapped (1973).

Representative money 118 Money (often paper) that symbolizes some valuable wealth (gold or silver) held in storage.

Republican 45-46 Of, relating to, characteristic of, or belonging to the Republican Party of the United States.

Reserve 125, 131 In banking, a percentage of deposited funds not to be used for loans and kept as a stockpile to cover withdrawals; also a legal minimum banks must keep as a safety margin against excessive lending.

Reserve requirements 131 State and FED restrictions on amounts banks must store (and not use for loans); FED alteration of reserves that change the money supply.

Return 133 To produce or yield (profit or interest) as a payment for labor, investment, or expenditure.

Revenue 13, 100, 158, 162-168 Income; usually refers to government income from taxation and fees.

Revolving credit (card) account 121 Credit card arrangement in which debtor need not pay total liability at end of billing period, but creditor can charge interest on unpaid balances.

Right-to-Work laws 109 State laws providing for open shop employment (union and nonunion employment); outlaws exclusive union shops.

Risk 133 The variability of returns from an investment.

Roosevelt, Franklin D. 9, 132, 148, 149, 150-151 32nd U.S. President (1933-1945); *New Deal* program attempted Keynesian approach to stimulating economy during the Great Depression.

S & L Crisis 132-133 Collapse of many Savings and Loan Association banks in the U.S. during the 1980s; bailout by federal government exceeded $600 billion.

Sales tax 162, 166 State and local government collects a percentage on nonessential items at point of sale.

Sanctions (trade sanctions) 216, 217 Embargoes, boycotts, high tariffs, and other regulations used to punish trade rivals.

Saturn 106 Semi-independent automotive firm launched by GM.

Savings and loan association (S&L) 132-133 Financial institution for small consumer savings and loan services (especially home mortgages) not always available in larger commercial banks.

Savings rate 192-193 Percentage of Personal Disposable Income stored in various savings accounts.

Say, Jean-Baptiste 154, 155 Late 18th - early 19th c. economist believed that supply created its own demand. Became base for supply-side school of thought in 20th c.

Scarcity 23-25, 28, 29, 134, 218 Lack of sufficient resources to meet needs and wants (demand exceeding supply); shortage.

Schedules 61 See Demand and Supply schedules.

Sears 63 Sears, Roebuck & Co.; Chicago-based clothing, general merchandising corp., national chain store (formerly catalog direct mail).

Securities and Exchange Commission 8, 151, 167, 169 Federal agency regulates activities of firms in stock, bond, and other financial markets.

Security 44, 45 Economic value of providing individuals with basic needs and a means to maintain a decent standard of living.

7-Eleven 81 Southland Corp.; convenience store franchisor.

Shareholder See stockholder.

Sherman Antitrust Act 88, 161, 171 Congressional law (1890) forbade certain business combinations which restricted a market (monopolies and near monopolies).

Shift in demand 65, 66, 100, 101 General change in the total amount of goods that producers are willing to provide at all price levels (shift to right = more, shift to left = less).

Shift in supply 65, 66, 100, 101, 102 General change in the total amount of goods that consumers are willing to buy at all price levels (shift to right = more, shift to left = less).

Shortage 63 Too few goods or labor available – gap between quantity demanded and quantity supplied.

Simple machines 30 Wheels, levers, screws, inclined planes when adapted to implements to mechanize them and make work efficient.

Smith, Adam 28, 42, 43, 88, 155, 218 18th c. Scots political economist whose *Wealth of Nations* (1776) articulated the basic philosophy of the classical market structure.

Socialist system 41, 44 A social system in which the means of producing and distributing goods are owned collectively and political power is exercised by the whole community.

Social Security 8, 9, 151, 152, 162, 164, 165, 189 A government program that provides economic assistance to persons faced with unemployment, disability, or agedness, financed by assessment of employers and employees.

Specialization 29 Becoming adept at performing a particular job or phase of an operation.

Split 137 To divide stock by issuing multiples of the existing stock with a corresponding reduction in the price of each share, so that the total value of the stock is unchanged.

Stability, economic 45 Basic economic value: even growth so that planning can occur.

Stabilization 152-153 Government actions to avoid serious declines or inflation; see monetary and fiscal policy.

Stagflation 10, 199 Unbalanced condition resulting from combination of inflation and no real economic growth.

Standard and Poor's Register of Corporations 139 Reference for obtaining corporate information; source for consumer complaints.

Standard of value 118 Money's use as a measure of an item's worth.

Standard and Poor's 135, 139 Independent firm that rates municipal bonds and other financial arrangements.

Stock exchange (market) 137 A place where stocks, bonds, or other securities are bought and sold; an association of stockbrokers who meet to buy and sell stocks and bonds according to fixed regulations.

Stockholder 78-79, 81 One who owns a share or shares of stock in a company; also shareholder.

Stocks 78-81, 136-139 Certificates of shared ownership in a corporation without liability; can be traded; earn dividends.

Store of wealth 118 Money's use as a consistent reserve of resources for future use.

Strike 103-105 Organized refusal of employees to work, usually in protest of some action by employer.

Structural unemployment 191 Unemployment stemming from basic changes (technological) which throws people out of work for lack of skill and training.

Subsidiary 84 A corporation wherein the majority of stock is owned by another corporation; usually allowed to operate under its own name.

Subsistence level 39 All the energy of the society devoted to producing bare essentials (no surplus to trade elsewhere).

Substitute goods 60 Goods used in place of others, ex. coffee v. tea.
Subway 82 Subway Sandwich Corp.; fast food franchisor.
Supply 56, 59, 61, 62, 64, 65, 184 Aggregate amount of goods producers are willing and able to produce.
Supply curve 59, 61, 62, 65 Graph line showing relation between price and quantity producers are willing and able to provide.
Supply, Determinants of 60, 64 Underlying factors motivating producers.
Supply, Law of 58 As P increases, Q will increase and vice versa.
Supply schedule 59, 62 Chart or table showing relation between price and quantity producers are willing and able to provide.
Supply-side economics 11-14, 153-155 School of thought which seeks to stimulate economic growth through fiscal policy of tax cuts and reduction of government spending levels, providing incentives for the private sector.
Surcharge 167, 199 An additional sum added to the usual amount of a tax.
Surplus 14, 28, 29, 39, 108, 198 An excess of goods available; overproduction – a gap between quantity demanded and quantity supplied; an extra amount of a good to be traded for others.

Taco Bell 82 Fast food franchisor; subsidiary of Pepsico.
Taft-Hartley Act 105, 109 Congressional act of 1947 gave President power to intervene in job actions which threatened national security; also outlawed closed (union only) shops.
Tariff 162, 164, 216, 217 A tax on imports (also customs duties).
Tax withholding system 162 Employers reduce employees' gross pay by taking out income tax owed on the gross and send to government.
Taxes 10, 11, 60, 158, 162-168, 183 Revenues collected by governments to fund activities; also fiscal policy tool to remedy adverse economic conditions; see Figures 7.6, 7.7, 7.8.
Tax Independence Day 159 Facetious May celebration by anti-tax groups as the day when the past 5 months of earnings would equal the average American's tax burden.
Technology 60, 96, 97, 191, 210 Application of scientific, electronic, and mechanical processes to production.
Tenth Amendment 147 Last of the *U.S. Constitution*'s *Bill of Rights* amendments reserves powers not assigned to federal government for states and localities; conflicts with the "Elastic Clause."
Terkel, Studs 15 Contemporary writer-journalist *Hard Times: An Oral History of the Great Depression* (1970), *Working* (1974), *The Good War: An Oral History of World War II* (1984), *The Great Divide: Second Thoughts on the American Dream* (1988).
Third world nation 181 See LDCs.
Tight money policy 13, 128-129 FED actions which constrict the money supply to offset inflation; contractionary actions.
Toyota 220 Toyota Automotive Corp.; Japanese based automotive multinational.
Trade barriers 216-219, 220 High tariffs, quotas, licenses, and other regulations used in protectionist trade policies.
Trade deficit 202 Balance of payments statements show a nation spends more on imports than it sells to other countries.

Trade-off 29, 29 Scarcity necessitates economic choices that entail a sacrifice of alternatives and opportunities as well as optimum gain.

Trade surplus 202 Balance of payments statements show a nation exports more than it buys from other countries.

Traditional system 39-40, 41 Economic decision-making based on past practices, or cultural or religious beliefs; see chart 65.

Transaction 117 Exchange of goods and services.

Transfer payments 160 Government payment of revenues to individuals (pensions, welfare, unemployment compensation, etc.).

"Trickle-Down" 13, 96 Approach to governmental aggregate economic stimulation of industry through loans and tax cuts to increase supply and jobs which, in turn, should stimulate personal consumption; See supply-side.

Trough 150, 182 Slump, depression; lowest phase of business cycle characterized by economic stagnation (low demand, rising unemployment); see Figure 7.1, 8.1.

Truman, Harry S 9 33rd President of U.S. after WW II (1945-1953), involved with economic conversion, *G.I. Bill*, and *Fair Deal*.

Truth in Lending Act 123 Congressional law (1968) outlining consumer rights to be apprised of finance charge, APR, and all pertinent details regarding loans and credit arrangements; see Figure 12.8.

UAW 103 United Auto Workers union.

Underemployed 8 When a person is working, but for fewer hours and at lesser pay than needed for survival.

Unearned income 189 Wealth gained from indirect sources such as gifts, investments, rents, etc.

Unemployment rate 14, 44, 108, 184, 190-192 Percentage of work force not actively engaged in wage-earning activity.

Union shop 109 A firm agrees to hire only union members (outlawed by right-to-work laws in some states).

Unionism 102 Drive to organize workers for collective bargaining purposes.

Usury 121 Lending money at excessive interest rates.

Utility tax 166 Government collects revenue on electric, telephone, CATV, water, etc.

Values See economic values.

Venezuela 219 Comparative advantage in petroleum production.

Verizon 78 Phone and communications giant (formerly Bell Atlantic).

Vertical merger 82-84 A business combines with another in the a different phase of same industry (e.g., chain of hamburger stands buys a beef cattle ranch).

Volume selling 63 Large-scale sale of items at lower profit margin.

Wage floor 108 minimum wage; either legislated or agreed to in a contract negotiation; see graph, Figure 6.8.

XYZ